Competition Culture and Corporate Finance

"I highly recommend "Competition Culture and Corporate Finance" to anyone interested in understanding the role of corporate culture in the field of finance. Dr. Terry Harris provides valuable insights into the impact of competition culture on various phenomena in corporate finance, including stock return performance, idiosyncratic stock price crash risk, meeting/beating analysts' earnings expectations, and earnings management activity. Using natural language processing to analyse firms' 10-K filings, the book introduces a measure of competition culture and provides evidence that transient institutional ownership intensifies firms' competition culture, while dedicated institutional ownership lessens it. The book's findings also suggest that firms with greater levels of competition culture achieve higher levels of short-term stock return performance and are more prone to meet/beat analysts' forecasts and engage in accruals-based earnings manipulation. Furthermore, the book examines the role played by competition culture in financial firms, specifically in the banking sector. The findings have significant policy implications and will be of interest to regulators, accounting standard-setters, managers, and those charged with firm governance, as well as career academics and researchers, graduates, and anyone interested in the impact of corporate culture on firms' economic outcomes. Dr. Harris's background in computer science, accounting, and finance provides a unique perspective on the subject matter, and his theoretical and applied research is evident throughout the book. "Competition Culture and Corporate Finance" is a well-written and well-researched book that is sure to become an essential resource for anyone interested in understanding the relationship between competition culture and corporate finance."

—Professor Laurence Ferry, *Professor of Accounting, Durham University, United Kingdom*

"If you're interested in understanding the complex relationship between corporate culture, competition, and financial outcomes, then Dr. Terry Harris's book, "Competition Culture and Corporate Finance," is a must-read. Using innovative methods like natural language processing (NPL) and textual analysis of firms' 10-K filings, Dr. Harris provides an insightful and detailed analysis of the impact of competition culture on various phenomena in corporate finance. The book's findings shed light on critical issues like institutional ownership structure, stock return performance, idiosyncratic stock price crash risk, meeting/beating analysts' earnings expectations, and earnings management activity. The evidence presented suggests that firms with higher levels of competition culture experience greater short-term stock return performance, are more prone to meeting/beating analysts' forecast, and engage in accruals-based earnings manipulation. In contrast, dedicated institutional ownership lessens competition culture, which is a crucial factor in shaping a firm's behaviour in a highly competitive market. The book's implications are significant for regulators, accounting standard-setters, managers, and those charged with firm governance. Dr. Harris's work will also be of interest to career academics and researchers, graduates, and anyone interested in the role of corporate culture in finance, economics, and accounting. In addition, the book examines the role of competition culture in financial firms and its effect on bank lending, providing a valuable perspective for policymakers and practitioners. All told, "Competition Culture and Corporate Finance" is a timely and insightful contribution to the field of corporate finance. Dr. Harris's rigorous research and analysis offer a wealth of information and insights into the complex relationship between competition culture and financial outcomes, making it a must-read for anyone interested in the intersection of finance, culture, and competition."

—Professor Omneya Abdelsalam, *Professor of Accounting & Finance, Durham University, United Kingdom*

Terry Harris

Competition Culture and Corporate Finance

A Measure of Firms' Competition Culture Based on a Textual Analysis of 10-K Filings

palgrave
macmillan

Terry Harris
Accounting Department
Durham University
Durham, UK

ISBN 978-3-031-30155-1 ISBN 978-3-031-30156-8 (eBook)
https://doi.org/10.1007/978-3-031-30156-8

This Palgrave Macmillan imprint is published by the registered company Springer Nature Switzerland AG
The registered company address is: Gewerbestrasse 11, 6330 Cham, Switzerland

To my dear mother Teresacita, father Timothy,
and love Virgil for her support and encouragement.

Contents

List of Figures

List of Tables

CHAPTER 1

Introduction

1.1 Introduction

Traditionally, researchers in finance (inclusive of empirical market-based accounting researchers) have tended to adopt a rather negative attitude towards the role played by culture in explaining firms' economic outcomes. According to Zingales (2015), this view has been historically taken because of the perception that culture was a "shoddy" way of dealing with economic problems, with many mainstream researchers in finance considering cultural explanations as a "cop-out" used by those unwilling to or incapable of unearthing the "real" economic reasons for the observations that they make (Guiso et al., 2006, 2015a, 2015b; Zingales, 2015). However, in recent years there has been increased acceptance of culture as a valid explanation for phenomena that are unexplained by traditional theories in finance and economics. This has led to an increasing body of work that has documented the significant role played by culture, and in particular corporate culture, in explaining a variety of firms' economic outcomes (see, for example, Andreou et al., 2020, 2021; Au et al., 2019; Audi et al., 2016; Barth, 2016; Barth & Mansouri, 2021; Bereskin et al., 2018; Bhandari et al., 2017; Callen & Fang, 2015; Cronqvist et al., 2007; Erhard et al., 2017; Fiordelisi & Ricci, 2014, 2021; Fiordelisi et al., 2019; Gorton et al., 2021; Graham et al., 2022; Grennan, 2019; Grieser et al., 2016; Groysberg et al., 2018; Guiso et al., 2006, 2015a, 2015b; Guo et al., 2022; Li et al., 2020; Luu et al.,

T. Harris, *Competition Culture and Corporate Finance*,
https://doi.org/10.1007/978-3-031-30156-8_1

2022; Nguyen et al., 2018, 2019; Thakor, 2015, 2020; Wang et al., 2021; Zingales, 2015, etc.). These studies suggest that corporate culture recites the operating philosophy that guides the top management teams' decision-making and influences the economic and policy outcomes of firms. To be sure, these works identify firms' culture as an important corporate attribute that governs managerial decision-making and hence impacts firms' performance in various domains (Quinn & Cameron, 1983; Quinn & Rohrbaugh, 1983).

This book extends the recent literature on the role played by corporate culture by first introducing a measure of firms' competition culture that is based on a textual analysis of 10-K filings. To develop our measure, we conceptualize firms' corporate culture by adopting the competing values framework (CVF), which suggests that there are four main cultural orientations that firms take; namely, *competition*, *collaboration*, *control*, and *creation*-oriented cultures (Cameron et al., 2014). Following this, we use our measure of firms' competition culture to explore the plausible antecedents and consequences of this corporate cultural orientation. In particular, following recent studies aiming to contribute to our understanding of the influence of institutional investors' preferences and interventions on firms' corporate governance (e.g., Bebchuk et al., 2015; Giannetti & Yu, 2016; Harford et al., 2018; McCahery et al., 2016), we first use the measure to investigate whether the composition of the institutional investor base influences firms' competition culture. Following this, we explore how firms' corporate culture relates to firms' financial performance as indicated by buy-and-hold returns, the propensity for firms to experience stock price crashes, and earnings manipulation behaviour. Additionally, using our measure of competition culture, we consider the nature of the relationship between banks' competition culture and bank lending.

The competition culture of a firm can be described as the combination of those firm attributes that focus on assimilating external information and responding to market conditions (Hartnell et al., 2011; Quinn & Cameron, 1983; Quinn & Rohrbaugh, 1983). Hence, the competition culture of a firm involves those value-creating practices and activities that entail an aggressive pursuit of competitiveness and achievement. Consequently, increase profitability, the speed of action, driving through barriers to deliver results, and building competition-focused decision-making, all typify firms with a competition culture (Cameron et al., 2014). In that vein, such firms have a proclivity towards being aggressive and moving fast, while assessing success based on indicators such as increased profit margins. Conversely, it is conceivable that a firm with greater levels of competition culture also faces increased pressure to perform from investors and therefore are more prone to make suboptimal decisions that can harm long-term shareholder value creation.

In this book, we follow the growing literature that applies textual analysis in finance-related research (see, for instance, Andreou et al., 2020, 2021; Barth & Mansouri, 2021; Bhandari et al., 2017; Fiordelisi & Ricci, 2014, 2021; Fiordelisi et al., 2019; Hoberg et al., 2014; Kearney & Liu, 2014; 2020; Loughran et al., 2009; Luu et al., 2022; Nguyen et al., 2018, 2019; Tetlock, 2007), to develop a measure of competition culture using the textual information in firms'10-K filings. Based on the intuition that the words used by management in firms' 10-K reports are reflective of the stated and latent values that they hold, we adopt this measurement approach as it provides an efficient way of capturing such values regarding firms' competition culture. What's more, by exploiting a large corpus of archival data which describes the current and expected future operations of US-listed firms we can circumvent severe data limitations associated with the measurement of latent corporate characteristics like corporate culture that has plagued past studies (Guiso et al., 2006, 2015a, 2015b; Zingales, 2015). We operationalize the measure by parsing 10-K filings to identify a set of lexical items relating to attributes that shape firms' competition culture.

We assess the validity of our measure by first relating it to alternative indicators of the firm's competition culture. In doing so, we note that according to existing theory, firms with a competition culture should be more in tune with and responsive to the external market environment and be more aggressive in the pursuit of profitability (Hartnell et al., 2011; Quinn & Cameron, 1983; Quinn & Rohrbaugh, 1983). Hence, if this is so, then one important indicator of firms with elevated levels of competition culture is high-profit margins (Cameron & Quinn, 2011; Cameron et al., 2014). Furthermore, it is reasonable to expect that the levels of a firm's competition culture will persist over time since it reflects the long-lived traits, practices, and attributes of the firm. Thus, we take advantage of these premises to assess the validity of our measure by exploring its relationship to other indicators of firms' competition culture (Cameron & Quinn, 2011; Cameron et al., 2014; Fiordelisi & Ricci, 2014, 2021), and by examining whether it reflects the theorized persistence. To consider these ideas, we conduct univariate and multivariate analyses that control for industry and year effects, and annual transition matrices analyses and find strong evidence that our measure of competition culture is positively related to firms' profit margins and an alternative text-based indicator of competition culture. Further, we find that our measure of the firm's competition culture reflects the slow-moving behaviour that is consistent with our expectations.[1]

Then, we use our measure of competition culture to first consider the overarching question; "*what is the influence of the composition of the institutional investor base on firms' competition culture?*" as this question is intriguing in many aspects. For instance, it can inform recent literature that documents strong links between institutional ownership and corporate outcomes such as earnings manipulation, R&D investments, M&As, and financing (see, for example, Chen et al., 2007; Elyasiani et al., 2010; Gaspar et al., 2005; Harford et al., 2018), as well as between institutional ownership and financial performance (see, for example, Cai & Zheng, 2004; Giannetti & Yu, 2016; Gompers & Metrick, 1998; Nofsinger & Sias, 1999). However, unlike most of the prior literature, that remains rather silent on exactly how institutional investors affect corporate outcomes and performance, in this book, we follow Andreou et al. (2021) and advance firms' competition culture as a channel through which institutional investors appear to influence corporate decision-making and outcomes. This proposition is consistent with recent evidence documenting that institutional investors regularly engage with management and the board of directors in behind-the-scenes interventions that can shape corporate objectives (Bebchuk et al., 2015; Brav et al., 2015; Edmans, 2014; McCahery et al., 2016, among others), and that the composition of firms' institutional investor base can create (or mitigate) implicit incentives for managers to over-allocate effort towards improving current performance, potentially at the expense of long-term firm value (e.g., Bushee, 1998; Dikolli et al., 2009). Based on these arguments, institutional investors could, therefore, influence firms' competition culture to create an operating environment that is more likely to fulfil their own goals at the expense of other investors. Thus, it is important to trace the effect of institutional investors on the firm's competition culture since it details the context in which organizational

[1] Please see Appendix A for the results of this analysis.

members prioritize activities that could deliver favourable (or adverse) financial results to investors (Hartnell et al., 2011; O'Reilly et al., 1996).

Accordingly, consistent with the prior findings of Andreou et al. (2021), we provide in Chapter 4 robust causal evidence that transient institutional ownership has a strong positive relationship with firms' one-year-ahead level of competition culture. As transient institutional investors invest based on the likelihood of reaping short-term trading profits (Bushee, 1998, 2001), this evidence supports that they intervene and exert pressure on managers to intensify their firms' competition culture, perhaps aiming for results-right-now and more immediate financial performance. As such, we argue that this behaviour is explained in part by the management of a firm with more transient institutional investors being more likely to succumb to such pressures under the threat that if these institutional investors become unhappy, then they will forcefully exit by selling shares, thereby suppressing the firm's stock price (Bernardo & Welch, 2004; Fos & Kahn, 2015).

Conversely, we demonstrate that dedicated institutional ownership has a negative relation to firms' one-year-ahead level of competition culture. This evidence supports the notion that dedicated institutional investors also intervene and influence managers but instead to lessen firms' competition culture, perhaps following their incentives to monitor and offset managerial myopia, and to assess performance by relying on information beyond the current period (Chen et al., 2007; Gaspar et al., 2005; Harford et al., 2018). Correspondingly, this evidence suggests that the managers of firms with more dedicated institutional investors feel less pressure to consistently meet market expectations and therefore ease their aggressive pursuit of short term performance objectives as they are less concerned about large price drops that can be spurred by the exit/selling strategies of these investors. This is reasonable since a large proportion of dedicated investors are in fact passive investors who simply invest in firms (directly or indirectly) based on an index. These investors are therefore usually unable or unwilling to directly sell specific firms that comprise the index. As a result, managers at firms with more dedicated investors are increasingly less likely to be concerned about selling pressure initiated by initial signals of underperformance (Cella et al., 2013; Giannetti & Yu, 2016).

Furthermore, in Chapter 5 we seek to address the question: *what is the effect of competition culture on a firm's stock return performance?* We find this question interesting for several reasons. Firstly, the seminal studies on the role of corporate culture posit that competition culture relates to the pursuit of robust performance through the processes of acquiring and evaluating market information and due to pressure from investors (Cameron et al., 2014; Harris & Ogbonna, 2001; Hartnell et al., 2011; Jaworski & Kohli, 1993; Kohli & Jaworski, 1990; Kotter & Heskett, 1992; O'Reilly et al., 2014; Quinn & Cameron, 1983; Quinn & Rohrbaugh, 1983; Reynolds, 1986; Sørensen, 2002). Therefore, competition culture enhances the firm's ability to adapt to a dynamic environment in a much more timely and efficient manner. Thus, we argue and find convincing evidence that competition culture is positively related to financial performance as indicated by one-year-ahead adjusted buy-and-hold stock returns.

Additionally, in Chapter 6 we use our measure of competition culture to investigate the relationship between it and engaging in "bad" news hoarding activity that increases crash risk. We argue that "bad" news hoarding makes firms vulnerable to adverse economic outcomes in the form of large idiosyncratic stock price declines, known as crash risk (Andreou et al., 2016, 2017, 2021; Callen & Fang, 2013, 2015; Hutton et al., 2009). For firms with an intense competition culture, managerial incentives to conceal negative information regarding poor operating performance would be naturally heightened, since such firms need to consistently deliver superior financial performance as such firms inherently have a proclivity to cater to market expectations. Thus, after controlling for known determinants of crash risk, we empirically test this proposition and show a strong positive relationship between competition culture and one-year-ahead measures of crash risk.

Combining the result that transient institutional ownership intensifies firms' competition culture with the evidence that competition culture heightens the propensity for crash risk, we postulate that competition culture might be a channel through which transient institutional ownership exerts direct intervention within firms to influence corporate policies and economic outcomes. To investigate this, we conduct subsample analyses and mediation test using seemingly unrelated regressions and the results are consistent with our expectations. Specifically, with regard to the subsample analysis, we find that the strong positive relationship between competition culture and future crash risk is present only within the subsample of firms that is dominated by high levels of transient institutional ownership and low levels of dedicated institutional ownership. Hence, consistent with the theoretical underpinnings in the CVF (see e.g., Cameron et al., 2014), the analysis shows that competition culture does not cause any adverse effects on shareholder value; rather, the striking result is that competition culture of a firm becomes harmful only when it is associated with a high proportion of transient and a low proportion of dedicated ownership structure. Further, the seemingly unrelated regression analyses are consistent with competition culture mediating the relationship between our measures of institutional ownership and stock price crash risk. By and large, these findings qualify institutional investors as key corporate governance agents which can (either curb or) exacerbate firms' competition culture as their preferences and interventions can lead the management to become highly susceptible to making suboptimal decisions and to prioritize activities that harm long-term firm value.

What's more, we use our measure to explore the relationship between competition culture and a firm's proclivity to meet and/or beat analysts' earnings expectations (please see Chapter 7) and engage in earnings manipulation activity (please see Chapter 8). We argue that at firms with more competition-orientated corporate cultures, it is expected that managers face greater pressures, have financial incentives, among other career motives, to extend themselves to consistently meet and/or beat analysts' earnings forecasts and engage in accruals-based earnings manipulation. Furthermore, it is plausible that managers at high competition culture firms face pressures to intentionally conceal "bad" news and to accelerate the disclosure of "good" news, hoping that poor current performance will be masked by stronger future performance (Kim & Zhang, 2011a, 2011b, 2016). Thus, consistent with this idea, we report evidence that competition culture increases the likelihood of meeting/beating analyst expectations and engaging in accruals-based earnings manipulation while diminishing the prospect of real earnings management activity.

In the final study of the book presented in Chapter 9, we use our measure to consider the role played by competition culture in explaining lending behaviour in US-based financial firms (from henceforth referred to as "banks"). While the prior studies of this book have explored the effect of competition culture on organizational outcomes in nonfinancial firms, the importance of bank's corporate culture in explaining phenomena cannot be overstated given the importance of the banking industry to the overall economy. This makes banking an interesting industry to study in its own right. Without a doubt, banks play a central role in the sound functioning of the entire financial system, and of particular concern to bank regulators is whether and how excessive lending and risk-taking by individual banks pose a threat to the financial system as a whole (see, e.g., Acharya et al., 2010; Hanson et al., 2011). In this vein, important undecided issues related to the extent to which banks' competition culture mitigates or exacerbates incentives for bank lending, particularly in crisis periods, and its effects on the overall stability of the financial system remain unaddressed. As a result, we are motivated to consider the following research questions; "*what is the relationship between banks' competition culture and bank lending*?" and "*how does banks' pre-crisis competition culture relate to crisis period lending*?".

The results suggest that greater competition culture banks are likely to engage in more lending activity. Additionally, we find that high competition culture banks are likely to engage in more procyclical lending, as they exhibit a more pronounced reduction in lending activity during the global financial crisis (GFC), given their pre-crisis period levels of competition culture.

This book contributes to the literature as follows. Firstly, the finding that the composition of institutional ownership base impacts managers' operating philosophy and decision-making as indicated by their firms' competition culture, adds direct knowledge to our understanding of how institutional investors engage with managers in behind-the-scenes interventions that leave an indelible mark on firms' culture. As such, our findings complement other recent studies (e.g., Bebchuk et al., 2015; Brav et al., 2015; Edmans, 2014) that endeavour to provide direct evidence of institutional investors' preferences and actions on their portfolio firms. Second, it contributes to the settling of the ongoing debate regarding the benefits and costs of institutional investors on corporate decision-making (e.g., Giannetti & Yu, 2016; Harford et al., 2018; Massa et al., 2015) by investigating the impact of transient and dedicated investors on firms' competition culture, which inherently encapsulates the managers' decision-making environment instead of simply relying only on corporate outcomes like R&D, dividends, investments, financial fraud, etc. Finally, this book also contributes to the burgeoning literature that focuses on the impact of firms' organizational values, norms, and principles to policies and economic outcomes (see, for example, Andreou et al., 2020, 2021; Barth & Mansouri, 2021; Callen & Fang, 2015; Erhard et al., 2017; Fiordelisi & Ricci, 2014, 2021; Fiordelisi et al., 2019; Graham et al., 2022; Guiso et al., 2006, 2015a, 2015b; Li et al.,

2020; Loughran et al., 2009; Luu et al., 2022; Nguyen et al., 2018, 2019; Zingales, 2015) by introducing competition culture as another organizational effectiveness factor that links to a firm's stock performance, idiosyncratic cash risk, earnings manipulation and bank lending activity, etc. As it is frequently very hard to measure such intangible corporate characteristics, we show how to operationalize such an empirical construct using textual analysis of the 10-K reports for all firms with such reports in the SEC Edgar database.

The book is presented as follows: In Chapter 2, we provide an overview of the literature surrounding the role played by corporate culture in finance. In addition, we provide a synthesis of the relevant theoretical and empirical works that explore the relationship between corporate culture and various economic outcomes.

Chapter 3 presents a review of the literature that discusses the textual analysis approach and how this method has been adopted by researchers in finance. Also, we highlight the main findings from works that used this approach and discuss whether and how it can be applied to measure corporate culture.

Chapter 4 provides the first study of the book. In this study, we develop a text-based measure of firms' corporate culture using the CVF. Also, we provide direct evidence that firms' institutional owner structure influences the level of competition culture, thereby providing confirmation that firms' institutional ownership structure is an important antecedent of corporate culture. In particular, we show that transient institutional ownership intensifies competition culture, while dedicated institutional ownership reduces it.

In Chapter 5 we explore the relationship between competition culture and performance as captured by one-year-ahead adjusted buy-and-hold stock returns. Using the text-based measure of firms' competition culture first developed in Chapter 4, we find strong evidence that firms with greater competition culture achieve superior short-term stock return performance.

Chapter 6 examines the relationship between competition culture and the stock price crash risk. We find strong evidence that competition culture firms systematically withhold negative news from the market and hence experience higher incidences of idiosyncratic stock price crashes. Further, we observe this phenomenon particularly among firms with a high proportion of transient and a low proportion of dedicated institutional ownership, and that is consistent with competition culture playing a mediating role.

In Chapter 7, we use the text-based measure of competition culture to show that firms with higher competition culture are more likely to meet and/or beat analysts' forecasts. We argue that this is in part explained by their propensity to engage in "bad" news hoarding activity which was previously reported to increase firms' stock price crash risk.

Chapter 8 examines whether competition culture serves to exacerbate manager's proclivity to engage in earnings manipulation. We find robust evidence that when competition culture is high managers engage in greater levels of accruals-based earnings management and lower levels of real earnings management behaviour.

Chapter 9 presents the final study of the book where we examine the effect of competition culture on bank lending. Consistent with expectations, we find evidence that banks with greater competition culture are generally more prone to engage in greater lending activity. However, we find that during the GFC banks with higher pre-crisis competition culture reduce lending more thereby feeding into a procyclical lending dynamic.

Chapter 10 concludes the book by providing a summary of the findings, and it also outlines the policy implications of the studies.

References

Acharya, V. V., Cooley, T. F., Richardson, M. P., & Walter, I. (2010). *Regulating Wall Street: The Dodd-Frank Act and the New Architecture of Global Finance.* Wiley.

Andreou, P. C., Antoniou, C., Horton, J., & Louca, C. (2016). Corporate Governance and Firm-Specific Stock Price Crashes. *European Financial Management, 22*, 916–956.

Andreou, P. C., Fiordelisi, F., Harris, T., & Philip, D. (2021). Institutional Ownership and Firms' Thrust to Compete. *British Journal of Management, 33*, 1346–1370.

Andreou, P. C., Harris, T., & Philip, D. (2020). Measuring Firms' Market Orientation using Textual Analysis of 10-K Filings. *British Journal of Management, 31*, 872–895.

Andreou, P. C., Louca, C., & Petrou, A. P. (2017). CEO Age and Stock-price Crash Risk. *Review of Finance, 21*, 1287–1325.

Au, S. Y., Dong, M., Tremblay, A. (2019). *When Culture Matters-Corporate Flexibility and Stock Returns.* Available at SSRN 2883353.

Audi, R., Loughran, T., & McDonald, B. (2016). Trust, but Verify: MD&A Language and the Role of Trust in Corporate Culture. *Journal of Business Ethics, 139*, 551–561.

Barth, A. (2016). *The Role of Corporate Culture in the Financial Industry*. Available at SSRN 2707078.

Barth, A., & Mansouri, S. (2021). Corporate Culture and Banking. *Journal of Economic Behavior & Organization, 186*, 46–75.

Bebchuk, L., Brav, A., & Jian, W. (2015). The Long-term Effects of Hedge Fund Activism. *Columbia Law Review, 115*, 1085–1155.

Bereskin, F. L., Byun, S. K., Officer, M. S., & Oh, J. M. (2018). The Effect of Cultural Similarity on Mergers and Acquisitions: Evidence from Corporate Social Responsibility. *Journal of Financial and Quantitative Analysis, 53*, 1995–2039.

Bernardo, A. E., & Welch, I. (2004). Liquidity and Financial Market Runs. *The Quarterly Journal of Economics, 119*, 135–158.

Bhandari, A., Mammadov, B., Thevenot, M., Vakilzadeh, S. H. (2017). *The Invisible Hand: Corporate Culture and Its Implications for Earnings Management* (Working Paper). Warrington College of Business.

Brav, A., Jiang, W., & Kim, H. (2015). The Real Effects of Hedge Fund Activism: Productivity, Asset Allocation, and Labor Outcomes. *Review of Financial Studies, 28*, 2723–2769.

Bushee, B. J. (1998). The Influence of Institutional Investors on Myopic R&D Investment Behavior. *Accounting Review, 73*, 305–333.

Bushee, B. J. (2001). Do Institutional Investors Prefer Near-Term Earnings Over Long-Run Value? *Contemporary Accounting Research, 18*, 207–246.

Cai, F., & Zheng, L. (2004). Institutional Trading and Stock Returns. *Finance Research Letters, 1*, 178–189.

Callen, J. L., & Fang, X. (2013). Institutional Investor Stability and Crash Risk: Monitoring Versus Short-Termism? *Journal of Banking and Finance, 37*, 3047–3063.

Callen, J. L., & Fang, X. (2015). Religion and Stock Price Crash Risk. *Journal of Financial and Quantitative Analysis, 50*, 169–195.

Cella, C., Ellul, A., & Giannetti, M. (2013). Investors' Horizons and the Amplification of Market Shocks. *Review of Financial Studies, 26*, 1607–1648.

Cameron, K. S., & Quinn, R. E. (2011). *Diagnosing and Changing Organizational Culture: Based on the Competing Values Framework*. Wiley.

Cameron, K., Quinn, R., DeGraff, J., & Thakor, A. (2014). *Competing Values Leadership*. Edward Elgar Publishing.

Chen, X., Harford, J., & Li, K. (2007). Monitoring: Which Institutions Matter? *Journal of Financial Economics, 86*, 279–305.

Cronqvist, H., Low, A., & Nilsson, M. (2007). *Does Corporate Culture Matter for Firm Policies?* (Working Paper). Fisher College of Business.

Dikolli, S. S., Kulp, S. L., & Sedatole, K. L. (2009). Transient Institutional Ownership and CEO Contracting. *The Accounting Review, 84*, 737–770.

Edmans, A. (2014). Blockholders and Corporate Governance. *Annual Review of Financial Economics, 6*, 23–50.

Elyasiani, E., Jia, J. J., & Mao, C. X. (2010). Institutional Ownership Stability and the Cost of Debt. *Journal of Financial Markets, 13*, 475–500.

Erhard, W., Jensen, M., & Zaffron, S. (2017). *Integrity: A Positive Model that Incorporates the Normative Phenomena of Morality, Ethics and Legality*. Available at SSRN 1542759.

Fiordelisi, F., & Ricci, O. (2014). Corporate Culture and CEO Turnover. *Journal of Corporate Finance, 28*, 66–82.

Fiordelisi, F., & Ricci, O. (2021). Corrigendum to "Corporate Culture and CEO Turnover." *Journal of Corporate Finance, 70*, 102064.

Fiordelisi, F., Renneboog, L., Ricci, O., & Lopes, S. S. (2019). Creative Corporate Culture and Innovation. *Journal of International Financial Markets, Institutions and Money, 63*, 101137.

Fos, V., & Kahn, C. (2015). *Governance through Threat of Intervention and Threat of Exit* (Working Paper). University of Illinois at Urbana–Champaign.

Gaspar, J. M., Massa, M., & Matos, P. (2005). Shareholder Investment Horizons and the Market for Corporate Control. *Journal of Financial Economics, 76*, 135–165.

Giannetti, M., & Yu, X. (2016). *The Corporate Finance Benefits of Short Horizon Investors*. Available at SSRN 2723357.

Gompers, P. A., & Metrick, A. (1998). *Institutional Investors and Equity Prices*. National Bureau of Economic Research.

Gorton, G. B., Grennan, J., & Zentefis, A. K. (2021). *Corporate Culture*. National Bureau of Economic Research.

Graham, J. R., Harvey, C. R., Grennen, J., & Rajgopal, S. (2022). Corporate Culture: Evidence from the Field. *Journal of Financial Economics, 146*, 552–593.

Grennan, J. (2019). *A Corporate Culture Channel: How Increased Shareholder Governance Reduces Firm Value*. Available at SSRN 2345384.

Grieser, W. D., Kapadia, N., Li, R., & Simonov, A. (2016). *Fifty Shades of Corporate Culture*. Available at SSRN 2843776.

Groysberg, B., Lee, J., Price, J., & Cheng, J. (2018). The Leader's Guide to Corporate Culture. *Harvard Business Review, 96*, 44–52.

Guiso, L., Sapienza, P., & Zingales, L. (2006). Does Culture Affect Economic Outcomes? *The Journal of Economic Perspectives, 20*, 23–48.

Guiso, L., Sapienza, P., & Zingales, L. (2015a). Corporate Culture, Societal Culture, and Institutions. *American Economic Review, 105*, 336–339.

Guiso, L., Sapienza, P., & Zingales, L. (2015b). The Value of Corporate Culture. *Journal of Financial Economics, 117*, 60–76.

Guo, H., Yin, C., & Zeng, Y. (2022). How Does Firm-Specific Investor Sentiment Affect the Value of Corporate Cash Holdings? *British Journal of Management, 34*, 410–441.

Hanson, S. G., Kashyap, A. K., & Stein, J. C. (2011). A Macro-prudential Approach to Financial Regulation. *Journal of Economic Perspectives, 25*, 3–28.

Harford, J., Kecskes, A., & Mansi, S. (2018). Do Long-Term Investors Improve Corporate Decision Making? *Journal of Corporate Finance, 50*, 424–452.

Harris, L. C., & Ogbonna, E. (2001). Strategic Human Resource Management, Market Orientation, and Organizational Performance. *Journal of Business Research, 51*, 157–166.

Hartnell, C. A., Ou, A. Y., & Kinicki, A. (2011). Organizational Culture and Organizational Effectiveness: A Meta-Analytic Investigation of the Competing Values Framework's Theoretical Suppositions. *Journal of Applied Psychology, 96*, 677.

Hoberg, G., Phillips, G., & Prabhala, N. (2014). Product Market Threats, Payouts, and Financial Flexibility. *The Journal of Finance, 69*, 293–324.

Hutton, A. P., Marcus, A. J., & Tehranian, H. (2009). Opaque Financial Reports, R 2, and Crash Risk. *Journal of Financial Economics, 94*, 67–86.

Jaworski, B. J., & Kohli, A. K. (1993). Competition Culture: Antecedents and Consequences. *The Journal of Marketing, 57*, 53–70.

Kearney, C., & Liu, S. (2014). Textual Sentiment in Finance: A Survey of Methods and Models. *International Review of Financial Analysis, 33*, 171–185.

Kim, J. B., Li, Y., & Zhang, L. (2011a). CFOs Versus CEOs: Equity Incentives and Crashes. *Journal of Financial Economics, 101*, 713–730.

Kim, J. B., Li, Y., & Zhang, L. (2011b). Corporate Tax Avoidance and Stock Price Crash Risk: Firm-Level Analysis. *Journal of Financial Economics, 100*, 639–662.

Kim, J. B., & Zhang, L. (2016). Accounting Conservatism and Stock Price Crash Risk: Firm-level Evidence. *Contemporary Accounting Research, 33*, 412–441.

Kohli, A. K., & Jaworski, B. J. (1990). Competition Culture: The Construct, Research Propositions, and Managerial Implications. *The Journal of Marketing, 54*, 1–18.

Kotter, J. P., & Heskett, J. (1992). *Corporate Culture and Performance*. The Free Press.

Li, K., Liu, X., Mai, F., & Zhang, T. (2020). The Role of Corporate Culture in Bad Times, Evidence from the COVID-19 Pandemic. *Journal of Financial and Quantitative Analysis, 56*, 1–68.

Loughran, T., McDonald, B., & Yun, H. (2009). A Wolf in Sheep's Clothing: The Use of Ethics-Related Terms in 10-K Reports. *Journal of Business Ethics, 89*, 39–49.

Luu, H., Nguyen, L., & Wilson, J. O. S. (2022). *Organizational Culture, Competition and Bank Loan Loss Provisions*. Available at SSRN 3921043.

Massa, M., Wu, F., Zhang, H., & Zhang, B. (2015). *Saving Long-Term Investment from Short-Termism: The Surprising Role of Short Selling*. Available at SSRN 2558876.

McCahery, J. A., Sautner, Z., & Starks, L. T. (2016). Behind the Scenes: The Corporate Governance Preferences of Institutional Investors. *The Journal of Finance, 63*, 1729–1775.

Nguyen, D. D., Hagendorff, J., & Eshraghi, A. (2018). Does a CEO's Cultural Heritage affect Performance under Competitive Pressure? *The Review of Financial Studies, 31*, 97–141.

Nguyen, D. D., Nguyen, L., & Sila, V. (2019). Does Corporate Culture affect Bank Risk-Taking? Evidence from Loan-Level data. *British Journal of Management, 30*, 106–133.

Nofsinger, J. R., & Sias, R. W. (1999). Herding and Feedback Trading by Institutional and Individual Investors. *The Journal of Finance, 54*, 2263–2295.

O'Reilly, C. A. I., Chatman, J., & Caldwell, D. F. (1996). People and Organizational Culture: A Profile Comparison Approach to Assessing Person-Organization Fit. *Academy of Management Journal, 34*, 487–516.

O'Reilly, C. A., III., Caldwell, D. F., Chatman, J. A., & Doerr, B. (2014). The Promise and Problems of Organizational Culture: CEO Personality, Culture, and Firm Performance. *Group and Organization Management, 39*, 595–625.

Quinn, R. E., & Cameron, K. (1983). Organizational Life Cycles and Shifting Criteria of Effectiveness: Some Preliminary Evidence. *Management Science, 29*, 33–51.

Quinn, R. E., & Rohrbaugh, J. (1983). A Spatial Model of Effectiveness Criteria: Towards a Competing Values Approach to Organizational Analysis. *Management Science, 29*, 363–377.

Reynolds, P. D. (1986). Organizational Culture as Related to Industry, Position and Performance: A Preliminary Report. *Journal of Management Studies, 23*, 333–345.

Sørensen, J. B. (2002). The Strength of Corporate Culture and the Reliability of Firm Performance. *Administrative Science Quarterly, 47*, 70–91.

Tetlock, P. C. (2007). Giving Content to Investor Sentiment: The Role of Media in the Stock Market. *The Journal of Finance, 62*, 1139–1168.

Thakor, A. V. (2015). *Corporate Culture in Banking*. Available at SSRN 2565514.

Thakor, A. V. (2020). Ethics, Culture and Higher Purpose in Banking: Post-Crisis Governance Developments. *International Journal of Central Banking, 17*, 1–31.

Wang, Y., Farag, H., & Ahmad, W. (2021). Corporate Culture and Innovation: A Tale from an Emerging Market. *British Journal of Management, 32*, 1121–1140.

Zingales, L. (2015). The 'Cultural Revolution' in Finance. *Journal of Financial Economics, 117*, 1–4.

CHAPTER 2

Literature Review: What Is Culture?

2.1 Introduction

What is culture? Culture is a broad and inherently complex concept that can be defined as those values, norms, customs, and beliefs held by particular societal groups (please see e.g., Graham et al., 2022; Guiso et al., 2006; Schein, 1990, 1992; Zingales, 2015). Put another way, culture can be said to represent the nexus of all implicit and explicit contracts that govern behaviour and human interaction within societal groups (Benabou & Tirole, 2003, 2011). With regard to the firm, culture can be defined as an intangible asset that is designed to meet unforeseen contingencies (Kreps, 1990). Simply put, culture can be said to be "*the way things get done around here*" (Deal & Kennedy, 1982).

In recent years, there has been an increased acceptance of culture as a valid explanation for economic behaviour in finance (Zingales, 2015). This has been aided in part by the development of new tools, methods, and methodologies aimed at measuring and analysing the effects of culture on various economic outcomes. To be sure, researchers in finance now have various seamless approaches for incorporating culture into empirical studies (Guiso et al., 2006). A central theme to all this is first the identification of a direct impact of culture or of a particular cultural orientation on the rational preferences and/or expectations of certain economic agents or groups. Following this, the researcher must show that those preferences and/or expectations, in turn, have a predictable and

T. Harris, *Competition Culture and Corporate Finance*,
https://doi.org/10.1007/978-3-031-30156-8_2

measurable impact on economic outcomes. Finally, the researcher must identify the cultural component of the said preference and expectation by instrumenting them with an appropriate measure of culture.

It is widely accepted that a particular group's culture reveals their preferences and expectations and that this is necessarily an important determinant of their behaviour. Clearly, this realization makes culture a seemingly important construct for explaining economic outcomes in finance. Nevertheless, despite this and other arguments that point to an economic impact of culture and social norms (e.g., Akerlof, 1980; Arrow, 1972; Becker, 1957; Hofstede et al., 1990), in past decades scholars in finance and economics have with very few exceptions (see for example Kreps, 1990), doggedly avoided investigations into the role played by culture when conducting research for mainstream consumption.

The negative attitude towards culture traditionally adopted by many researchers in finance was in part due to the perceived notion that it was a "sloppy" way of dealing with economic problems in finance. In fact, many have considered cultural explanations as a "cop-out" used by individuals unwilling or unable to discover the "true" economic reasons for the empirical results that they obtain (Zingales, 2015). However, in recent years there has been increased acceptance of culture as a valid explanation for observed phenomena that are unexplained by traditional theories in finance and economics. This has led to an increasing body of work that has documented the critical role of culture in explaining a wide array of economic outcomes and phenomena (see, for example, Ahern et al., 2015; Andreou et al., 2021; Callen & Fang, 2015; Callen et al., 2011; Cameron et al. 2014; Chui et al., 2010; Dang et al., 2018; Doupnik, 2008; Erhard et al., 2017; Eun et al., 2015; Fiordelisi & Ricci, 2014, 2021; Giannetti & Yafeh, 2012; Graham et al., 2022; Gray, 1988; Grennan, 2019; Guiso et al., 2006, 2008, 2009, 2015a, 2015b; Hofstede, 1980, 2001; Hofstede et al., 1990; Kanagaretnam et al., 2013; Li et al., 2013; Luu et al., 2022; Schwartz, 1992, 1994; Wang et al., 2021; Zingales, 2015).

In this chapter, we review the finance-related literature centred on the role played by corporate culture to answer economically meaningful research questions. In particular, we focus on the various theoretical frameworks and taxonomics that can be used to describe a firm's "culture" and the empirical studies that discuss the role of corporate culture in finance.

2.2 Corporate Culture

Previous finance and economics-based works on corporate culture provide theoretical insights into the role that it plays within the organization. For instance, Kreps (1990) motivates corporate culture as an important economic concept and develops a model in which corporate culture can be used as a "coordination" mechanism that is designed to meet unforeseen contingencies. Furthermore, Cremer (1993) views corporate culture as the shared knowledge of organizational members that is unavailable to outsiders. Similarly, Hermalin (2001) models the choice of corporate culture as the decision between high fixed cost and low marginal cost (strong culture) and low fixed cost and high marginal cost (weak culture). Meanwhile, Van den Steen (2010a, 2010b) interprets corporate culture as being concerned with the shared values and beliefs that can reduce belief heterogeneity and disagreement among organizational members. More recently, Lo (2015) introduced the "Adaptive Market Hypothesis" view of corporate culture, which suggests that firm's culture represent the core traits of an organization that survive various evolutionary processes.

In recent times, the increased data available on firms, managers, and those charged with governance has made it possible to quantify various aspects of corporate culture and to use these measures to answer questions motivated by past theoretical work (Fiordelisi & Ricci, 2014, 2021; Graham et al., 2022; Grennan, 2019; Guiso et al., 2015a, 2015b). In particular, these firm-level measures of culture have made it possible to address questions such as; "*does corporate culture affect firms' economic outcomes, and if so how?*". Further, the thrust to explore the role of corporate culture is also explained by the fact that in corporations rational agents have a greater ability to shape the distinct norms and preferences of the organization (Guiso et al., 2015a, 2015b; Zingales, 2015). This makes corporate culture a fertile ground to explore such design choices in relation to existing finance and economic theories. What is more, at the corporate level there is greater data available with which to undertake large-scale studies and hence it should come as no surprise that researchers in finance are increasingly focusing on corporate culture.

2.2.1 *Taxonomies of Corporate Culture*

To study the role of corporate culture in finance, we first make use of the extensive body of work that has explored the broader concept that is organizational culture. This approach makes sense since past decades have seen a number of theoretical frameworks for organization culture proposed and developed by esteemed researchers of organizational behaviour (see for example, Cameron & Quinn, 2011; Cameron et al., 2014; Deal & Kennedy, 1982; Denison, 1990; Handy, 1976; Hofstede, 1980, 2001, 2011; Johnson, 1988; O'Reilly et al., 1991; Reynolds, 1986; Schein, 1990, 1992). Furthermore, in recent years these taxonomies for organizational culture have provided researchers in finance, interested in pursuing questions related to the role of corporate culture, with broad overviews of the many variations that exist between the different conceptualization of organizational culture that can manifest within firms. Therefore, to get a better understanding of these notions of organizational culture and how they are reflected in the corporate form of business organization, we next consider some of the noted typologies of organizational culture that have emerged in the organizational behaviour literature.

2.2.1.1 *Handy (1976)*

Early work by Handy (1976) provides a coherent framework for thinking about organizational culture. Based on a scheme originally introduced by Harrison (1972) he links organizational structure to firm culture and identifies four distinct types of organizational culture; namely, the *power culture*, *role culture*, *task culture*, and *person culture*. The *power culture* captures the degree to which tactical and strategic decision-making authority within the organization is concentrated on a key central person or among a small group of individuals. The *role culture* seeks to delegate decision-making authority to individuals with defined functions and specialties within a highly defined organizational structure. In the *task culture*, decision-making authority resides with a small collaborative team of individuals with varying expertise who collectively solve problems and execute tasks. Finally, Handy identifies the *person culture* where the individual is the central focal point and thus, they believe themselves to be set apart from the organization as a whole.

2.2.1.2 Deal and Kennedy (1982)

Another popular taxonomy for organizational culture that can be used to explore corporate culture was introduced by Deal and Kennedy (1982), who defined organizational culture as simply "*the way things get done around here*". In their work, Deal and Kennedy identify six interlocking cultural elements that help to define the firms' culture. These cultural elements are the institution's *history*, *values and beliefs*, *rituals and ceremonies*, *stories*, *heroic figures*, and *cultural network*. By examining these cultural elements across a variety of organizations they identify two factors that influence observed cultural patterns. These factors are (i) the degree of risk that accompanies the organization's activities, and (ii) the speed at which organizations learn and provide feedback concerning whether particular actions and strategies are successful. These two dimensions combine to define four types of organizational culture; namely, *work-hard, play-hard culture*, *tough-guy, macho culture*, *process culture*, and *bet-the-company culture*. In the *work-hard, play-hard culture* speed of action and speed of recreation all typify this culture. Organizations with a *work-hard, play-hard culture* focus on swift learning and the delivery of rapid feedback to members as it relates to their performance; these members are encouraged to take the low risk. The *tough-guy, macho culture* also emphasizes rapid learning and feedback but encourages members to take on high degrees of risk. In the *process culture* learning and feedback are slow and members take on low risk. The *bet-the-company culture* also provides slow learning and feedback but members within organizations that have this culture are encouraged to take on higher levels of risk.

2.2.1.3 Reynolds (1986)

Reynolds (1986) argues that the various dimensions of culture introduced by previous researchers (for example, Deal & Kennedy, 1982; Handy, 1976) overlap. Synthesizing the past literature, he presents 14 independent dimensions of organizational culture. These are *external versus internal*, *task versus social*, *risk versus safety*, *conformity versus individuality*, *individual versus group rewards*, *individual versus collective decision-making*, *ad hockery versus planning*, *stability versus innovation*, *cooperation versus competition*, *simple versus complex organization*, *informal versus formalize procedures*, *high versus low loyalty*, and *ignorance versus knowledge of organizational expectations.*

In the *external versus internal* emphasis domain, organizations with greater external emphasis are said to focus on satisfying customers and other external stakeholders, while those organizations with an internal emphasis concentrate on enhancing the efficiency and effectiveness of internal activities. The *task versus social* dimension measures the degree to which organizations view either task completion or meeting the social needs and desires of members/employees is more important. In the *risk versus safety* dimension, how willing individuals in the organization are to accept and adapt to changing environments and ways of doing work is measured. The *conformity versus individuality* domain measures the degree to which the members are forced to kowtow their distinctive behaviour to the group. The *individual versus group rewards* domain captures how the organization rewards all members whether as a group and/or individually based on their contribution. The *individual versus collective decision-making* dimension measures the degree to which decisions are made by individuals or as a group. The *centralized versus decentralized decision-making* dimension captures whether decisions are made by those in senior positions in the organization or by those with the day-to-day responsibility for the implementation of the decided course of action. The *ad hockery versus planning* domain reveals the degree to which the organization develops in an unplanned manner or whether detailed plans are made. The *stability versus innovation* dimension captures whether the organization is open to adopting new and unique goods, services, and processes. The *cooperation versus competition* domain reflects the attitude of individuals in the institution towards internal competition with other members of the organization for rewards and status versus their attitude towards teamwork and collaboration to enhance the effectiveness of external competition with outsiders. The *simple versus complex organization* dimension measures the degree of complexity of the internal political processes of the firm as well as the formal and informal structures of the organization. The *informal versus formalize procedures* domain reflects the tendency within the firm to have detailed rules and procedures for making decisions. In the *high versus low loyalty* dimension, the degree of loyalty individuals have to the organization compared to other relevant groups is captured. Finally, the *ignorance versus knowledge of organizational expectations* domain reveals the degree to which organizations communicate performance expectations to members and the level to which members are aware of these expectations and how they, in turn, contribute to the achievement of organizational goals.

2.2.1.4 *The Cultural Web*

The cultural web proposed by Johnson (1988) is another noteworthy organizational cultural framework that is useful for understanding corporate culture. Their framework identifies a number of elements that describe and influence organizational culture. According to them, these elements may overlap to form the culture of the organization; and they point out that a greater level of cultural coherence among these elements is a likely source of competitive advantage. The first element of culture that they identify is the organization's *paradigm*; this cultural element describes what the institution is all about, what it does, its values, its mission, and its objectives. Next, they describe the *control systems* of the organization as the processes that are put in place to monitor internal activities. They also identify the *organizational structures* of the entity, which defines the internal reporting lines that describe the way that workflows through the organization. Further, they identify the *power structures* of the entity as the degree to which individuals or groups of individuals make the decisions in the organization. *Symbols* include the organizational logos and designs as well as those internal symbols of power. The *rituals and routines* of the firm are those habitual organizational practices that occur as a matter of habit rather than necessity. Finally, they categorize the institution's *stories and myths* as those narratives accumulated about people and events that communicate what is valued within the organization.

2.2.1.5 *Denison (1990)*

Similarly, Denison (1990) proposes a model of organizational culture that is useful for understanding how corporate culture manifests within businesses. In particular, this model allows the culture of organizations to be defined broadly as being either externally or internally focused as well as being flexible or stable. Further, this model suggests that organizational culture and organizational effectiveness can be described by four dimensions; namely, *involvement*, *consistency*, *adaptability*, and *mission*. The *involvement* domain refers to the degree to which the organization is able to create a sense of ownership and responsibility. This sense of ownership engenders greater levels of commitment to the institution. The *consistency* dimension involves the relationship between aspects of organizational culture and organizational effectiveness. In particular, this perspective emphasizes the positive impact that culture can have on effectiveness by reinforcing core values, engendering agreement, and promoting greater inter-functional coordination. The *adaptability* domain refers to the system of norms and beliefs which support the capacity of an organization to receive, interpret, and translate signals from the environment to internal behaviours. Finally, the *mission* dimension captures the degree to which there is a shared purpose and direction for the organization and its members.

2.2.1.6 O'Reilly et al. (1991, 1996, 2014)

O'Reilly et al. (1991, 1996, 2014) advance a model of organizational culture that has proved popular in the finance-related literature (see e.g., Grennan, 2019; Grieser et al., 2016; Guiso et al., 2015b). First, based on the idea that an organization's culture is distinguished by the values held and reinforced from inside, they propose the Organizational Cultural Profile (OCP). Hence, this model of culture gauges organizational climate and measures the degree of compatibility between individuals and the organization, i.e., the person-organizational fit. They argue that this model can be used to identify the most efficient persons suited to join the institution.

Then, consistent with the OCP, O'Reilly et al. (1991, 1996, 2014) identify seven main components of organizational culture; namely, *adaptability*, defined as the willingness to experiment, take risk, and innovate; *collaboration*, which denotes the attitude individuals within the organization have towards working with others; *customer-orientation*, this indicates the degree to which customers are listened to; *detail-orientation*, which refers to the attention paid to detail; *integrity*, this signifies the regard held for honesty and high ethical standards; *results-orientation*, denotes emphasis placed on performance; and *transparency*, refers to the degree to which the information concerning the organization's goals and practices are shared freely with interested parties.

2.2.1.7 Schein (1990, 1992)

Yet another important framework for organizational culture was proposed by Schein (1990, 1992), who identifies *external adaptation* and *internal integration* as the two main reasons why cultures develop within organizations. In his work, he posits that *external adaptation* suggests that cultures develop and are maintained because they help organizations to survive and do well. Thus, if the organization's culture is valuable and presents the potential for engendering sustained competitive advantages, then it is retained. The other main explanation for the development of organizational culture, *internal integration*, is identified as a function since cohesive social structures are important for the existence of organizations. According to Schein (1992), organizational practices are learned through socialization at work. Further, the work environment serves to support the prevailing culture by encouraging members to adopt the prevailing cultural values and norm‘s. In addition, he develops the dimensions of organizational culture and introduces three levels of the organizational culture; namely, *artefacts*, *espoused values*, and *assumptions*.

At the *artefact* level, aspects of the organization's culture are visible to those external to the institution. These cultural factors may include the organization's formal and informal infrastructures and the language used in the organization's messages. An organization may claim certain values; however, its infrastructure may serve to undermine those espoused values. In this case, the *artefacts* show that the values held by organizational leaders have not been effectively shared or transmitted such that they affect the organization's activities. Furthermore, once the external environment changes the organization's *artefacts* are the first level of culture to be affected. In turn, changes to this outer level of organizational culture may gradually affect the deeper cultural levels—*espoused values* and *assumptions*.

The *espoused values* of organizations represent the middle layer of the three levels of organizational culture posited by Schein (1992). This level denotes the philosophies, goals, objectives, and strategies of the organization. Also, the *espoused values* represent those unwritten norms and customs that members understand and follow self-consciously. Those individuals not adhering to the *espoused values* of the group are made to feel ostracized. The *espoused values* themselves are comprised of the *working environment* and the *leadership style*. The *working environment* reflects the nature of relationships in the organization. In particular, it entails how supervisors relate to their subordinates, the relations between members, and how conflicts are managed, etc. In contrast, the *leadership style* reflects the approach of the leader in the execution of the organization's strategies in the achievement of organizational goals and objectives.

Assumptions are the core values that are shared by members of the group but that are often imperceptible even to these members. The core values take a long time to develop and are hard to remove once established. The essence of the core values is conveyed by communicating their key facets into the espoused values and artefacts of the organization. Hence, to determine the *assumptions* of an organization, it is important to identify the values that are comprehended and followed by members of the institution. Further, these core values should not just be slogans or even the speech/writings of the directors, but they are reflected in the other cultural levels of the organization. Put another way, the core values manifest themselves as automatic reactions and unconscious perceptions and/or opinions of organizational members.

2.2.1.8 Hofstede (2011)

In yet another important work that presents a taxonomy of organizational culture, Hofstede (2011) introduces a framework that identifies six dimensions to describe organizational culture; namely, *process-oriented* versus *results-oriented*, *job-oriented* versus *employee-oriented*, *professional* versus *parochial*, *open system* versus *closed system*, *tight* versus *loose control*, and *pragmatic* versus *normative* dimensions. A further discussion of these six dimensions follows.

The *process-oriented* versus *results-oriented* dimension is closely linked to the operational success of the organization. Organizations with a *process-oriented* culture focus on the technical and bureaucratic aspects of *how* the work is done. On the other hand, organizations that are results-oriented are concerned with outcomes, where members are focused on what is to be done. *Process-oriented* and *results-oriented* organizations also differ with respect to the level of risk-taking. In particular, *process-oriented* organizational cultures seek to avoid risk, while *results-oriented* cultures tend to take on more risk in order to achieve the organization's goals and objectives.

In Hofstede's (2011) organizational culture framework, the *job-oriented* versus *employee-oriented* dimension relates to the operating philosophy of management. In *job-oriented* organizational cultures, members are held responsible for their performance without much regard for their individual well-being. In contrast, organizations with an *employee-oriented* culture take both performance and the welfare of individual members into consideration.

The *professional* versus *parochial* domain relates to how members are perceived by others within the organization and how they view themselves. In the *professional* culture, members are identified with their profession or job category/type. Conversely, in institutions that adopt a *parochial* culture, members are identified with their various organizational subunits/groups (i.e., departments, teams, and/or work units).

The *open system* versus *closed system* dimension reveals the ease of access to information about the organization. In particular, it reflects the internal and external communication style of the institution and how easily insiders and outsiders have access to information of particular interest. In an *open system*, information is accessible to both insiders and outsiders, while in a *closed system* this information is not as accessible to outsiders.

The *tight control* versus *loose control* cultural domain refers to the level of discipline exercised within the organization. Specifically, this dimension is concerned with the amount of control exercised over organizational members in terms of the level of formality and punctuality expected of them. In a *tight control* culture, organizational members are exposed to more control and discipline, while in a *loose control* culture members are expected to be less formal.

Hofstede's (2011) *pragmatic* versus *normative* dimension is concerned with the external–internal drive of the organization. In a *pragmatic* culture, the organization is focused on satisfying the needs, wants, and demands of end users (i.e., customers) without much regard for other organizational norms. Thus, such institutions are said to be externally driven. Conversely, in a *normative culture,* the organization is said to be more internally driven since they place greater emphasis on their internal processes, and ethical and compliance issues.

2.2.1.9 The Competing Values Framework

The final taxonomy for organizational culture that we will discuss is the competing values framework (CVF). Modelled by Quinn and Rohrbaugh (1981, 1983), Cameron and Quinn (2011), and Cameron et al. (2014), this organizational culture framework has been widely cited in the literature and has been used in a number of recent finance-related studies to conceptualize firms' organizational culture (see e.g., Andreou et al., 2021; Barth, 2016; Bhandari et al., 2017; Fiordelisi & Ricci, 2014, 2021; Nguyen et al., 2018, 2019; Thakor, 2015, 2020; Tremblay, 2020).

Like previous taxonomies (see for example Denison, 1990), this framework for organizational culture differentiates between those competing values and attitudes within the firm that focuses on the external environment from those that focus on internal effectiveness—the *external–internal* domain. Further, it distinguishes between those organizational attributes that emphasize effectiveness criteria that focus on flexibility and discretion from those that are centred on stability and internal control—i.e., the *flexibility–stability* domain. These two dimensions intersect to define four distinct types of orientations that comprise the CVF, namely the *competition culture*, *creation culture*, *collaboration culture*, and *control culture*.

Organizations with the *competition culture* value the accomplishment of measurable and stretch goals. These types of organizations place particular emphasis on finance-based and market-based goals and objectives such as enhanced financial performance and increased market share. In such institutions, the relationship between members and organization is contractual and members are individually held accountable for achieving a pre-agreed level of performance. Furthermore, a spirit of competitiveness permeates throughout the organization. The entity focuses on the external environment and the formal control orientation reflects stability.

A *creation culture* is a cultural form that is characterized by high levels of creativity and risk-taking behaviour. The members of such organizations are committed to being innovative and on being on the leading edge of whatever endeavour the group is pursuing. This type of organization reacts rapidly to change and in fact, creates it via individual initiative and flexibility that promotes growth that is reinforced by rewards. This type of organization focuses on providing new and unique products and/or services. Thus, the organization focuses on the external environment and the formal control orientation is flexible.

In organizations defined by the *collaboration culture*, traits such as loyalty, cooperation, and teamwork are all valued. Organizations with this type of culture place greater emphasis on internal effectiveness, while allowing for a flexible form of control. Members of such institutions exhibit a commitment to others in the group and to the organization as a whole that is beyond their mere job descriptions. In response to the long-term levels of commitment (i.e., loyalty) by members to the "clan", the organization reciprocates with a long-term commitment to the members. In organizations with the collaborative/clan culture, there is a strong peer pressure to abide by the norms that are valued by the group. Thus, normative pressures within the institution generate enhanced levels of the valued traits. Further, in such organization success is assumed to depend on cooperation and teamwork, as well as concern for other people.

Finally, organizations with the *control culture* value rules, hierarchy, ordered coordination, and standardized operating procedures that are clearly defined. These types of organizations are concerned with long-term efficiency, predictability, and stability. Thus, managers within a bureaucratic institution are organizers and are required to police the rules and procedures to ensure that they are enforced. The tasks, responsibilities, and authority of all members are also clearly defined. However, this type of culture can impede their effectiveness and efficiency of the organization as it is likely to dampen flexibility. The emphasis of attention of this organization is internal, and the formal control is stable.

2.2.2 *Implications of Corporate Culture for Finance*

Recent empirical works have documented the importance of corporate culture for the behaviour of so-called "economic man" in organizations (see e.g., Andreou et al., 2021; Bhandari et al., 2017; Callen & Fang, 2015; Cronqvist et al., 2007; Erhard et al., 2017; Fiordelisi & Ricci, 2014, 2021; Graham et al., 2022; Grennan, 2019; Grieser et al., 2016; Guiso et al., 2006, 2015a, 2015b; Zingales, 2015). In much of this strand of literature, corporate culture is conceptualized as a type of intangible asset of the firm that is designed to meet unforeseen contingencies (Kreps, 1990). In this way, corporate culture is said to reflect those intrinsic and informal institutions of the firm that help to shape employee behaviours (Graham et al., 2022; Grennan, 2019). Thus, using this and other related definitions of corporate culture, hitherto unaddressed questions such as; "*does corporate culture matter?*", and "*what is the role of corporate culture?*" are increasingly being answered by mainstream researchers in finance despite these relationships being largely unaccounted for in traditional finance and economic theories.

For instance, in an extensive and influential work, Graham et al. (2022) conduct a survey and interview-based analysis of 1,348 North American firms and use this information to investigate whether differences in firms' corporate culture help to explain why otherwise similar firms experience divergence in terms of success and failure. They find that half of the senior executives believe that corporate culture is a top-three driver of firm value and 92% believe that improving their culture would increase firm value. Somewhat surprisingly, they find that a mere 16% of senior executives believe that their firm's culture is where it should be. Furthermore, they find that senior executives link firms' corporate culture to ethical choices (e.g., compliance and short-termism), innovation (e.g., creativity and taking the appropriate risk), and value creation (e.g., productivity and acquisition premia). They assess these links within a framework that implies that cultural effectiveness depends on interactions between the corporate culture, which is theorized as an informal attribute of firms, and those formal institutions. In doing so, they find evidence that firms' corporate culture is as important as their stated values in achieving success.

The drive to investigate culture in the corporate setting is explained in part because the corporation provides a unique environment within which to examine the role played by culture. This is so since corporations are in fact micro-societies that have the ability to actively shape distinct norms, values, and preferences (Guiso et al., 2015a, 2015b; Zingales, 2015). Thus, in this vein researchers in finance who study corporate culture often embed it within the broader literature that surrounds corporate institutions and theorize corporate culture as a type of informal institution that helps to shape employee behaviours and hence firm outcomes (e.g., Guiso et al., 2015a, 2015b; Graham et al., 2022). In this way, corporate culture is thought to be a fruitful area for research into the role of culture more broadly since it is more likely to reflect the specific design choices of those economic agents who first instilled these informal arrangements. Also, in the corporate setting, there is greater data availability, and this fact coupled with the increased precision of variables measured at the firm level makes corporate culture an important and rich area for research into the impact of culture. In fact, recent results suggest that management and those charged with governance help to shape the corporate culture of the firm (Andreou et al., 2021; Benmelech & Frydman, 2015; Biggerstaff et al., 2015; Bushman et al., 2017); further, the results reveal the corporate culture has implications for firm performance (Fiordelisi & Ricci, 2014, 2021; Guiso et al., 2015b; Mironov, 2015; Sørensen, 2002), firm value (Au et al., 2019; Benmelech & Frydman, 2015; Grennan, 2019), earnings manipulation activity (Benmelech & Frydman, 2015; Bhandari et al., 2017; Biggerstaff et al., 2015; Braguinsky & Mityakov, 2015; Davidson et al., 2015; DeBacker et al., 2015; Grieser et al., 2016; Liu, 2016), bank behaviour (Barth, 2016; Bushman et al., 2017; Luu et al., 2022; Nguyen et al., 2019), and merger and acquisition activity (Bereskin et al., 2018; Tremblay, 2020).

2.2.2.1 Performance

Prior literature suggests that strong types of corporate cultures can improve firms' performance since they can help to enhance the internal consistency of management and staff behaviours (see, e.g., Deal & Kennedy, 1982; Kotter & Heskett, 1992; O'Reilly & Chatman, 1996).

Given this, Sørensen (2002) explores the impact of having a strong corporate culture on the variability of firms' performance. Using a sample of firms from a broad variety of US industries, he hypothesizes and finds that firms with a strong corporate culture do indeed perform well during times of incremental change. However, he finds that relationship between corporate culture and firms' performance is weaker in more volatile environments.

Fiordelisi and Ricci (2014, 2021) also consider the implications of corporate culture to firms' performance by examining the role it plays in the relationship between firm performance and CEO turnover. In particular, they examine the question; "*what role does corporate culture play in the decision to fire a CEO after [a] poor performance?*". To answer this question, they adopt the competing values framework of culture proposed by Quinn and Rohrbaugh (1981, 1983), Cameron and Quinn (2011), and Cameron et al. (2014). They find that the probability of a CEO change is increased when firms exhibit greater levels of compete- and create-oriented corporate cultures. Further, their results suggest that the negative relationship between firm-specific performance and CEO turnover is strengthened by the control culture and diminished by the create culture. Finally, they observe that firms with a create culture are less likely to replace the CEO with an outsider as opposed to an internal promotion.

Guiso et al. (2015b) consider whether and why certain dimensions of corporate culture are related to firms' performance. They find that firms' declared values are irrelevant for predicting corporate outcomes; however, they note that when employees identify top managers as being more ethical and trustworthy (i.e., managers have more "integrity") firms' performance is indeed stronger. In addition, they find that when employees perceive managers as having more integrity the attractiveness of job offerings is increased and the degree of unionization among employees is decreased. Further, they explore how differences in firms' corporate governance structures affect the ability to sustain integrity as a corporate value. They find that while traditional measures of corporate governance do not seem to have an effect, privately held firms are better able to sustain integrity compared to publicly listed companies.

Also examining the role that corporate culture plays in relation to firms' performance, Mironov (2015) explores the relationship between a culture of managerial corruption, as indicated by managements' propensity to corrupt (PTC), and firm performance. Using data on Moscow traffic violations, he constructs the PTC of every licensed driver in Moscow. Assuming that some traffic violations were not recorded due to bribe-taking activity, Mironov constructs individual PTC by taking the difference between the expected and actual number of recorded traffic violations, given observed driver characteristics. Following this, they determine the PTC for the top management of over 58,000 privately held firms and find that a one standard deviation increase in managements' PTC corresponds to a 3.6% increase in income diversion among firms. Interestingly, given the previous results of Guiso et al. (2015b), he finds that firms with more corrupt managers in fact significantly outperform their less corrupt counterparts.

2.2.2.2 Firm Value

Grennan (2019), using the O'Reilly et al. (1991, 1996, 2014) model of corporate culture, shows that corporate culture is an important channel through which shareholder governance is able to affect firm value. In particular, she finds that greater shareholder governance significantly increases results-orientation but lessens customer-orientation, integrity, and collaboration. Furthermore, consistent with a positive link between shareholder governance and firm value, she finds that stronger shareholder governance increases tangible financial results in the short term. However, she finds that by focusing on the tangible aspects of the firm's performance, the firm's intangible assets associated with customer satisfaction and employee integrity declines, and this partially reverses the gains from greater results-orientation. She argues that these results are consistent with a model of multitasking where stronger governance encourages managers to focus on easy-to-observe short-term targets at the expense of the harder-to-measure intangibles, even though to do so is not in the long-run interest of the firm.

Likewise, Au et al. (2019) identify employee flexibility as an important dimension of corporate culture that leads to higher firm value. Further, they note that this is particularly true for those firms that are exposed to high exogenous risk. In particular, they estimate firms' employee flexibility scores using a textual analysis of job reviews published by a career intelligence website for a sample of S&P 1500 firms. They find that firms with a strong employee flexibility score earn abnormally high stock returns. Moreover, consistent with their hypothesis that firms with proactive and resilient employees respond best to unexpected situations, they find that the benefits of greater employee flexibility are concentrated on those firms with an elevated exposure to systematic risk and in periods of policy uncertainty. Also, they find that firms with a culture of flexibility have higher gross profitability. All told, their results suggest that a culture of employee flexibility is valuable, but market participants do not fully value this intangible asset.

2.2.2.3 Earnings Manipulation

Considering the impact of firm's culture on earnings manipulation, Benmelech and Frydman (2015) explore how personal traits of CEOs can help to shape the corporate culture and effect that this can have on firms' propensity to commit financial fraud. To achieve this, they take advantage of exogenous variation in the propensity to serve in the military (see, for example, Angrist, 1990, 1991, 1998) and find that military service is associated with conservative corporate policies and ethical behaviour. In particular, they find that CEOs with military service pursue lower levels of corporate R&D investment and are less likely to be involved in fraudulent corporate activity. Further, they find that firms which have Military CEOs have superior performance during industry downturns. Taken together, their finding suggests that CEOs with military service are able to shape the corporate environment and firm outcomes.

Furthermore, Biggerstaff et al. (2015) explore the ability of management to shape corporate culture and the implications that this can have on fraudulent activities by examining the culture of firms' top executives and whether this affects corporate malfeasance. To do this, they explore the relationship between those firm CEOs who personally benefit from options backdating (i.e., "suspect CEOs") and various forms of corporate misbehaviour and find that such CEOs are more likely to engage in financial fraud and to overstate earnings. Thus, they argue that whether CEOs personally benefit from options backdating is suggestive of an unethical corporate culture. Further, they find that private companies are more likely to be acquired by suspect CEOs and that this is possible in an effort to hide the frauds that such CEOs commit. Also, they note that when suspect CEOs make acquisitions the market response is more muted. They also find that the relationship between suspect CEOs and corporate misbehaviour is acuter for externally hired CEOs and this is consistent with outside CEOs having a greater ability to help shape firms' corporate culture (Hambrick & Mason, 1984). Importantly, they point out that the cost of such corporate misbehaviours is reflected in larger stock price declines/crashes during market corrections and increased CEO turnover rates.

Focusing on the implications of corporate culture to financial fraud, Braguinsky and Mityakov (2015) consider differences in corporate culture between multinational corporations and privately held domestic firms in Russia. They note that firms from developed countries usually have a culture of transparency and that this is in contrast with firms from transition economies, such as Russia, where a culture of hiding and insider dealing persists. To examine whether firms' corporate culture of transparency affects firms' proclivity to commit fraud, they make use of Russian administrative data on reported earnings and the market values of cars. Based on the intuition that reported earnings can be more easily falsified relative to car values in Moscow, they measure transparency as the difference in employees' reported earnings and car values. Using this measure of transparency, they find that the employees' earnings reported by foreign-owned firms are, on average, four times higher than those reported by domestic firms for employees with the same car values. Further, they show that closer ties with multinational firms lead to increased wage reporting transparency by privately held Russian companies. Also, they find a positive relationship between a corporate culture of transparency and increased hiring from multinational firms.

Likewise, Davidson et al. (2015) examine the influence of corporate culture on financial reporting by considering how executives' behaviour external to the workplace is related to financial reporting risk. In particular, they explore whether executives' ownership of luxury goods, including expensive cars, boats, real estate, etc., (their "frugality") and whether they have prior legal infractions predicts fraudulent activity and material mistakes in corporate reporting. They find that CEOs and CFOs who have a legal record are more likely to engage in fraudulent reporting. However, they find no relationship between executives' frugality and their likelihood to engage in fraudulent corporate reporting. Instead, they note that less frugal CEOs generally administer over a relatively weak internal control environment that is characterized by a comparatively high likelihood of fraud being committed by others. They also find that unintentional material reporting mistakes are also more likely when CEOs are less frugal. Further, they find that cultural changes that are consistent with an increased risk of fraud are associated with less frugal CEOs.

Moreover, DeBacker et al. (2015) explore how corporate cultural norms affect illicit corporate activities. Using confidential US data obtained from Internal Revenue Service (IRS) audits and Corruption Perception Index (CPI) published by Transparency International, they find that foreign-owned/controlled US-based firms are more likely to evade taxes when the owners are from countries that have higher levels of corruption norms. They also note that this effect is more pronounced among smaller firms and is decreasing in firm size. Furthermore, they find that enforcement efforts aimed at reducing tax evasion are less effective in corporations whose owners are from corrupt countries.

What's more, Liu (2016) considers the role played by corporate culture in influencing corporate misconduct. Using a large sample of US publicly listed firm-year observations, she examines whether a firm's corruption culture influences corporate misbehaviour. To measure corruption culture, she adopts the epidemiological approach as described in Fernández (2011), where it is assumed that when individuals emigrate to a new country, their prior cultural values, norms, and beliefs travel with them and are passed down to their descendants (Guiso et al., 2015b). Thus, corruption culture is proxied as the average corruption values for all insiders, where individuals' corruption values are based on the corruption index in the insiders' country of ancestry identified using their surnames (Lauderdale & Kestenbaum, 2000). Using this measure, she finds that firms with high corruption culture are more likely to engage in earnings management, accounting fraud, option backdating, and opportunistic insider trading. Further, she finds evidence that corruption culture operates both as a selection mechanism and by having a direct effect on individual behaviour.

In a recent and thought-provoking paper, Grieser et al. (2016) explore the effects of firms' culture on earnings manipulation by moving beyond the self-reported measures of integrity used in previous studies (see e.g., Guiso et al., 2015b), to a measure based on individual employee action. Specifically, they use the frequency of employees' decision to register for, and use, AshleyMadison.com, a website that facilitates extramarital affairs, as a measure of integrity. They find that in those firms that score low on integrity, as their employees have a high number of active accounts with AshleyMadison.com, are associated with a greater probability of SEC enforcement actions for accounting misstatements, lower corporate ethics ratings by external analysts, and a greater propensity for tax-avoidance. However, they also report that such firms also have higher research and development output, more patents and patent citations, and greater patent diversity, thereby suggesting a link between a lack of integrity and higher levels of creativity.

Bhandari et al. (2017) examine the effect of firms' corporate culture on earnings management practices. To quantify culture, they follow past studies (e.g., Fiordelisi & Ricci, 2014, 2021) by adopting the competing values framework and implementing a textual analysis of firms' 10-K filings for a large sample of US firms. They measure firms' earnings management practices using an accruals-based model of earnings management, real activities-based model of earnings management, and the presence of a GAAP violation. They find that firms with collaboration (competition) oriented corporate cultures are more (less) likely to manage earnings, while firms with the control culture are more prone to engage in real activities-based earnings manipulation only. Further, they find that auditors price the risk of culture-driven earnings manipulation since firms with collaboration and control culture face on average higher audit fees, while since firms with the competition culture face on average lower audit fees.

2.2.2.4 *Bank Behaviour*

In an examination of the relevance of corporate culture to bank behaviour, Barth (2016) utilizes the competing values framework of corporate culture proposed by Quinn and Rohrbaugh (1981, 1983), Cameron and Quinn (2011), and Cameron et al. (2014). In particular, following the theoretical literature which suggests that corporate culture plays an important role in the sorting process of workers into firms (see e.g., Friebel & Giannetti, 2009; Van den Steen, 2010a, 2010b), he examines whether banks that differ in terms of their corporate culture also differ in terms of the compensation schemes that they deploy, plausibly in an effort to attract a particular type of staff. Consistent with this, he finds that at banks with a stronger competition culture CEOs' total compensation have a larger proportion of variable elements. Furthermore, investigating the impact of corporate culture on banks' risk-taking and performance, he finds that banks with more competition culture are associated with higher levels of credit risk and higher buy-and-hold stock market return.

Furthermore, Bushman et al. (2017) explore the role of corporate culture in banking by considering whether and how bank CEO materialism influences bank culture. In particular, they measure CEO materialism using a revealed preference approach similar to that previously adopted by Davidson et al., (2015) for nonfinancial firms which suggest that executives' personal ownership of luxury goods can be viewed as a manifestation of relatively high materialism. Consistent with the "Upper Echelons Theory" (see Hambrick & Mason, 1984), they expect these manifestations of CEO materialism to have implications for the behaviour of non-CEO executives. Specifically, they examine the extent to which bank CEOs exert influence on the corporate cultures of banks by exploring how bank CEO materialism has evolved over time. Further, they explore how bank CEO materialism is associated with observed risk management policies, the behaviour of non-CEO executives and bank tail risk. They find that the percentage of banks run by materialistic CEOs has increased during the 1994–2004 period and that this has coincided with a significant amount of deregulation in the banking industry. Moreover, using an index that reflects the strength of the bank's risk management functions (RMI), they find that RMI is significantly lower for banks with materialistic CEOs. Further, they provide evidence consistent with non-CEO executives in such banks being more aggressive in exploiting inside trading opportunities around government interventions during the global financial crisis (GFC). Finally, they find that banks with materialistic CEOs have considerably more downside tail risk compared to those banks with more frugal (i.e., less materialistic) CEOs and that the difference between downside tail risk for these two groups of banks increased significantly during the GFC.

In a related study, Nguyen et al. (2019) explore the effect of banks' corporate culture on bank lending decisions. Using the CVF, they find that compete culture banks are associated with riskier lending behaviour. That is, these banks have higher approval rates, lower borrower quality, and fewer covenant requirements. Further, these banks exhibit higher loan growth but incur larger loan losses. As a result, they find that such banks make greater contributions to overall systemic risk. However, they find the opposite result among banks with the control culture.

2.2.2.5 *Mergers and Acquisitions*

Recent papers in finance have also studied the impact of corporate culture on the likelihood and success of M&A activity. For instance, Tremblay (2020) uses a textual analysis of firms' annual reports to develop an estimate of the cultural similarity of combining firms. In particular, she quantifies the dimensions of corporate culture by counting the frequency of words in a firm's 10-K filing that correspond to the competing values framework (Cameron et al., 2014). Tremblay (2020) then measures the cultural similarity between two merging firms using the correspondence of these word counts. Based on this measure, she finds that when the cultural distance between the firms is greater, this leads to higher synergistic gains post-merger, but only when the acquiring firm has a stronger culture than that of its target. Further, she finds that the synergy gains are concentrated among deals where the acquirer's values are not antagonistic to those of the target firm.

Similarly, Bereskin et al. (2018) examine the effects of corporate cultural similarity on M&A decisions and outcomes. They hypothesize that the similarity between two firms in terms of corporate social responsibility (CSR) practices reflects cultural similarity between them and that this is positively related to the probability that such firms will form merger pairs, and that post-merger performance will be superior. They note that an essential feature of this hypothesis is that firms with analogous CSR behaviour have similar corporate cultures and will experience less post-merger integration challenges. To measure of CSR similarity, they adopt a textual analysis-based approach where they apply Jaffe's (1986) distance measure a given pair of firms' CSR policies obtained from the KLD database. Using this measure of firms' CSR similarity, they find that firms with similar corporate culture are indeed more likely to merge. Furthermore, consistent with the notion that cultural similarity eases post-deal integration, they find that these mergers are associated with greater synergies, superior long-run operating performance, and fewer write-offs.

2.3 Summary

In this chapter, we define the term culture as a broad, inherently complex, and intangible concept that reflects group values and decision-making environment. In so doing, we introduce it as an important, economically valid, and significant empirical construct, particularly at the corporate level, that is of increasing relevance and interest to researchers in finance and economics. We then review a wide array of taxonomies for corporate (i.e., organizational) culture, where we focus on those better documented theoretical frameworks that have emerged in the rich organization behaviour literature on the theme.

Following this, we supplement our understanding of the implication of firms' corporate culture by perusing and highlighting the key findings from the empirical finance-related literature that documents the role of firms' corporate culture as an important explanatory variable for explaining firms' economic policies and outcomes. And, as we have seen, this past literature suggests that corporate culture impacts firms' level of performance (Fiordelisi & Ricci, 2014, 2021; Guiso et al., 2015a; Mironov 2015), firm value (Au et al., 2019; Benmelech & Frydman, 2015; Grennan, 2019), earnings manipulation activity (Benmelech & Frydman, 2015; Bhandari et al., 2017; Biggerstaff et al., 2015; Braguinsky & Mityakov, 2015; Davidson et al., 2015; DeBacker et al., 2015; Grieser et al., 2016; Liu, 2016), bank behaviour (Barth, 2016; Bushman et al., 2017; Nguyen et al., 2019), and merger and acquisition activity (Bereskin et al., 2018; Tremblay, 2020), among many other outcomes.

References

Ahern, K. R., Daminelli, D., & Fracassi, C. (2015). Lost in Translation? The Effect of Cultural Values on Mergers Around the World. *Journal of Financial Economics, 117*, 165–189.

Akerlof, G. A. (1980). A Theory of Social Custom, of Which Unemployment May Be One Consequence. *The Quarterly Journal of Economics, 94*, 749–775.

Andreou, P. C., Fiordelisi, F., Harris, T., & Philip, D. (2021). Institutional Ownership and Firms' Thrust to Compete. *British Journal of Management, 33*, 1346–1370.

Angrist, J. (1990). Lifetime Earnings and the Vietnam Era Draft Lottery: Evidence from Social Security Administrative Records. *The American Economic Review, 80*, 313–336.

Angrist, J. (1991). The Draft Lottery and Voluntary Enlistment in the Vietnam Era. *Journal of the American Statistical Association, 86*, 584–595.

Angrist, J. (1998). Estimating the Labor Market Impact of Voluntary Military Service Using Social Security Data on Military Applicants. *Econometrica, 66*, 249–288.

Arrow, K. (1972). Some Mathematical Models of Race in the Labor Market. In A. H. Pascal (Ed.), *Racial Discrimination in Economic Life*. Lexington Books.

Au, S. Y., Dong, M., & Tremblay, A. (2019). *When Culture Matters-Corporate Flexibility and Stock Returns*. Available at SSRN 2883353.

Barth, A. (2016). *The Role of Corporate Culture in the Financial Industry*. Available at SSRN 2707078.

Becker, G. S. (1957). *The Economics of Discrimination*. University of Chicago Press.

Benabou, R., & Tirole, J. (2003). Intrinsic and Extrinsic Motivation. *The Review of Economic Studies, 70*, 489–520.

Benabou, R., & Tirole, J. (2011). Identity, Morals, and Taboos: Beliefs as Assets. *The Quarterly Journal of Economics, 126*, 805–855.

Benmelech, E., & Frydman, C. (2015). Military CEOs. *Journal of Financial Economics, 117*, 43–59.

Bereskin, F. L., Byun, S. K., Officer, M. S., & Oh, J. M. (2018). The Effect of Cultural Similarity on Mergers and Acquisitions: Evidence from Corporate Social Responsibility. *Journal of Financial and Quantitative Analysis, 53*, 1995–2039.

Bhandari, A., Mammadov, B., Thevenot, M., & Vakilzadeh, S. H. (2017). *The Invisible Hand: Corporate Culture and Its Implications for Earnings Management* (Working Paper). Warrington College of Business, Gainesville, FL.

Biggerstaff, L., Cicero, D. C., & Puckett, A. (2015). Suspect CEOs, Unethical Culture, and Corporate Misbehavior. *Journal of Financial Economics, 117*, 98–121.

Braguinsky, S., & Mityakov, S. (2015). Foreign Corporations and the Culture of Transparency: Evidence from Russian Administrative Data. *Journal of Financial Economics, 117*, 139–164.

Bushman, R. M., Davidson, R. H., Dey, A., & Smith, A. (2017). Bank CEO Materialism: Risk Controls, Culture and Tail Risk. *Journal of Accounting and Economics, 65*, 191–220.

Callen, J. L., & Fang, X. (2015). Religion and Stock Price Crash Risk. *Journal of Financial and Quantitative Analysis, 50*, 169–195.

Callen, J. L., Morel, M., & Richardson, G. (2011). Do Culture and Religion Mitigate Earnings Management? Evidence from a Cross-country Analysis. *International Journal of Disclosure and Governance, 8*, 103–121.

Cameron, K. S., & Quinn, R. E. (2011). *Diagnosing and Changing Organizational Culture: Based on the Competing Values Framework*. Wiley.

Cameron, K., Quinn, R., DeGraff, J., & Thakor, A. (2014). *Competing Values Leadership*. Edward Elgar Publishing.

Chui, A. C., Titman, S., & Wei, K. J. (2010). Individualism and Momentum Around the World. *The Journal of Finance, 65*, 361–392.

Cremer, J. (1993). Corporate Culture and Shared Knowledge. *Industrial and Corporate Change, 2*, 351–386.

Cronqvist, H., Low, A., & Nilsson, M. (2007). *Does Corporate Culture Matter for Firm Policies?* (Working Paper), Fisher College of Business, Columbus, OH.

Dang, T., Faff, R., Luong, H., & Nguyen, L. (2018). *Individualistic Cultures Crash Risk*. Available at SSRN 2711204.

Davidson, R., Dey, A., & Smith, A. (2015). Executives' "off-the-job" Behaviour, Corporate Culture, and Financial Reporting Risk. *Journal of Financial Economics, 117*, 5–28.

Deal, T. E., & Kennedy, A. A. (1982). *Corporate Cultures: The Rites and Rituals of Organizational Life*. Addison-Wesley.

DeBacker, J., Heim, B. T., & Tran, A. (2015). Importing Corruption Culture from Overseas: Evidence from Corporate Tax Evasion in the United States. *Journal of Financial Economics, 117*, 122–138.

Denison, D. R. (1990). *Corporate Culture and Organizational Effectiveness*. Wiley.

Doupnik, T. S. (2008). Influence of Culture on Earnings Management: A Note. *Abacus, 44*, 317–340.

Erhard, W., Jensen, M., & Zaffron, S. (2017). *Integrity: A Positive Model That Incorporates the Normative Phenomena of Morality, Ethics and Legality*. Available at SSRN 1542759.

Eun, C. S., Wang, L., & Xiao, S. C. (2015). Culture and R2. *Journal of Financial Economics, 115*, 283–303.

Fernández, R. (2011). Does Culture Matter? In J. Benhabib, A. Bisin, M. O. Jackson (Eds.), *Handbook of Social Economics*. North Holland Publishing.

Fiordelisi, F., & Ricci, O. (2014). Corporate Culture and CEO Turnover. *Journal of Corporate Finance, 28*, 66–82.

Fiordelisi, F., & Ricci, O. (2021). Corrigendum to "Corporate Culture and CEO Turnover". *Journal of Corporate Finance, 70*, 102064.

Friebel, G., & Giannetti, M. (2009). Fighting for Talent: Risk-Taking, Corporate Volatility and Organisation Change. *The Economic Journal, 119*, 1344–1373.

Giannetti, M., & Yafeh, Y. (2012). Do Cultural Differences Between Contracting Parties Matter? Evidence from Syndicated Bank Loans. *Management Science, 58*, 365–383.

Graham, J. R., Harvey, C. R., Grennen, J., & Rajgopal, S. (2022). Corporate Culture: Evidence from the Field. *Journal of Financial Economics, 146*, 552–593.

Gray, S. J. (1988). Towards a Theory of Cultural Influence on the Development of Accounting Systems Internationally. *Abacus, 24*, 1–15.

Grennan, J. (2019). *A Corporate Culture Channel: How Increased Shareholder Governance Reduces Firm Value*. Available at SSRN 2345384.

Grieser, W. D., Kapadia, N., Li, R., & Simonov, A. (2016). *Fifty Shades of Corporate Culture*. Available at SSRN 2843776.

Guiso, L., Sapienza, P., & Zingales, L. (2006). Does Culture Affect Economic Outcomes? *The Journal of Economic Perspectives, 20*, 23–48.

Guiso, L., Sapienza, P., & Zingales, L. (2008). Trusting the Stock Market. *The Journal of Finance, 63*, 2557–2600.

Guiso, L., Sapienza, P., & Zingales, L. (2009). Cultural Biases in Economic Exchange? *The Quarterly Journal of Economics, 124*, 1095–1131.

Guiso, L., Sapienza, P., & Zingales, L. (2015a). Corporate Culture, Societal Culture, and Institutions. *American Economic Review, 105*, 336–339.

Guiso, L., Sapienza, P., & Zingales, L. (2015b). The Value of Corporate Culture. *Journal of Financial Economics, 117*, 60–76.

Hambrick, D., & Mason, P. (1984). Upper Echelons: The Organization as a Reflection of its Top Managers. *Academy of Management Review, 9*, 193–206.

Handy, C. B. (1976). *Understanding Organizations*. Oxford University Press.

Harrison, R. (1972). *Organization's Character*. Harvard Business Review.

Hermalin, B. E. (2001). Leadership and Corporate Culture. In C. A. Cooper, S. Cartwright & P. C. Earley (Eds.), *The International Handbook of Organizational Culture and Climate*. Blackwell Publishers.

Hofstede, G. (1980). Culture and Organizations. *International Studies of Management and Organization, 10*, 15–41.

Hofstede, G. (2001). *Cultural Consequences*. Sage Publications.

Hofstede, G. (2011). *Dimensionalizing Cultures: The Hofstede Model in Context*. Online Readings in Psychology and Culture. Available at https://doi.org/10.9707/2307-0919.1014.

Hofstede, G., Neuijen, B., Ohayv, D. D., & Sanders, G. (1990). Measuring Organizational Cultures: A Qualitative and Quantitative Study Across Twenty Cases. *Administrative Science Quarterly, 35*, 286–316.

Jaffe, A. B. (1986). Technological Opportunity and Spill-Overs of R&D: Evidence from Firms' Patents, Profits and Market Value. *American Economic Review, 76*, 984–1001.

Johnson, G. (1988). Rethinking Incrementalism. *Strategic Management Journal, 9*, 75–91.

Kanagaretnam, K., Lim, C. Y., & Lobo, G. J. (2013). Influence of National Culture on Accounting Conservatism and Risk-Taking in the Banking Industry. *The Accounting Review, 89*, 1115–1149.

Kotter, J. P., & Heskett, J. (1992). *Corporate Culture and Performance*. The Free Press.

Kreps, D. M. (1990). Corporate Culture and Economic Theory. In J. E. Alt & K. A. Shepsle (Eds.), *Perspectives on Positive Political Economy*. Cambridge University Press.

Lauderdale, D., & Kestenbaum, B. (2000). Asian American Ethnic Identification by Surname. *Population Research and Policy Review, 19*, 283–300.

Li, K., Griffin, D., Yue, H., & Zhao, L. (2013). How Does Culture Influence Corporate Risk-Taking? *Journal of Corporate Finance, 23*, 1–22.

Liu, X. (2016). Corruption Culture and Corporate Misconduct. *Journal of Financial Economics, 122*, 307–327.

Lo, A. W. (2015). *The Gordon Gekko Effect: The Role of Culture in the Financial Industry*. National Bureau of Economic Research.

Luu, H., Nguyen, L., & Wilson, J. O. S. (2022). *Organizational Culture, Competition and Bank Loan Loss Provisions*. Available at SSRN 3921043.

Mironov, M. (2015). Should One Hire a Corrupt CEO in a Corrupt Country? *Journal of Financial Economics, 117*, 29–42.

Nguyen, D. D., Hagendorff, J., & Eshraghi, A. (2018). Does a CEO's Cultural Heritage Affect Performance Under Competitive Pressure? *The Review of Financial Studies, 31*, 97–141.

Nguyen, D. D., Nguyen, L., & Sila, V. (2019). Does Corporate Culture Affect Bank Risk-Taking? Evidence from Loan-Level Data. *British Journal of Management, 30*, 106–133.

O'Reilly, C. A., & Chatman, J. A. (1996). Culture as Social Control: Corporations, Cults, and Commitment. In B. M. Staw & L. L. Cummings (Eds.), *Research in Organizational Behavior: An Annual Series of Analytical Essays and Critical Reviews*. Elsevier Science/JAI Press.

O'Reilly, C. A., Chatman, J., & Caldwell, D. F. (1991). People and Organizational Culture: A Profile Comparison Approach to Assessing Person-Organization Fit. *Academy of Management Journal, 34*, 487–516.

O'Reilly, C. A. I., Chatman, J., & Caldwell, D. F. (1996). People and Organizational Culture: A Profile Comparison Approach to Assessing Person-Organization Fit. *Academy of Management Journal, 34*, 487–516.

O'Reilly, C. A., III., Caldwell, D. F., Chatman, J. A., & Doerr, B. (2014). The Promise and Problems of Organizational Culture: CEO Personality, Culture, and Firm Performance. *Group and Organization Management, 39*, 595–625.

Quinn, R. E., & Rohrbaugh, J. (1981). A Competing Values Approach to Organizational Effectiveness. *Public Productivity Review, 5*, 122–140.

Quinn, R. E., & Rohrbaugh, J. (1983). A Spatial Model of Effectiveness Criteria: Towards a Competing Values Approach to Organizational Analysis. *Management Science, 29*, 363–377.

Reynolds, P. D. (1986). Organizational Culture as Related to Industry, Position and Performance: A Preliminary Report. *Journal of Management Studies, 23*, 333–345.

Schein, E. H. (1990). Organizational Culture: What It Is and How to Change It. In *Human Resource Management in International Firms*. Palgrave Macmillan.

Schein, E. H. (1992). *Organizational Culture and Leadership: A Dynamic View*. Jossey-Bass.

Schwartz, S. H. (1992). Universals in the Content and Structure of Values: Theoretical Advances and Empirical Tests in 20 Countries. In M. Zanna (Ed.), *Advances in Experimental Social Psychology*. Academic Press.

Schwartz, S. H. (1994). Beyond Individualism and Collectivism: New Cultural Dimensions of Values. In U. Kim, H. C. Triandis, C. Kagit-cibasi, S. C. Choi, & G. Yoon (Eds.), *Individualism and Collectivism: Theory, Method, and Applications*. Sage.

Sørensen, J. B. (2002). The Strength of Corporate Culture and the Reliability of Firm Performance. *Administrative Science Quarterly, 47*, 70–91.

Thakor, A. V. (2015). *Corporate Culture in Banking*. Available at SSRN 2565514.

Thakor, A. V. (2020). Ethics, Culture and Higher Purpose in Banking: Post-Crisis Governance Developments. *International Journal of Central Banking*.

Tremblay, A. (2020). *Cultural Differences, Synergies and Mergers and Acquisitions*. Available at SSRN 2895110.

Van den Steen, E. (2010a). On the Origin of Shared Beliefs (and Corporate Culture). *The RAND Journal of Economics, 41*, 617–648.

Van den Steen, E. (2010b). Culture Clash: The Costs and Benefits of Homogeneity. *Management Science, 56*, 1718–1738.

Wang, Y., Farag, H., & Ahmad, W. (2021). Corporate Culture and Innovation: A Tale from an Emerging Market. *British Journal of Management, 32*, 1121–1140.

Zingales, L. (2015). The 'Cultural Revolution' in Finance. *Journal of Financial Economics, 117*, 1–4.

CHAPTER 3

Literature Review: What Is Textual Analysis, and Can We Use It to Measure Corporate Culture?

3.1 Introduction

The textual analysis approach also sometimes referred to as content analysis, computational linguistics, information retrieval, natural language processing, etc., refers to the systematic and objective quantification of the semantic content contained in a body of text. This notion of the parsing text to discover patterns allows for the unearthing of valuable information in text and has a long history and has been applied in many different contexts and disciplines. For instance, in a recent comprehensive review on the topic, Loughran and McDonald (2016) note that in the 1300s Catholic priest to provide indexes of common biblical phrases. However, Loughran and McDonald (2016) point out that it wasn't until the 1960s that textual analysis achieved wider popularity with Mosteller and Wallace's (1964) reliance on it to determine the disputed authorship of the Federalist Papers.

In the years since, the publication of a large corpus of unstructured textual information that is available online in news articles, conference calls, Security and Exchange Commission (SEC) filings, and text generated by social media outlets like Twitter and Facebook, coupled with the significant increases in computational power and the accuracy of statistical parsing techniques has led to researchers in finance and related fields exploring whether textual analysis can be used to extract valuable information from these sources (see for example, Andreou et al., 2020, 2021;

T. Harris, *Competition Culture and Corporate Finance*,
https://doi.org/10.1007/978-3-031-30156-8_3

Antweiler & Frank, 2004; Audi et al., 2016; Bushman et al., 2016; Das & Chen, 2007; Fiordelisi & Ricci, 2014, 2021; Fiordelisi et al., 2019; Guo et al., 2022; Hoberg & Phillips, 2010, 2016; Hoberg et al., 2014; Kearney & Liu, 2014; Li, 2008, 2010a, 2010b, 2010c; Li et al., 2013a, 2013b, 2020; Loughran & McDonald, 2011, 2016; Loughran et al., 2009; Luu et al., 2022; Nguyen et al., 2018, 2019; Tetlock, 2007).

Of particular importance to researchers in finance is whether the corporate disclosures provide economically meaningful information. A relationship between the textual content of firms' corporate disclosures and firms' economic outcomes is plausible since it is likely that information contained in such documents provide insights into managements' operating philosophies, societal norms, design characteristics, incentives, and private information sets, that in turn guide the data generation process which creates the financial numbers. Thus, it is reasonable to expect that the textual information provided in corporate disclosures offers an important context for interpreting the financial data produced, and can be used to answer important research questions and test economically interesting hypotheses.

To be sure, the transmission of firm-specific qualitative information to the public has a paramount importance for the efficiency of stock markets (Feldman et al., 2010; Li, 2010a; Li & Ramesh, 2009), firm's information environment (Kothari et al., 2009), and the behaviour of investors and financial analysts (Lehavy et al., 2011; Miller, 2010). Textual disclosures do not only affect how investors react to and trade on the obtained information, but also reveal particular managerial characteristics (Li, 2010a, 2011), various management incentives (Simon, 1997), and firm's behaviour in a potentially litigious environment (Nelson & Pritchard, 2007). Hence, understanding the short- and long-run value of the firm through the prism of corporate disclosures among other pieces of firm-related text is of broad interest both to academics and practitioners and has become possible due to the technological breakthrough of textual analysis techniques. However, to date, the application of textual analysis to analyse a firm's corporate disclosures remains an emerging area in the finance literature. In the subsequent sections, we discuss the main techniques used and how these have been applied in finance-related research.

3.2 Textual Analysis Techniques and Applications

In this section, we discuss the techniques that are designed to extract relevant information from a body of text and explore how these tools have been applied. Generally, textual analysis can be thought of as a three-step process that involves (i) collecting text data, (ii) preparing and cleaning text data, and (iii) analysing text data. During the collecting phase, the researcher collates the necessary text data on firms from one or more of a varied range of sources (e.g., corporate disclosures, Twitter, web forms, etc.). After collecting the text data, which is unstructured in nature, the researcher pre-processes the text. This may involve converting words into lowercase so that capitalization is ignored, removing (or replacing) any URLs embedded in the document to ensure that the analysis is not biased due to web addresses, removing (or replacing) all non-words and punctuations, and trimming to a single space all white spaces (e.g., tabs and newlines). Finally, during the analysis phase, the researcher further processes the data using a variety of techniques to derive information from the body of text. Broadly speaking, such techniques can be divided into two approaches: namely, lexicon-based approaches and statistical learning approaches.

3.2.1 Lexicon-Based Approaches

3.2.1.1 Readability

Lexicon-based approaches rely on the direct use of the words contained in a body of text. One such methodology makes use of the quantity and complexity of these words to examine the ease with which an investor can read and understand the corporate disclosures. In so doing, these methods seek to quantify the readability of firms' corporate disclosures using an algorithm that produces a score based on the quantity and complexity of the words in each sentence in the text (see e.g., Bonsall et al., 2017; Li, 2008; Loughran & McDonald, 2014). Researchers document that firms with reports that are difficult to read tend to exhibit higher stock volatility, analyst dispersion, and earnings surprises. These implications are more likely to reflect the complexity of a firm's business.

Li (2008) introduces the first well-known measure of readability for 10-K reports; namely, the "Fog Index". This index is based on the average sentence length and the percentage of complex words (i.e., words with more than two syllables). They show that firms with difficult-to-read reports exhibit lower documented earnings. Following Li (2008), a large number of studies exploit the Fog Index and link it with capital investment efficiency (Biddle et al., 2009), small investors' trading behaviour (Miller, 2010), retail investors' ownership (Lawrence, 2013), and analyst coverage and dispersion (Lehavy et al., 2011).

However, the recent study of Loughran and McDonald (2014) identifies a number of weaknesses of the Fog Index and proposes a new easy to construct and intuitive measure of readability. In particular, they point out that the number of complex words and sentence length are negatively related to each other; hence, the Fog Index is likely to be misspecified. Furthermore, the definition of complex words used by Li (2008) is more likely to reflect the industry-specific component rather than the complexity of 10-K reports. For example, such words as "financial, company, operations, and management" can be easily digested by investors and do not reflect the difficult-to-interpret information in business documents. Hence, as an easy to replicate and straightforward proxy for readability, Loughran and McDonald (2014) introduce the natural logarithm of gross 10-K file size and show that it can serve as a good proxy.

Another measure of readability for financial reports was proposed by Bonsall et al. (2017). Particularly, they posit the "Bog Index", which consists of three multifaceted components (i) average sentence length scaled by a standard long sentence limit of 35 words, (ii) plain English style problems (frequent use of passive and hidden verbs, overwriting, legal terms, clichés) along with word difficulty (heavy words, specialist terms), and (iii) good writing attributes (frequent usage of names and interesting words). The important finding of the paper is that among all readability measures, the Bog Index has the strongest effect on post-10-K filing stock volatility.

3.2.1.2 *Dictionary Methods*

Dictionary methods seek to reduce the dimensionality of a body of text by assuming that the order and sequence of words, as well as the context of sentences, carry no meaningful information. Such methods are typically termed "bag-of-words" approaches and consist of parsing the texts into vectors of words and word counts and the construction of a "term-document matrix".

Using the "term-document matrix", a "mapping" algorithm is applied which allocates the words into different categories based on specifically developed word lists. Finally, following the literature on information retrieval, a term weighting scheme is routinely used to scale the raw word counts since these are likely to be strongly related to document length. Further, such term weighting schemes also account for the word frequency by putting less weight on commonly occurring words.

Target Words

The collection and processing of certain words in the text constitute one of the most parsimonious and powerful approaches to textual analysis. The advantage of this approach is its simplicity and a lower likelihood of extracting a misspecified proxy for a certain firm characteristic. For instance, Li et al. (2013a) derive a measure of firms' competition from 10-K reports by counting the number of occurrences of "competition", "competitor", "competitive", "compete", "competing" and then scaling this count by the total number of words in the 10-K filings.

Dictionaries and Word Lists

A collection of words with similar sentiment, tone, and/or meaning is typically called a "dictionary", "word lists", or "lexicon". Put another way, a dictionary is an array of words with common characteristics and interpretations that are intentionally created to determine a certain attribute of the report. The lexicon methodology is applied to the "term-document" matrix when counting the number of words pertaining to a certain lexicon category (e.g., words with positive, negative, or neutral meaning) relative to the total number of words in the document. This approach allows the researcher to gauge the tone and sentiment of a financial document, with, for example, a higher proportion of positive words in the file associated with a more optimistic tone of the report. The dictionary approach has several advantageous properties including the applicability to large samples, easy replicability by other researchers; however, it is clear that the success of any dictionary-based procedure in extracting the meaning from the text critically depends on the words selected for the dictionary (Li, 2010a; Loughran & McDonald, 2011).

The most frequently used dictionaries in finance for textual analysis are the Henry's (2008) word list, the Harvard's General Inquirer dictionaries, the Diction word list, and the Loughran and McDonald's (2011) word list. These dictionaries contain subcategories of words that share common thematic sentiments such as optimism, pessimism, uncertainty, constraints, pleasure, emotion, or pain. In the following sections, we will discuss each of these dictionaries, which are frequently used in finance to analyse the tone and sentiment of a body of text.

The Harvard's General Inquirer

The most popular set of dictionaries that have been widely used by researchers in finance due to their rich thematic vocabulary in multiple subcategories and availability are the Harvard's General Inquirer line of dictionaries. Tetlock (2007), in arguably one of the more innovative papers in this area, uses the Harvard IV-4's (Harvard Psychological Dictionary) positive and negative lexicon categories to examine the prospective impact on the stock market of negative and positive words found in the "Abreast of the Market" Wall Street Journal (WSJ) column. Specifically, in this study, Tetlock finds that when journalistic pessimism is high, this relates to both lower subsequent stock price returns and higher stock market volatility in later periods. What is more, he observes that the pressure on stock prices is not as a result of the "Abreast of the Market" WSJ column revealing new value relevant information; however, he suggests that the "Abreast of the Market" WSJ column is nevertheless a good proxy for investor sentiment. Following Tetlock's (2007) seminal work, a number of papers use the Harvard IV-4 dictionary among other word lists to measure the sentiment and tone of corporate disclosures, news articles, and other pieces of communication (see for example, Andreou et al., 2020, 2021; Da et al., 2015; Fiordelisi & Ricci, 2014, 2021; Fiordelisi et al., 2019; Hanley & Hoberg, 2010; Heston & Sinha, 2015; Hoberg & Phillips, 2010, 2016; Hoberg et al., 2014; Kearney & Liu, 2014; Kothari et al., 2009; Li et al., 2020; Loughran & McDonald, 2011, 2016; Luu et al., 2022; Nguyen et al., 2018, 2019; Tetlock et al., 2008).

For instance, using the Harvard IV-4 dictionary's word categories, Tetlock et al. (2008) conduct a textual analysis on news stories for several listed S&P 500 firms that appear in WSJ and the Dow Jones News Service. In this work, they find that a greater frequency of negative words in firm-specific news is associated with lower earnings in subsequent periods even after controlling for other well-known determinants of earnings such as prior period financial data and analyst forecasts. Likewise, Kothari et al. (2009) rely on the Harvard IV-4 dictionary's negative and positive word lists to analyse the information content of disclosures made by firms, analysts, and various media outlets. They find that the tone of such content is related to both the volatility of stock returns and analyst forecast error dispersion. In particular, they find that a more positive tone in such disclosures is associated with lower stock return volatility and analyst forecast error dispersion. Conversely, they find that when the tone of news content in such disclosures is negative, that this is associated with significantly higher stock return volatility and analyst forecast error dispersion.

Furthermore, Hanley and Hoberg (2010) use the Harvard IV-4 dictionary's negative and positive word categories to explore the impact on future stock price returns of the tone of the initial prospectus form (Form S-1) for a large sample of initial public offerings (IPOs). They find that the tone of this form impacts stock price returns on the first day of trading. Specifically, they locate in the "Risk Factors" section of the initial prospectus form, a link between firms with an increasingly positive score on their net tone measure, computed as the percentage of positive tone words minus the percentage of negative tone words, and lower stock price returns on the first day. Furthermore, they find a positive relationship between this measure of net tone and smaller changes in the offer price revision. Their finding suggests that investors, likely reassured that managers and underwriters face strict legal penalties for material misstatements when making IPOs, take a favourable view of the content contained in the initial prospectus form, and in particular the Risk Factors section, when the tone of such disclosure is positive.

Da et al. (2015) use the Harvard IV-4 dictionary (and the Lasswell Value Dictionary) to construct their Financial and Economic Attitudes Revealed by Search (FEARS) index. They argue that the FEARS index is able to capture investor sentiment. They operationalize the FEARS index by collating the volume of queries documented by Google Trends that relate to the Harvard IV-4 dictionary words that are indicative of economic sentiment. They find the FEARS index is able to predict short-term return reversal, temporary increases in stock price volatility, and mutual fund outflows from mutual funds to bonds and other safe havens.

Similarly, Heston and Sinha (2015) adopt the Harvard IV-4 dictionary's negative and positive word classifications to examine the effect of the sentiment of news articles published by Thomson Reuters and stock price returns. Using a sample of more than 900,000 articles, they find that a higher score on their net tone measure, calculated as positive tone words frequencies minus negative tone words frequencies, relates to high stock price returns for the specific firms mentioned in such articles for up to one to two days after the article has been published. On the other hand, they find that firms with greater negative sentiment news articles experience lower short-term stock price returns.

The use of the Harvard IV-4 dictionary's negative and positive word classification to detect sentiment and tone in finance-related research is not without its critics. Some researchers suggest that more accurate general word lists are appropriate when seeking to capture the tone of a document (see for example Davis et al., 2012; Rogers et al., 2011). Further, some (see for example Li, 2010a; Loughran & McDonald, 2011) suggest that the Harvard IV-4 dictionary word list is not appropriate in the context of textual analysis applied to documents related to financial information since this word list was not designed to deal with this specialized subject area. In particular, Loughran and McDonald (2011) argue that the Harvard IV-4 word list misclassifies as negative words such as "cost", "depreciation", and "liability". Furthermore, researchers find that about 75% of negative words according to the Harvard dictionary classification are typically not negative in the case of financial disclosures. For example, words such as "mine, cancer, tire or capital" tend to describe industry-specific characteristics of the firm rather than indicate a negative tone, as suggested by Harvard list, whereas such words as "felony, litigation, misstatement or unanticipated", which are clearly associated with negative sentiment, are missing in the Harvard IV-4 lexicon. Testing whether the proposed word classification categories indeed capture the tone of 10-K reports, Loughran and McDonald (2011) document strong relations between the constructed word lists and next-day stock returns, trading volume, return volatility, and earnings surprises. For instance, portfolio sorts based on the frequency of Harvard IV-4 negative words in 10-K filings do not generate a significant predictability for 10-K filing returns, whereas using the suggested financial negative word list to rank firms produces a strong return pattern.

As a result, word list other than the Harvard IV-4 dictionary has been developed and used in finance research to assess the sentiment or tone of news releases, corporate disclosures, and other pieces of communication pertaining to the firm (Davis et al., 2012; Loughran & McDonald, 2011, 2016; Price et al., 2012; Rogers et al., 2011).

The Diction Word List

In a critique of the Harvard IV-4 word list-based approach to measuring the sentiment of financial documents, Rogers et al. (2011) suggest that the Diction Optimism and Pessimism ("the Diction") word list, although not created with financial text in mind, nevertheless allows for a more suitable measure of tone in firms' corporate releases. In their paper, Rogers et al. rely on this word list to study the relationship between net tone and the likelihood of shareholder litigation. They find that firms with higher positive net tone (i.e., more optimism), measured as the percentage of Diction optimism words minus the percentage of Diction pessimism words, in their earnings announcements experience an increased likelihood of subsequent shareholders litigation action.

Similarly, Davis et al. (2012) use the Diction Optimism and Pessimism word list to explore the relationship between firms' earnings announcements and performance as measured by return on assets (ROA) in subsequent quarters. They find that firms with a more positive net tone in earnings releases achieve significantly higher subsequent ROA.

What is more, Davis and Tama-Sweet (2012) complement the prior studies of Rogers et al. (2011) and Davis et al. (2012) and find an association between the net tone (using the Diction word list) of the management discussion and analysis (MD&A) section of firm's 10-K and ROA in subsequent periods. In particular, they find that the more negative (i.e., more pessimistic) this section of a firm's 10-K is, the poorer ROA results are for the firm.

As with the use of the Harvard IV-4 dictionary word list, several authors in finance criticize the practice of using the Diction Optimism and Pessimism word list to measure tone since this list has not been developed to specifically deal with financial information (Li, 2010a; Loughran & McDonald, 2011). Loughran and McDonald (2011) suggest that in fact some Diction word list positive (optimism) words, for example "necessary", "power", and "trust" do not usually have a positive connotation in financial disclosures, while words that classified as negative (pessimism), such as "gross", "no", and "not", do not typically have negative meanings in financial releases. These authors (among others) call for the use of finance-specific word lists when undertaking a textual analysis of finance-related disclosures.

The Henry (2008) Word List

Perhaps the earliest example of a word list specifically developed to detect tone in financial disclosures is the Henry (2008) word list. In particular, Henry (2008) develops her financial dictionary for words classification in earnings press releases for high-tech industries. Since its introduction, this word list has been shown to provide valuable insight into managerial sentiment particularly during conference calls. For instance, Price et al. (2012) find that when presenters adopt a more positive tone in the question-and-answer segments of the conference call such firms exhibit significantly higher stock price returns during both three-day and two-month windows. On the other hand, Price et al. (2012) find that when presenters adopt a more negative tone during this segment, such firms suffer negative abnormal stock price returns. Similarly, Doran et al. (2012) utilize the Henry (2008) word lists to study the effect of the tone of earnings conference calls for Real Estate Investment Trusts on stock price returns. Like Price et al. (2012), they find that the tone of earnings conference calls is related to stock price returns and that this is so even during the conference call when they control for earnings surprises.

However, despite being more appropriate for finance-related studies, Loughran and McDonald (2011) note several limitations of the use of Henry (2008) word lists to detect sentiment and tone. For instance, this word list consists of 85 words compared to the over 4,100 words that make up the Harvard IV-4 dictionary and Loughran and McDonald raise this limited number of words as a potential shortcoming. They further point out that Henry's (2008) word list ignores commonly occurring negative words in financial disclosures, such as "adverse", "impairment", and "loss".

The Loughran and McDonald (2011) Word List

As an alternative to both the Harvard VI-4 and Diction word lists, Loughran and McDonald (2011) develop what they argue is a more comprehensive taxonomy of words to capture the sentiment in financial disclosures and other pieces of corporate communication. In the Loughran and McDonald (LM) word list, in addition to the main "positive" and "negative" word classifications, Loughran and McDonald also create additional word classes, namely, "uncertainty", "litigious", "strong modal", and "weak modal" words. To produce these tonal classes, Loughran and McDonald (2011) develop a dictionary of words from all 10-Ks filed during 1994–2008. After carefully examining all words occurring in at least 5% of the documents they classify each word according to its most likely usage and sentiment in a financial context. As such, those words classified as "negative" are indicative of some adverse financial implication. Conversely, "positive" words are those that carry a favourable connotation in business. Those words classified as "uncertainty" are indicative of imprecision and/or risk, while those that reflect the potential for legal contestation are denoted as "litigious". Those words that express either strong or weak levels of confidence are classified as strong modal and weak modal words.[1] The LM word list was then used by them to evidence a relationship between managerial sentiments detected in firms' 10-K reports and market reaction around the 10-K filing date, trading volume, unexpected returns, and subsequent stock price volatility.

Since its release, the LM word list has seen widespread acceptance and application in a range of finance and accounting-related research (see, e.g., Chen et al., 2014; Dougal et al., 2012; Feldman et al., 2010; Garcia, 2013; Kearney & Liu, 2014; Solomon et al., 2014). For example, Feldman et al. (2010) use the LM word list to explore market reaction to changes in the sentiment and tone of the Management, Discussion, and Analysis (the "MD&A") section of firm's 10-K/Q filings. They find that even after controlling for known determinants of stock price changes when the tone of the MD&A section of 10-K/Qs are more positive and a firm's stock price return is higher immediately after the 10-K/Q release.

Similarly, Dougal et al. (2012), expanding on the work of Tetlock (2007), use the LM word list to consider the relationship between the authorship of the WSJ's "Abreast of the Market" column and stock market reaction. They find that individual journalists who are associated with a more pessimistic column tone are related directly to more negative stock market returns on the day following the column's publication.

The LM word list has also been applied to uncover the tone of news releases beyond the WSJ's "Abreast of the Market" column. For instance, Garcia (2013) use it to measure the sentiment of two columns in the New York Times (NYT) for the period 1905–2005. He finds that the tone of this column predicts future stock price returns and that this is especially true during recessionary periods. Similarly, Chen et al., (2014) use the LM word list to explore the link between stock price returns and the tone of the commentary section of the Seeking Alpha (SA) website. They find that the tone of opinions contained in the SA commentary is related to future stock price returns and subsequent earnings surprises.

[1] In later work, Bodnaruk et al. (2015) adopt a similar methodology to that used in Loughran and McDonald (2011) and propose "constraining" words, which are those words that suggest some financial constraint, for inclusion in the Loughran and McDonald word list.

In works reminiscent of Hanley and Hoberg (2010), Ferris et al. (2013) and Loughran and McDonald (2013) both use the LM word list to explore the impact of the tone of IPO prospectus releases. Ferris et al. (2013) investigate the impact of IPO prospectus "conservatism" on IPO pricing and subsequent operating performance and stock price returns, where they define conservatism as the proportion of negative LM words to the total words contained in the documents. In this work, they find that IPO prospectus conservatism is positively related to IPO underpricing and that this is more pronounced for technology firms. Further, they find that when nontechnology IPO prospectuses are more conservative, this has a negative impact on the firm's post-IPO operating performance. In addition, they find evidence that for nontechnology IPOs conservatism is negatively related to abnormal stock price returns in the post-IPO period.

In this same direction, Loughran and McDonald (2013) used the LM word list to investigate the relationship between IPO prospectus "uncertainty" and firms' first-day returns, offer price revisions, and aftermarket volatility. They proxy uncertainty as the document frequencies of weak modal and negative words and using this measure find that when firms' IPOs prospectuses have high levels of uncertain in the text, such firms tend to experience greater first-day returns. They also find a positive relationship between text uncertainty and absolute offer price revisions and subsequent volatility.

Further consideration of investors' reaction to news tone is provided by Solomon et al. (2014), who use the LM word list to explore the relationship between newspaper sentiment and investors' proclivity to invest in particular funds. They find that when funds receive newspaper coverage that is more positive in tone this results in them receiving higher capital inflows. In a similar fashion, Hillert et al. (2014) use the LM word lists to measure the tone of mutual fund letters to shareholders and find that they are responsive to the tone of these letters.

What is more, Ahern and Sosyura (2014) use the LM word list to explore whether the tone of firm press releases can affect the stock prices of acquiring firms during merger negotiations. They find that some bidders try to increase the value of their stock prices during the private negotiation phase by making press releases. In particular, they note that press releases by bidders can result in increased media coverage that is, in fact, more positive in tone and this in turn slightly increases the bidder's stock price. These findings have motivated additional research activity into whether and how managers' tone can inform or mislead investors by the tone of the language used in press releases (see, for example, Mayew & Venkatachalam, 2012; Huang et al., 2014b).

Term Weighting Schemes

The development of tailored dictionaries, that become suitable for financial documents, makes the word classification process easier, faster, and more transparent. However, once the words are classified into different thematic subcategories, it is crucial to impose a proper normalization on the word counts. Loughran and McDonald (2011) demonstrate that the attenuation bias caused by misclassifications can be considerably reduced by applying a term weighting scheme to word occurrences. More specifically, as shown by Loughran and McDonald (2011), some negative words appear very frequently in 10-K reports (e.g., "loss" appears 179,000 times), while the word "aggravates" appears only 10 times. Term weighting helps to dampen the effect of high-frequency words on sentiment measurement and put more weight on rare but important words in 10-K filings. Researchers exploit a log transformation of the word count and adjust the document for its length. This weighting scheme takes into account the relevance of a term in a document, the document length, and the significance of a term in the entire corpus. In this case, the log transformation of raw word count and average word count in the document mitigates the effect of high-frequency words, whereas the log difference between the total number of 10-Ks in the sample and the number of documents with at least one occurrence of a term changes the effect of a word based on its commonality.

In summary, the dictionary-based approach has proved a very popular technique for textual analysis in finance; however, one noted limitation is that such approaches tend to ignore the context of the document. Furthermore, such wordlists have been criticized for frequently misclassifying words due to the limited availability of thematic dictionaries for corporate statements (Li, 2010a).

3.2.2 *Statistical Learning Approaches*

In this section, we discuss some alternative statistical and machine learning techniques for textual analysis. In particular, we focus on statistical and machine learning approaches such as Naïve Bayes (Antweiler & Frank, 2004) and semantic analysis (Blei et al., 2003; Boukus & Rosenberg, 2006), which attempt to classify a message based on the grammatical structure of the language, and similarity analysis (Hoberg and Phillips, 2016; Cohen et al., 2020), which aims to measure how alike two or more documents/paragraphs/sentences, etc., are. We focus on these three techniques as they have proven to be historically popular in the finance-related textual analysis literature and provide an overview of the statistical learning approaches that have been taken in the field. We note however that deep learning models such as artificial neural networks, recurrent neural networks, transformers, and large language models like ChatGPT/GPT4 are also emerging as important and powerful statistical learning approaches for textual analysis in finance. In general, compared to lexicon approaches, all statistical learning methodologies seek to extract the relevant information content from a document/paragraph/sentence etc by learning the latent structure in the text data. For instance, when applied to sentiment analysis, statistical learning algorithms undertake in-sample training to "learn" grammar-dependent classification rules and then define the positive, negative, or neutral tone of the out-of-sample message by examining the distance between word/phrase and grammar vectors that capture these tones, or a discriminant function based on word counts (Das & Chen, 2007).

3.2.2.1 Naïve Bayes

According to Huang et al. (2014a), Naïve Bayes classification is a statistical learning method that can be used to categorize text documents into their most likely class based on a statistical relation, i.e., model, that is based on words and category relations that is learned from a training sample of text documents. The algorithm is called naïve since it ignores the word sequence and treats each word independently. Hence, like the dictionary-based approaches this method disregards the grammatical structure of the document; however, it enables the researcher to process huge volumes of qualitative data, accurately measure the context of documents through training the Naïve Bayes learning algorithms, and classifying the entire document and or sentences into positive, negative, or neutral categories. In particular, this procedure can be considered as a prediction algorithm since it maximizes the probability that a message belongs to a certain category or type conditional on the stream of words in the document.

The input parameters in this algorithm, the likelihood of word occurrences conditional on the particular category, are obtained through training on an initial dataset, which usually represents a limited number of randomly selected sentences from financial reports. As a result of this in-sample learning, the Naïve Bayes model is developed and is then used to classify out-of-sample sentences in reports as either negative, positive, or neutral.

In an early and important study that asks the question "does message tone matter?", Antweiler and Frank (2004) apply Naïve Bayes to explore the influence of "Yahoo Finance" message boards postings for companies listed on the Dow Jones Industrial Average (Dow). In particular, they use this approach to classify tone of the posted messages. They find that these financial messages do indeed matter and they can predict the volatility of the index as a small degree of negative return predictability is generated by bullishness, while disagreement among messages generates higher trading activity.

Another important study in this area by Huang et al. (2014a) exploits the Naïve Bayes learning approach to measure the sentiment from more than 350,000 analyst reports. In fact, their training procedure processes about 27 million sentences from analyst reports. The findings from this large-scale study illustrate that even a few positive sentences make a significant impact on the earnings growth rate of a company.

3.2.2.2 Semantic Analysis

Another method for classifying the content of documents into certain thematic groups, which is free of using any lexicon is semantic analysis. This approach is specifically designed to define the themes within a corpus of reports by reducing the dimensionality of the term-document matrix through the assignment of each word to latent factors. The most frequently used techniques for semantic analysis are latent semantic indexing, which reduces the dimension of the term-document matrix using singular value decomposition (SVD), and latent Dirichlet allocation (LDA), that utilizes a Bayesian model with a variety of latent topics.

In particular, latent semantic analysis reduces the dimensionality of the "term-document" matrix using singular value decomposition. Applying a latent semantic analysis, Boukus and Rosenberg (2006) investigate market reaction to Federal Reserve policy as reflected in the Federal Open Market Committee (FOMC) meeting minutes. They show that themes, derived from the minutes, are correlated with current and future macroeconomic and financial indicators, with, for instance, FOMC minutes strongly affecting Treasury yields.

Similarly, latent Dirichlet allocation aims to discern the latent structure from the array of documents by applying the Bayesian model to shrink the dimensionality of the "term-document" matrix. This procedure helps to analyse a large corpus of lengthy documents in a clear and replicable manner and infer the content of documents with multiple topics. The recent study of Dyer et al. (2017) examines the changing content of 10-K filings and demonstrates that these reports become more lengthy, redundant, sticky, less readable, and specific. Bellstam et al. (2019) propose a new measure of text-based innovation by applying a topic modelling tool such as latent Dirichlet allocation to the large corpus of financial reports and capture innovation by the intensity with which analysts mention innovation topics in the reports. The paper finds that this proxy for innovation is strongly related to R&D expenditures and forecasts future R&D spending.

3.2.2.3 *Similarity Analysis*

There also exist tools that aim to measure the semantic similarity across documents. For example, Hoberg and Phillips (2016) establish new time-varying measures of product similarity based on firms' 10-K product descriptions. In particular, Hoberg and Phillips (2016) construct proxies of product similarity across firms using 10-K product descriptions and cosine similarity measure. To explore the relatedness between firms, researchers collect unique words in 10-K business descriptions that specify the characteristics of the firm's products and estimate pair-wise word similarity scores for each pair of companies within a year. These researchers document that a higher firm's expenditure on R&D is associated with a significant decrease in measures of product similarity and a substantial increase in future profitability.

Similarly, Cohen et al. (2020) propose the use of various measures of document similarity to capture the effect of active changes in a firm's reports on asset prices. Specifically, Cohen et al. (2020), using the history of 10-K and 10-Q reports over the period from 1995 to 2014, examine the changes in the language structure of corporate reports across time by applying four commonly used similarity measures; namely, cosine similarity, Jaccard similarity, minimum edit distance, and simple similarity. The essence of these measures lies in converting two documents into vectors of word counts (or a number of occurrences of a certain term) and exploiting various geometrical formulas for measuring the closeness of two vectors. This paper finds a strong return predictability pattern stemming from firms that change significantly their reporting style. Particularly, a portfolio that buys "non-changers" and short "changers" generate a monthly abnormal return of 30–60 basis points.

3.3 Can Textual Analysis Be Used to Measure Corporate Culture?

As we have discussed in Chapter 2, corporate culture remains difficult to observe and measure force within firms that explains variations in firms' performance and other corporate behaviour. In fact, one reason often given for the limited empirical research that concerns the role of corporate culture has been the absence of large-scale samples with high-quality data about this construct (Andreou et al., 2020, 2021; Fiordelisi & Ricci, 2014, 2021; Fiordelisi et al., 2019; Graham et al., 2022; Guiso et al., 2015a, 2015b; Luu et al., 2022; Nguyen et al., 2018, 2019). Traditionally, corporate culture has been measured using various survey instruments that seek to capture managements' and/or employees' perceptions and opinions about the firm (Graham et al., 2022; Guiso et al., 2015a). This approach for detecting corporate culture is a commonly used research strategy as it allows for easy comparisons and the appearance of authoritativeness.

For instance, Graham et al. (2022) conduct a survey and interview-based analysis of 1,348 North American firms to investigate the question, "*does corporate culture matter?*", and use this information to investigate whether differences in corporate culture explains why similar firms experience divergence in terms of success and failure. However, although the survey designs adopted by Graham et al. (2022) allow researchers to capture corporate culture from a relatively large cross-section of respondents, in practice this approach is limited due to the response availability of survey participants and the costs of administering questionnaires on a large scale. Further, sampling and non-sampling errors pose a challenge to the accuracy of the results. What is more, disadvantages stemming from the social interaction of the researcher and the respondents, and the potential inaccuracy of responses all remain potential sources of errors for survey research designs.

In addition to survey-based methods, the textual analysis of firms' corporate disclosures and other documents has emerged as an increasingly popular approach to quantify various aspects of corporate culture (Andreou et al., 2020, 2021; Barth, 2016; Bhandari et al., 2017;

Fiordelisi & Ricci, 2014, 2021; Graham et al., 2022; Grennan, 2019; Luu et al., 2022; Nguyen et al., 2019). This is because, unlike the survey approach, this method of quantifying firms' corporate culture is more practical for large-scale research studies as it allows for the measurement of the key dimensions of the construct in a manageable and objective way using firms' archival documents. Furthermore, given the large increase in the number of corporate disclosures and other related documents in recent years, it should come as no surprise that this has led to researchers in finance leveraging tools developed in computer science and linguistics to parse the words contained in these documents to unearth firm features and traits. In doing so, researchers actively adopt the assumption that the expressions and words were chosen by management in producing firms' disclosures are representative of the firms' culture that has been developed. Thus, the finance-related literature on corporate culture has begun to make increasing use of various textual analysis techniques in order to understand how a firm's culture relates to various economic phenomena.

For instance, Grennan (2019) applies a textual analysis approach to an original dataset consisting of over 1.8 million employee reviews to quantify corporate culture based on the O'Reilly et al. (1991, 1996, 2014) model (please see Chapter 2). Similarly, Fiordelisi and Ricci (2014, 2021) utilize the textual analysis method to measure from firms' readily available corporate reports (i.e., the 10-K filings). In doing this, Fiordelisi and Ricci (2014, 2021) adopt the competing values framework of culture.

In fact, the ease and extendibility of the approach taken by Fiordelisi and Ricci (2014, 2021) have seen their textual analysis-based approach to quantifying culture become increasingly popular with researchers in finance. For example, Barth (2016), Nguyen et al. (2019), and Luu et al. (2022) utilize this method to explore the role played by corporate culture in banks, while Bhandari et al. (2017) and Andreou et al. (2020, 2021) adopt a similar textual analysis approach to examine firms' corporate culture in nonfinancial firms.

Hence, given the previous studies (Andreou et al., 2020, 2021; Barth, 2016; Bhandari et al., 2017; Fiordelisi & Ricci, 2014, 2021; Fiordelisi et al., 2019; Graham et al., 2022; Grennan, 2019; Luu et al., 2022; Nguyen et al., 2019), it seems reasonable to suggest that a textual analysis of the certain firm-related text represents a suitable approach to measuring corporate culture; however, it should also be mentioned that this approach to capturing corporate culture has also been criticized. For example, Guiso et al. (2015b) shed some doubt on whether firms stated values, such as those contained in firms' disclosures, should be used to measure firms' corporate culture as they find that firms' stated values are in fact not indicative of corporate culture.

Furthermore, the finding that firms' proclaimed values should be viewed with suspicion is also supported by the prior work of Loughran et al. (2009) who investigate the occurrence of ethics-related terms in firms' 10-K reports and find that firms that use more ethics-related terms in these reports are more likely to have an unethical corporate culture. That is, these firms are more prone to be the subject of class action lawsuits and are expected to have inadequate corporate governance policies (e.g., entrenched managers). Their results suggest that managers who portray their firm as being more "ethical" in 10-K reports are in fact more likely to be systematically misleading the public.

Nevertheless, despite these limitations in this book we adopt a textual analysis-based approach to quantify the firm's competition culture as we maintain consistent with past literature (see, e.g., Andreou et al., 2020, 2021; Barth, 2016; Bhandari et al., 2017; Fiordelisi & Ricci, 2014, 2021; Fiordelisi et al., 2019; Luu et al., 2022; Nguyen et al., 2019) that the textual analysis of firm's 10-K filings represents an efficient way of capturing the latent (and proclaimed) values of the management of the firm. Furthermore, this method allows us to exploit a large corpus of archival data that are available for firms and thereby overcome the severe data limitation problem that would otherwise be associated with the intended study had we adopted an alternative research design (e.g., surveys).

3.4 Summary

In summary, textual analysis has recently been proven to be a valuable tool in finance to measure relevant information from various texts (see, e.g., Antweiler & Frank, 2004; Audi et al., 2016; Hoberg & Phillips, 2010; Kearney & Liu, 2014; Li, 2008; Loughran & McDonald, 2011; Tetlock, 2007; Tetlock et al., 2008). Further, we have discussed the relevance of this approach for quantifying corporate culture and although it remains questionable as to whether corporate culture is best measured using this approach, it seems reasonable since the words used by the management of a firm and the meanings that they carry should reflect the values that these individuals have developed over time. Therefore, by analysing the corporate disclosures produced by the firm, we argue that we are able to detect the elusive but distinctive features of firms' corporate culture that are reflected in such documents.

References

Ahern, K. R., & Sosyura, D. (2014). Who Writes the News? Corporate Press Releases During Merger Negotiations. *The Journal of Finance, 69*, 241–291.

Andreou, P. C., Fiordelisi, F., Harris, T., & Philip, D. (2021). Institutional Ownership and Firms' Thrust to Compete. *British Journal of Management, 33*, 1346–1370.

Andreou, P. C., Harris, T., & Philip, D. (2020). Measuring Firms' Market Orientation Using Textual Analysis of 10-K Filings. *British Journal of Management, 31*, 872–895.

Antweiler, W., & Frank, M. Z. (2004). Is All That Talk Just Noise? The Information Content of Internet Stock Message Boards. *The Journal of Finance, 59*, 1259–1294.

Audi, R., Loughran, T., & McDonald, B. (2016). Trust, but Verify: MD&A Language and the Role of Trust in Corporate Culture. *Journal of Business Ethics, 139*, 551–561.

Barth, A. (2016). *The Role of Corporate Culture in the Financial Industry*. Available at SSRN 2707078.

Bellstam, G., Bhagat, S., & Cookson, J. A. (2019). *A Text-Based Analysis of Corporate Innovation*. Available at SSRN 2803232.

Bhandari, A., Mammadov, B., Thevenot, M., & Vakilzadeh, S. H. (2017). *The Invisible Hand: Corporate Culture and Its Implications for Earnings Management* (Working Paper). Warrington College of Business, Gainesville, FL.

Biddle, G. C., Hilary, G., & Verdi, R. S. (2009). How does Financial Reporting Quality Relate to Investment Efficiency? *Journal of Accounting and Economics, 48*, 112–131.

Blei, D. M., Ng, A. Y., & Jordan, M. I. (2003). Latent Dirichlet Allocation. *Journal of Machine Learning Research, 3*, 993–1022.

Bodnaruk, A., Loughran, T., & McDonald, B. (2015). Using 10-K Text to Gauge Financial Constraints. *Journal of Financial and Quantitative Analysis, 50*, 623–646.

Bonsall, S. B., IV., Leone, A. J., Miller, B. P., & Rennekamp, K. (2017). A Plain English Measure of Financial Reporting Readability. *Journal of Accounting and Economics, 63*, 329–357.

Boukus, E., & Rosenberg, J. V. (2006). *The Information Content of FOMC Minutes*. Available at SSRN 922312.

Bushman, R. M., Hendricks, B. E., & Williams, C. D. (2016). Bank Competition: Measurement, Decision-Making, and Risk-Taking. *Journal of Accounting Research, 54*, 777–826.

Chen, H., De, P., Hu, Y. J., & Hwang, B. H. (2014). Wisdom of Crowds: The Value of Stock Opinions Transmitted Through Social Media. *The Review of Financial Studies, 27*, 1367–1403.

Cohen, L., Malloy, C., & Nguyen, Q. (2020). Lazy prices. *The Journal of Finance, 75*, 1371–1415.

Da, Z., Engelberg, J., & Gao, P. (2015). The Sum of All FEARS Investor Sentiment and Asset Prices. *The Review of Financial Studies, 28*, 1–32.

Davis, A. K., Piger, J. M., & Sedor, L. M. (2012). Beyond the Numbers: Measuring the Information Content of Earnings Press Release Language. *Contemporary Accounting Research, 29*, 845–868.

Davis, A. K., & Tama-Sweet, I. (2012). Managers' Use of Language Across Alternative Disclosure Outlets: Earnings Press Releases Versus MD&A. *Contemporary Accounting Research, 29*, 804–837.

Das, S. R., & Chen, M. Y. (2007). Yahoo! for Amazon: Sentiment Extraction from Small Talk on the Web. *Management Science, 53*, 1375–1388.

Doran, J. S., Peterson, D. R., & Price, S. M. (2012). Earnings Conference Call Content and Stock Price: The Case of REITs. *The Journal of Real Estate Finance and Economics, 45*, 402–434.

Dougal, C., Engelberg, J., Garcia, D., & Parsons, C. A. (2012). Journalists and the Stock Market. *The Review of Financial Studies, 25*, 639–679.

Dyer, T., Lang, M., & Stice-Lawrence, L. (2017). The Evolution of 10-K Textual Disclosure: Evidence from Latent Dirichlet Allocation. *Journal of Accounting and Economics, 64*, 221–245.

Feldman, R., Govindaraj, S., Livnat, J., & Segal, B. (2010). Management's Tone Change, Post Earnings Announcement Drift and Accruals. *Review of Accounting Studies, 15*, 915–953.

Ferris, S. P., Hao, Q., & Liao, M. Y. (2013). The Effect of Issuer Conservatism on IPO Pricing and Performance. *Review of Finance, 17*, 993–1027.

Fiordelisi, F., & Ricci, O. (2014). Corporate Culture and CEO Turnover. *Journal of Corporate Finance, 28*, 66–82.

Fiordelisi, F., & Ricci, O. (2021). Corrigendum to "Corporate Culture and CEO Turnover". *Journal of Corporate Finance, 70*, 102064.

Fiordelisi, F., Renneboog, L., Ricci, O., & Lopes, S. S. (2019). Creative Corporate Culture and Innovation. *Journal of International Financial Markets, Institutions and Money, 63*, 101137.

Garcia, D. (2013). Sentiment During Recessions. *The Journal of Finance, 68*, 1267–1300.

Graham, J. R., Harvey, C. R., Grennen, J., & Rajgopal, S. (2022). Corporate Culture: Evidence from the Field. *Journal of Financial Economics, 146*, 552–593.

Grennan, J. (2019). *A Corporate Culture Channel: How Increased Shareholder Governance Reduces Firm Value*. Available at SSRN 2345384.

Guiso, L., Sapienza, P., & Zingales, L. (2015a). Corporate Culture, Societal Culture, and Institutions. *American Economic Review, 105*, 336–339.

Guiso, L., Sapienza, P., & Zingales, L. (2015b). The Value of Corporate Culture. *Journal of Financial Economics, 117*, 60–76.

Guo, H., Yin, C., & Zeng, Y. (2022). How Does Firm-Specific Investor Sentiment Affect the Value of Corporate Cash Holdings? *British Journal of Management*.

Hanley, K. W., & Hoberg, G. (2010). The Information Content of IPO Prospectuses. *The Review of Financial Studies, 23*, 2821–2864.

Henry, E. (2008). Are Investors Influenced by How Earnings Press Releases Are Written? *The Journal of Business Communication, 45*, 363–407.

Heston, S. L., & Sinha, N. R. (2015). *News Versus Sentiment: Predicting Stock Returns from News Stories*. Available at SSRN 2311310.

Hillert, A., Niessen-Ruenzi, A., & Ruenzi, S. (2014). *Mutual Fund Shareholder Letter Tone-Do Investors Listen?* (Working Paper). University of Mannheim, Mannheim, Germany.

Hoberg, G., & Phillips, G. (2010). Product Market Synergies and Competition in Mergers and Acquisitions: A Text-Based Analysis. *Review of Financial Studies, 23*, 3773–3811.

Hoberg, G., & Phillips, G. (2016). Text-Based Network Industries and Endogenous Product Differentiation. *Journal of Political Economy, 124*, 1423–1465.

Hoberg, G., Phillips, G., & Prabhala, N. (2014). Product Market Threats, Payouts, and Financial Flexibility. *The Journal of Finance, 69*, 293–324.

Huang, A. H., Zang, A. Y., & Zheng, R. (2014a). Evidence on the Information Content of Text in Analyst Reports. *The Accounting Review, 89*, 2151–2180.

Huang, X., Teoh, S. H., & Zhang, Y. (2014b). Tone Management. *The Accounting Review, 89*, 1083–1113.

Kearney, C., & Liu, S. (2014). Textual Sentiment in Finance: A survey of Methods and Models. *International Review of Financial Analysis, 33*, 171–185.

Kothari, S. P., Li, X., & Short, J. E. (2009). The Effect of Disclosures by Management, Analysts, and Business Press on Cost of Capital, Return Volatility, and Analyst Forecasts: A Study Using Content Analysis. *The Accounting Review, 84*, 1639–1670.

Lawrence, A. (2013). Individual Investors and Financial Disclosure. *Journal of Accounting and Economics, 56*, 130–147.

Lehavy, R., Li, F., & Merkley, K. (2011). The Effect of Annual Report Readability on Analyst Following and the Properties of Their Earnings Forecasts. *The Accounting Review, 86*, 1087–1115.

Li, E. X., & Ramesh, K. (2009). Market Reaction Surrounding the Filing of Periodic SEC Reports. *The Accounting Review, 84*, 1171–1208.

Li, F. (2008). Annual Report Readability, Current Earnings, and Earnings Persistence. *Journal of Accounting and Economics, 45*, 221–247.

Li, F. (2010a). Textual Analysis of Corporate Disclosures: A Survey of the Literature. *Journal of Accounting Literature, 29*, 143.

Li, F. (2010b). The Information Content of Forward-Looking Statements in Corporate Filings: A Naive Bayesian Machine Learning Approach. *Journal of Accounting Research, 48*, 1049–1102.

Li, F. (2011). *Managers' Self-serving Attribution Bias, Overconfidence, and Corporate Financial Policies* (Working Paper). University of Michigan, Ann Arbor, MI.

Li, F., Lundholm, R., & Minnis, M. (2013a). A Measure of Competition Based on 10-K Filings. *Journal of Accounting Research, 51*, 399–436.

Li, K., Griffin, D., Yue, H., & Zhao, L. (2013b). How Does Culture Influence Corporate Risk-Taking? *Journal of Corporate Finance, 23*, 1–22.

Li, K., Liu, X., Mai, F., & Zhang, T. (2020). The Role of Corporate Culture in Bad Times, Evidence from the COVID-19 Pandemic. *Journal of Financial and Quantitative Analysis*, 1–68.

Li, X. (2010c). The Impacts of Product Market Competition on the Quantity and Quality of Voluntary Disclosures. *Review of Accounting Studies, 15*, 663–711.

Loughran, T., McDonald, B., & Yun, H. (2009). A Wolf in Sheep's Clothing: The Use of Ethics-Related Terms in 10-K Reports. *Journal of Business Ethics, 89*, 39–49.

Loughran, T., & McDonald, B. (2011). When Is a Liability Not a Liability? Textual Analysis, Dictionaries, and 10-Ks. *The Journal of Finance, 66*, 35–65.

Loughran, T., & McDonald, B. (2013). IPO First-Day Returns, Offer Price Revisions, Volatility, and Form S-1 Language. *Journal of Financial Economics, 109*, 307–326.

Loughran, T., & McDonald, B. (2014). Measuring Readability in Financial Disclosures. *The Journal of Finance, 69*, 1643–1671.

Loughran, T., & McDonald, B. (2016). Textual Analysis in Accounting and Finance: A Survey. *Journal of Accounting Research, 54*, 1187–1230.

Luu, H., Nguyen, L., & Wilson, J. O. S. (2022). *Organizational Culture, Competition and Bank Loan Loss Provisions*. Available at SSRN 3921043.

Mayew, W. J., & Venkatachalam, M. (2012). The Power of Voice: Managerial Affective States and Future Firm Performance. *The Journal of Finance, 67*, 1–43.

Miller, B. P. (2010). The Effects of Reporting Complexity on Small and Large Investor Trading. *The Accounting Review, 85*, 2107–2143.

Mosteller, F., & Wallace, D. (1964). *Inference and Disputed Authorship: The Federalist*. Addison-Wesley.

Nelson, K. K., & Pritchard, A. C. (2007). *Litigation Risk and Voluntary Disclosure: The Use of Meaningful Cautionary Language*. Available at SSRN 998590.

Nguyen, D. D., Hagendorff, J., & Eshraghi, A. (2018). Does a CEO's Cultural Heritage Affect Performance Under Competitive Pressure? *The Review of Financial Studies, 31*, 97–141.

Nguyen, D. D., Nguyen, L., & Sila, V. (2019). Does Corporate Culture Affect Bank Risk-Taking? Evidence from Loan-Level Data. *British Journal of Management, 30*, 106–133.

Price, S. M., Doran, J. S., Peterson, D. R., & Bliss, B. A. (2012). Earnings Conference Calls and Stock Returns: The Incremental Informativeness of Textual Tone. *Journal of Banking & Finance, 36*, 992–1011.

Rogers, J. L., Van Buskirk, A., & Zechman, S. L. (2011). Disclosure Tone and Shareholder Litigation. *The Accounting Review, 86*, 2155–2183.

Simon, A. (1997). *Administrative Behaviour* (4th ed.). The Free Press.

Solomon, D. H., Soltes, E., & Sosyura, D. (2014). Winners in the Spotlight: Media Coverage of Fund Holdings as a Driver of Flows. *Journal of Financial Economics, 113*, 53–72.

Tetlock, P. C. (2007). Giving Content to Investor Sentiment: The Role of Media in the Stock Market. *The Journal of Finance, 62*, 1139–1168.

Tetlock, P. C., Saar-Tsechansky, M., & Macskassy, S. (2008). More Than Words: Quantifying Language to Measure Firms' Fundamentals. *The Journal of Finance, 63*, 1437–1467.

CHAPTER 4

Institutional Investors and Competition Culture

4.1 Introduction

In recent decades, a growing literature has emphasized the importance of corporate culture for influencing a firm's economic outcomes (see, for example, Andreou et al., 2021; Bhandari et al., 2017; Callen & Fang, 2015; Cronqvist et al., 2007; Erhard et al., 2017; Fiordelisi & Ricci, 2014, 2021; Fiordelisi et al., 2019; Graham et al., 2022; Grennan, 2019; Grieser et al., 2016; Guiso et al., 2006, 2015a, 2015b; Li et al., 2013b; Luu et al., 2022; Wang et al., 2021; Zingales, 2015). However, with the exception of Andreou et al. (2021), very little work has explored the antecedence of firms' corporate culture and in this chapter, we extend the existing literature in this direction by investigating whether the composition of the institutional investor base influences corporate competition culture. To do this, we utilize textual analysis of 10-K filings to develop a measure of corporate competition culture using the competing values framework of corporate culture (e.g., Quinn & Cameron, 1983; Quinn & Rohrbaugh, 1983). In so doing, we also follow recent studies that aim to contribute to the understanding of institutional investors' preferences and interventions on firms' governance (e.g., Bebchuk et al., 2015; Giannetti & Yu, 2016; Harford et al., 2018; McCahery et al., 2016).

The competing values framework emerged from studies of the factors that account for highly effective organizational performance and has been

T. Harris, *Competition Culture and Corporate Finance*,
https://doi.org/10.1007/978-3-031-30156-8_4

named as one of the 40 most important frameworks in the history of business (Ten Have et al., 2003). This framework (Cameron & Quinn, 2011; Cameron et al., 2014; Hartnell et al., 2011; Quinn & Cameron, 1983; Quinn & Rohrbaugh, 1983) theorizes the competition culture of a firm to be a concatenation of attributes that focus on achieving superior financial performance by assimilating external information and catering to capital market expectations. The competition culture of a firm therefore reflects aggressiveness in the pursuit of profitability. Hence, speed of action to achieve results characterize firms with a competition culture (Cameron et al., 2014). In that vein, such firms have a proclivity towards being aggressive and moving fast, while assessing success based on indicators such as increased profitability.

Following the growing literature that applies textual analysis in finance research (see, for instance, Hoberg & Phillips, 2010, 2016; Hoberg et al., 2014; Kearney & Liu, 2014; Li et al., 2013a; Loughran et al., 2009; Tetlock, 2007), we develop a measure for corporate competition culture using information in the 10-K filings for the period 1994–2014. We adopt this measurement approach as it provides an efficient way to capture firm's competition culture by exploiting a large corpus of archival data that describe the current and future operations of US-listed firms. Further, by relying on the information environment portrayed in the 10-K filings creates a leeway to circumvent data limitation problems that are regularly associated with the measurement of latent corporate characteristics, like the competition culture. We operationalize our measure by parsing 10-K filings to identify a set of lexical items relating to attributes that shape firms' competition culture. In particular, we focus on attributes that feature firms' external effectiveness to pursue enhanced competitiveness, emphasized organizational achievements, setting of goals and being aggressive, growth in profitability, superior financial performance, etc. For instance, it is sensible to expect firms using in their 10-K filings a relatively high frequency of words pertaining to "achievement", "aggressive", "compete", "goal", "profits", and "performance", among others, to be highly driven by corporate attributes geared towards the competition culture.

Having developed our text-based measure, we consider the overarching question; "*what is the influence of the composition of the institutional investor base on corporate competition culture?*", as this question is intriguing in many aspects. For instance, it can inform recent literature that documents strong links between institutional ownership and organizational outcomes such as earnings manipulation, R&D investments, M&As, and financing (see, for example, Chen et al., 2007; Elyasiani et al., 2010; Gaspar et al., 2005; Harford et al., 2018), as well as between institutional ownership and financial performance (see, for example, Cai & Zheng, 2004; Giannetti & Yu, 2016; Gompers & Metrick, 1998; Nofsinger & Sias, 1999). However, unlike the prior literature that remains rather silent on exactly how institutional investors affect corporate outcomes and performance, we posit firms' competition culture as a channel through which institutional investors appear to influence corporate philosophy, decision-making, and outcomes. This proposition is consistent with recent evidence documenting that institutional investors regularly engage with management and the board of directors in behind-the-scene interventions that can shape corporate objectives (Bebchuk et al., 2015; Brav et al., 2015; Edmans, 2014; McCahery et al., 2016, among others), and that the composition of firms' institutional investor base can create (or mitigate) implicit incentives for managers to over-allocate effort towards improving current performance, potentially at the expense of shareholder value creation (e.g., Bushee, 1998; Dikolli et al., 2009). Further, it is well known that corporate goals and decision-making processes can be altered so as to reflect certain (desired) sets of management behaviours, priorities, shared norms, and beliefs (Giannetti & Yu, 2016; Guiso et al., 2015b), and if institutional investors engage with management to change their decision-making environment via their "voice" and "exit" then it is conceivable that these investors affect firms' outcomes via alteration to firms' decision-making environment. Based on these arguments, institutional investors could, therefore, influence firms' competition culture so as to fulfil their own objectives and thereby leave an indelible mark on their values and norms. Hence, it is important to trace the effects of institutional investors' interventions on firms' culture since this provides the context in which organizational members (particularly managers) prioritize activities that could deliver lucrative (or devastating) financial results to investors (Hartnell et al., 2011; O'Reilly et al., 1996).

Our investigation provides robust causal evidence that transient institutional ownership has a strong positive relation to the one-year-ahead level of corporate competition culture. As transient institutional investors invest based on the likelihood of reaping short-term trading profits (Bushee, 1998, 2001) this evidence supports that they intervene and exert pressure on managers to intensify their firms' competition culture, perhaps aiming for results-right-now and more immediate financial performance. As such, the management of a firm with more transient institutional investors would succumb to such pressures under the threat that if these institutional investors become unhappy, they will forcefully exit by selling shares, thereby suppressing the firm's stock price (Bernardo & Welch, 2004; Fos & Kahn, 2015). Indeed, Graham et al. (2005) report that the majority of managers would avoid commencing projects with positive NPVs and sacrifice long-term shareholder value creation for short-term profits in exchange for being able to cater to investors' expectations.

Conversely, we demonstrate that dedicated institutional ownership has a negative relation to the firm's one-year-ahead level of firm's competition culture. This evidence supports that dedicated institutional investors also intervene and influence managers but instead to lessen firms' competition culture, perhaps following their incentives to monitor and offset managerial myopia and to assess financial performance by relying on information beyond that provided in the current earnings period to assess managers' performance (Chen et al., 2007; Gaspar et al., 2005; Harford et al., 2018). Furthermore, this evidence might reveal that the managers of firms with more dedicated institutional investors feel less pressure to consistently cater to investors and ease their thrust of being aggressive and forceful in the pursuit of performance as they are unconcerned about large price drops that can be spurred by the exit/selling strategies of these investors.[1] Overall, this evidence lends further credence to the view that institutional investors are far from homogeneous, whereby their investment horizon and performance-related objectives and preferences incentivize them to exert much different governance on firms' operating philosophy, priorities, and decision-making processes.

In terms of econometric methods, our regression approaches are carefully implemented to tackle identification issues that may cloud the interpretation of the results. For instance, since firms' competition culture and the level of institutional ownership are rather persistent over time,

[1] This is reasonable since a large proportion of dedicated investors are in fact passive investors who simply invest in firms (directly or indirectly) based on an index. These investors are therefore usually unable or unwilling to directly sell specific firms that comprise the index. As a result, managers at firms with more dedicated investors are increasingly less likely to be concerned by selling pressure brought about by initial signals of underperformance (Cella et al., 2013; Giannetti & Yu, 2016).

following prior studies that derive their key variables using textual analysis (e.g., Hoberg & Phillips, 2010; Hoberg et al., 2014; Li, 2010c; Li et al., 2013a), we utilize pooled cross-sectional models for our primary analyses including time and industry fixed effects.[2] At the same time, in the spirit of the competing values framework, we adopt a scaling scheme designed to account for other corporate cultures that may co-exist with the competition culture, to mitigate omitted variable issues. In addition, to safeguard against simultaneous causality issues, our main baseline regression models rely on a one-year time-lag between the independent and dependent variables. Additionally, we conduct further analysis to confirm the causal relationship by ranking firms into deciles based on their competition culture at time t and test whether institutional ownership structure can explain the t to $t + 1$ changes in a firm's decile rank of competition culture. We also adopt an instrumental variables approach by using a firm's inclusion or exclusion in the Russell 1000/2000 indexes as a source of exogenous variation in institutional ownership (Appel et al., 2016; Crane et al., 2015). In addition, we estimate additional instrumental variable models, dynamic panel generalized methods of moments (GMM) estimation, as well as firm random- a fixed effects estimation. Irrespective of the approach, all econometric estimates confirm the robustness of our main findings and lend credence to the idea that the composition of the institutional investor base influences the firms' competition culture.

Our study contributes to the literature as follows. First, our main finding that the composition of institutional ownership base impacts firms' competition culture and hence managers' operating philosophy and decision-making, adds direct knowledge to our understanding of how institutional investors engage with managers and reveal their interactions in behind-the-scenes interventions that leave an indelible mark

[2] We also conduct random effects estimates for the main relations, as this approach allows us to capture the effects of slow-moving variables and permits an efficient estimation of model parameters. For our analysis, we refrain from relying on firm fixed effect estimations, which depend solely on within-firm variations and are thus inapplicable in our case due to the slow-changing behaviour of some of our main variables. Such behaviours resemble, for example, the well-known stickiness nature of the corporate governance attributes, in which, following the intuition in Wintoki et al. (2012), the firm fixed effects approach is also not the optimal choice. However, for the sake of completeness, we report firm fixed effects in Appendix A which show similar conclusions, lending in this way more credence to the overall conclusions of this chapter.

on firms' corporate culture. As such, our findings complement other recent studies (e.g., Andreou et al., 2021; Bebchuk et al., 2015; Brav et al., 2015; Edmans, 2014; McCahery et al., 2016) that endeavour to provide direct evidence of institutional investors' preferences and actions on their portfolio firms. Second, it contributes to the settling of the ongoing debate regarding the benefits and costs of institutional investors on corporate decision-making (e.g., Giannetti & Yu, 2016; Harford et al., 2018) by investigating the impact of transient and dedicated investors on firms' competition culture, which inherently encapsulates the managers' decision-making environment instead of relying only on corporate outcomes like R&D, dividends, investments, financial fraud, etc. Also, as it is frequently very hard to measure corporate characteristics, we show how to operationalize such an empirical construct using textual analysis of the 10-K reports for all firms with such reports in the SEC Edgar database. Further, we also complement other recent studies as in our analysis we demonstrate that firms' competition culture remains distinct from other conceptualizations of market competitiveness that centre on product market competition (for example, Bushman et al., 2016; Li et al., 2013a).

The remainder of this chapter is presented as follows: the hypotheses are developed in Sect. 4.2, details of the data and summary statistics are presented in Sect. 4.3; Sect. 4.4 presents the empirical results, and Sect. 4.5 concludes.

4.2 Measurement and Hypotheses

4.2.1 Measuring Competition Culture

It has long been argued that corporations are micro-societies that have the ability to shape distinct norms, values, and practices i.e., cultures (Guiso et al., 2015a, 2015b; Zingales, 2015). These principles shape the essence of a company's identity as defined by beliefs, priorities, and operating philosophy. In measuring such corporate culture, a strand of the literature relies on the competing values framework (CVF) (see, for example, Cameron et al., 2014; Hartnell et al., 2011; Schneider et al., 2013). This framework differentiates between competing values that emphasize an external orientation from those that focus on internal capability, integration, and effectiveness—the external–internal domain. Further, it distinguishes between corporate attributes that emphasize effectiveness criteria that focus on flexibility and discretion from those that are centred on stability and internal control—i.e., the flexibility–stability domain. These two dimensions intersect to define four distinct types of orientations that comprise the CVF, namely the *competition culture*, *creation culture*, *collaboration culture*, and *control culture*. Schematic representations of the attributes that characterize the competing values associated with the CVF are depicted in Fig. 4.1.

Organizations with the competition culture are externally focused and performance-driven and are therefore more likely to encourage organization-wide generation, dissemination, and integration of external environmental information in the pursuit of profitability (Kohli & Jaworski, 1990; Narver & Slater, 1990). Success is assessed on the basis of indicators such as increased revenues and profitability. As a result, corporate

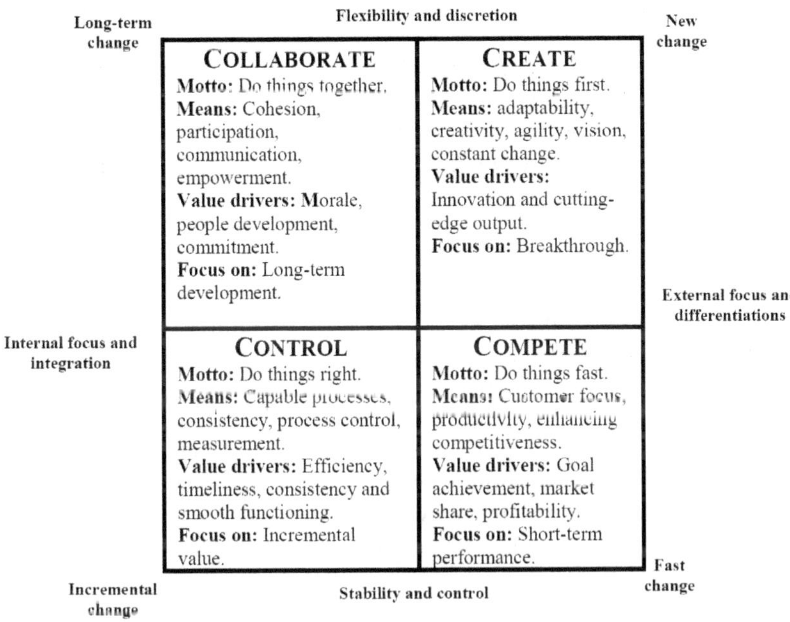

Fig. 4.1 Schematic representation of the four corporate cultures (*Note* Associated with the competing values framework [CVF]. *Source* Adapted from Cameron et al. [2014])

attributes of this kind are strongly associated with financial effectiveness and are important determinants of reported financial performance (Harris & Ogbonna, 2001; Jaworski & Kohli, 1993). Overall, speed is an indispensable component in maintaining a competitive edge, so *results-right-now* is a characteristic demand; hence, firms with an orientation towards the competition culture emphasize competitiveness and the aggressive pursuit of profits (Cameron et al., 2014; Hartnell et al., 2011; Quinn & Cameron, 1983; Quinn & Rohrbaugh, 1983).

As a comparison, corporate attributes associated with the creation culture are focused externally and centre on creating future opportunity through innovation and cutting-edge output. These elements within the organization are supported by a flexible organizational structure which stipulates freedom of thought and action among employees and allows the firm to effectively handle discontinuity, change, and risk (Cameron et al., 2014; Hartnell et al., 2011). Conversely, the collaboration and control cultures are internally focused and place emphasis on integration. However, while the collaboration culture stresses employee development and consensus building that is facilitated by a flexible organizational structure aiming to long-term development, corporate attributes that pertain to the control culture focus on creating value through internal improvements in efficiency supported by a stable organizational structure driven by strong internal control mechanisms (Cameron et al., 2014; Hartnell et al., 2011; Quinn & Cameron, 1983; Quinn & Rohrbaugh, 1983).

In this chapter, we measure corporate attributes relating to a firm's competition culture using a textual analysis of 10-K filings obtained from the SEC's Edgar database. Textual analysis permits the systematic and objective quantification of semantic content recited in a specific body of text.[3] As such, we assume that the 10-K filings encapsulate useful information regarding corporate values that firms have developed over time which is not easy to observe using other data sources. Thus, parsing 10-K filings for specific lexical items allows us to quantify corporate attributes associated with the four cultures exemplified by the CVF.

To estimate annual frequencies for each firm's competition culture, we create a list of selected lexical items that best describe this culture, as theorized in the CVF. This is achieved by a two-step procedure that

[3] There are numerous empirical studies to suggest that textual analysis of the 10-K filings is a source of semantics with useful information for finance and accounting research (refer to the review study by Loughran and McDonald [2016] and references therein).

minimizes subjectivity in the selection process (Andreou et al., 2020, 2021; Fiordelisi & Ricci, 2014, 2021; Fiordelisi et al., 2019; Luu et al., 2022). First, we select certain keywords suggested by Cameron et al. (2014) to identify corporate attributes associated with the competition culture. Second, all keywords selected in the first step are looked up in the Harvard IV-4 Psychosocial Dictionary to identify other synonyms. For instance, a relatively high frequency of keywords in 10-Ks describing "achievement", "profit", "performance", "competitiveness", "market", etc. should be associated with the competition culture. In that respect, the set of synonyms comprises the bag of words that describe the firms' competition culture. We account for suffixes (forming grammatical and derivational variants of the same lexical item) by reducing these words to their stemmed form (e.g., "competitiveness" becomes "compet*"). This helps to ensure that when we conduct our word search, we count all variants of words that make up our list. We then investigate the items so as to exclude terms consistent with firm names, industries, and other words likely to systematically bias our results. We follow similar steps to create the corresponding bag of words for the other three corporate cultural orientations (*creation culture*, *collaboration culture*, and *control culture*) as theorized by the CVF. The bag of words with all lexical items used to parse the 10-Ks are listed in Appendix A.

Specifically, we measure competition culture (COMP) by counting the number of times that the lexical items included in the bag of words describing corporate attributes for the competition culture are found in the 10-K filings. Since firms' 10-Ks can reflect other corporate attributes associated with create, collaborate, and control cultural orientations, we likewise apply our word count algorithm to also estimate frequencies on these alternative orientations and scale our measure as follows[4]:

$$\text{COMP} = \frac{\text{Number of lexical items describing the competition culture}}{\text{Total number of lexical items for all types of cultures}}. \quad (4.1)$$

As we have discussed in Chapter 3, similar textual analysis approaches have been shown to extract valuable information from firms' reports (Andreou et al., 2020, 2021; Audi et al., 2016; Bushman et al., 2016; Fiordelisi & Ricci, 2014, 2021; Fiordelisi et al., 2019; Kearney & Liu, 2014; Li et al.,

[4] While conducting our count we exclude negation of the lexical items by ignoring occasions when the word is preceded by "no", "non", "not", "less", "few", or "limited" by three or fewer words.

2013a; Li, 2010a, 2010b; Loughran & McDonald, 2011, 2016; Luu et al., 2022). What is more, some authors (e.g., Bushman et al., 2016; Li et al, 2013a) have used textual analysis to measure product market competition, which is a concept close in terminology to our own. These studies capture the relevant information extracted from discussions of competition in the 10-K filings primarily by counting the number of occurrences of word inflections relating to the lexical item "competition".[5]

However, unlike these prior works we carefully construct our measurement approach to capture corporate attributes that describe a firm's competition culture by using a comprehensive bag of words that elicit the full array of firms' corporate cultures as theorized under the CVF in Cameron et al. (2014) and Hartnell et al. (2011). Scaling the frequency of lexical items describing a firm's competition culture by the total number of lexical items in the bags of words for all four cultural orientations allows us to construct a relative intensity measure of the competition culture that does not neglect the intensity of the rest of the corporate cultures that exist within firms.

Figure 4.2 presents some of the properties of our measure. In particular, it highlights the frequency of the competition culture related words used per 10-K report. We observe lexical items such as customer*, market*, result*, and performanc* ranking highest, with 10 to 15 occurrences on average per 10-K report. This distribution across words is consistent with the theoretical underpinnings in the CVF and is suggestive that our empirical measure is able to capture important facets of the competition culture.

In introducing our measure, we do not claim that our method or chosen framework represents the one best approach to assess culture in firms. To do so would be of course unreasonable since as we have discussed in Chapter 2 other authors have proposed alternative approaches to measuring organizational culture (see for example, Deal & Kennedy, 1982; Denison, 1990; Handy, 1976; Hofstede, 1980, 2001, 2011; Johnson, 1988; O'Reilly et al., 1991, 1996; Reynolds, 1986; Schein, 1990, 1992). However, we argue that our technique is practical as it allows us to quantify the key dimensions of organizational culture that have been found to matter and to do so in a manageable

[5] The studies by Li et al. (2013a) and Bushman et al. (2016) rely on a measure that counts the number of occurrences of the words, competition, competitor, competitive, compete, and competing, and scaled by the total number of words in the document.

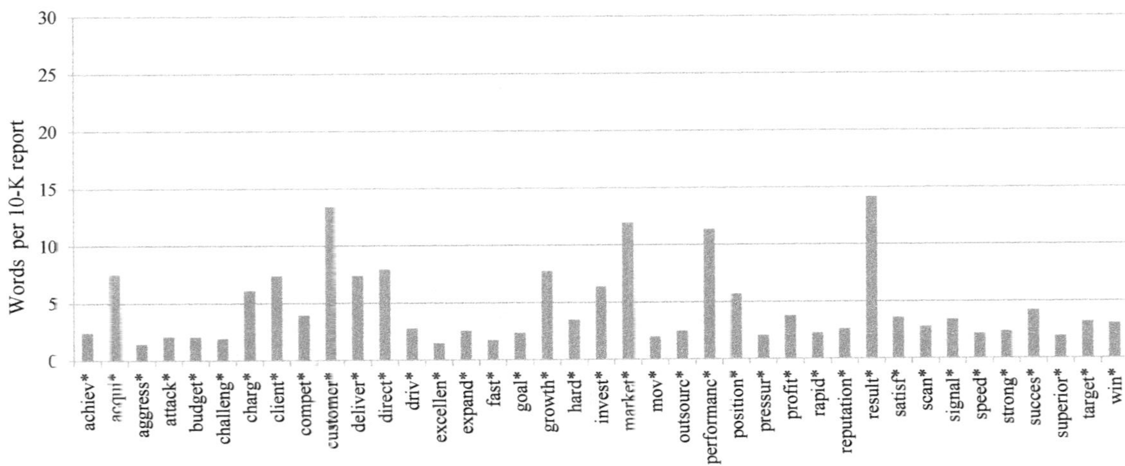

Fig. 4.2 Lexical items per 10-K report for a firm's competition culture (*Note* This figure presents the per 10-K report frequency of the lexical items used to identify the competition Culture)

way for a large sample of firms. Further, our approach is objective as it permits the capture of firms' competition culture in a manner that is unlikely to be influenced by subjective biases. What is more, our measure and the framework upon which it is built do not only make sense, but they are both valid. In particular, the competing values framework is supported by empirical literature and the underlying dimensions have a verified scholarly foundation (Quinn & Rohrbaugh, 1983). Beyond this, we assess the validity of our measure of firms' competition culture by relating it to other measures of firms' competition culture. Further, we show that our measure of competition culture is distinct from managerial short-termism and does not significantly overlap with product market competition as captured by Li et al.'s (2013a) text-based firm-specific competitive environment measure.[6]

4.2.2 *Hypotheses*

In this study, we use our measure of competition culture to investigate whether and how transient and dedicated institutional ownership is related to firms' competition culture. Based on past literature and our own reasoning we expect that since transient institutional owners emphasize short-term performance, these investors should propel a firm towards adopting more competition culture relative to the other cultural orientations. Furthermore, consistent with past literature, we argue that such investors are more likely to intervene and exert pressure on managers to intensify their competition culture, aiming for *results-right-now* and more immediate financial performance (Bernardo & Welch, 2004; Fos & Kahn, 2015). Consequently, it is reasonable to expect that the management of a firm with more transient institutional investors will yield to such pressures in order to avoid these investors becoming unhappy and forcefully exiting the firm, thereby suppressing the firm's stock price. Hence, we propose the following hypothesis in alternate form;

H1: Transient institutional ownership is positively associated with firm's competition culture.

[6] Please see the Appendix A for univariate and multivariate validation and sanity checks on our measure of firms' competition culture.

Conversely, it is widely accepted that dedicated institutional investors are more likely to stress long-term performance (see e.g., Bushee, 1998). Thus, we can expect that these investors will be motivated to dampen a firm's competition culture when management's overinvestment in this type of operating environment is likely to undermine the long-term performance and success of the firm. This proposition is plausible since it supports the notion that dedicated institutional investors also intervene and influence managers, but unlike transient investors, do so in line with their incentives to monitor and offset managerial myopia and to assess financial performance based on information beyond the current period (Chen et al., 2007; Gaspar et al., 2005; Harford et al., 2018). Thus, we propose the following hypotheses in alternate form;

H2: Dedicated institutional ownership is negatively associated with firm's competition culture.

4.3 Data, Variables, and Sample Selection

4.3.1 Data

To conduct our empirical analysis, we build a unique dataset by merging information from various data sources. We obtain annual firm-level data of US publicly traded firms for the period 1994 to 2014 from Compustat. To measure the competition culture through textual analysis we obtain firms' 10-K reports from the SEC's Edgar database. For the institutional ownership variables, we employ data from the Thomson Reuters Institutional Holdings Database. Finally, we acquire Russell 1000 and Russell 2000 index constituents for the period 2003 until 2006 from the Russell Corporation.

Our analysis is carried out on all firms included in the Compustat database excluding financials (SIC 6000–6999) and utilities (SIC 4900–4999). To limit survivorship bias, firms that are inactive and/or acquired by another firm during the period of study are retained in the sample. We also delete from our sample all firm-year observations with missing data on the variables of interest. This results in a final main sample consisting of 31,223 firm-year observations. Table 4.1 reports the definition of all the variables used in the empirical analysis.

Table 4.1 Definition of variables

	Symbol		*Definitions*
Competition culture			
	COMP	=	the intensity of a firm's competition culture estimated for each fiscal year using the text-analysis approach
Institutional ownership			
	TRA	=	the percentage of stock ownership in the firm by transient institutional investors relative to total shares outstanding
	DED	=	the percentage of stock ownership in the firm by dedicated institutional investors relative to total shares outstanding
Other variables			
	AGE	=	number of years since the firm first appears in CRSP
	DTURN	=	average monthly turnover for the current fiscal year, minus the average monthly share turnover for the previous year;
	DYIELD	=	annual dividend yield
	FLOAT	=	the difference between rank implied by the observed market capitalization and the rank assigned by Russell in June
	HHI	=	the Herfindahl–Hirschman concentration ratio computed using total assets for each firm by FF 48 index and state;
	LEV	=	long-term debt by total assets
	MKTCAP	=	natural logarithm of market capitalization at May 31 for each calendar year
	MTB	=	market to book value of equity at the end of the fiscal year
	RANK	=	the rank order of the Russell index based on market capitalizations on May 31 of each calendar year
	RET	=	average weekly returns for the fiscal year

(continued)

Table 4.1 (continued)

Symbol		*Definitions*
ROA	=	return on assets defined as income before extraordinary items divided by total assets
R2000	=	equal to 1 if the firm is in the Russell 2000 index and is 0 if the firm is a member of the Russell 1000 index
SGROWTH	=	sales for the fiscal year divided by sales for the prior fiscal year
SIZE	=	natural logarithm of the market value of equity at the end of the fiscal year
SP500	=	equal to 1 if the firm is included in the S&P 500 index, and is 0 otherwise; and
STDEV	=	the volatility of firm-specific weekly returns

4.3.2 *Measuring Institutional Ownership*

We adopt two measures of institutional ownership, namely transient and dedicated institutional ownership, as in Bushee (1998) and subsequently studied in numerous works.[7] Transient institutional ownership, TRA, is defined as the percentage of stock ownership in the firm by transient institutional investors relative to total shares outstanding. Transient investors focus on short-term performance and invest based on the likelihood of earning short-term trading profits (Bushee, 1998, 2001; Callen & Fang, 2013). Dedicated institutional ownership, DED, is defined as the percentage of stock ownership in the firm by dedicated institutional investors relative to total shares outstanding. Dedicated investors are defined as those that hold large stakes in a limited number of firms and have strong incentives to monitor the long-term performance of management (Bushee, 1998, 2001; Chen et al., 2001).

[7] An incomplete list of studies includes Shleifer and Vishny (1986), Gompers and Metrick (1998), Bushee (2001), Cai and Zheng (2004), Gaspar et al. (2005), Chen et al. (2007), Yan and Zhang (2009), Elyasiani and Jia (2010), Elyasiani et al. (2010), Callen and Fang (2013), and Andreou et al. (2016, 2017).

4.3.3 Control Variables

Next, we select a series of control variables for our empirical analysis based on the prior literature that has considered these variables (please see e.g., Andreou et al., 2021; Bushee, 1998, 2001; Callen & Fang, 2013; Chen et al., 2001). Firstly, we include in all models controls to capture firm-specific characteristics. Specifically, we include the following variables: the number of years since the firm was first included in the CRSP/Compustat database, AGE; financial leverage as indicated by total liabilities scaled by total assets, LEV; market value of equity divided by book value of equity, MTB; income on total assets, ROA; and the natural logarithm of market value of equity, SIZE.

Further, in our main specifications, we control for investor heterogeneity since it is argued that this construct influences both variables. We control for investor heterogeneity by including the detrended average weekly stock trading volume, DTURN, average weekly returns, RET, and volatility of weekly returns, STDEV, over the fiscal year (Bushman et al., 2016; Hong & Stein, 2003).

4.3.4 Descriptive Statistics and Correlations

Table 4.2 presents the descriptive statistics of the variables used in our empirical analysis.[8] In particular, the mean value of our competition culture variable, COMP, is 0.49. The institutional ownership variables TRA and DED have respective mean values of 0.15 and 0.06. We observe that the summary statistics on the variables are largely comparable to the values reported in previous studies using these data (Andreou et al., 2017, 2021; Bushee, 2001; Callen & Fang, 2013).

We compute Pearson correlation coefficients for the variables used in our empirical analysis and report these in Table 4.3. Some of the more interesting correlations include the relationship between COMP and TRA (DED), where we find a positive and significant correlation between COMP and TRA (correlation = 0.0958) and a negative and significant correlation between COMP and DED (correlation = −0.0621). These

[8] To mitigate the effects of outliers, all continuous variables are winsorized at the 1% and 99% levels.

Table 4.2 Descriptive statistics for the variables used in the empirical analyses

Variable	*Obs*	*Mean*	*Std. Dev*	*25th Pctl*	*Median*	*75th Pctl*
COMP	31,223	0.49	0.06	0.45	0.49	0.54
TRA	31,223	0.15	0.12	0.06	0.13	0.22
DED	31,223	0.06	0.09	0	0.01	0.09
AGE	31,223	23.64	12.98	14	20	32
DTURN	31,223	1.19	23.18	−5.97	0.4	7.76
DYIELD	31,223	0.01	0.05	0	0	0.01
FLOAT	2,608	103.45	132.92	−485	3	78
HHI	31,223	0.43	0.29	0.2	0.35	0.6
LEV	31,223	0.47	0.29	0.28	0.46	0.62
MKTCAP	2,900	20.66	1.57	16.91	19.53	20.41
MTB	31,223	3.38	55.44	1.32	2.13	3.58
RANK	2,900	413.88	830.87	−999	−314	415
RET	31,223	−0.2	0.21	−0.25	−0.12	−0.06
ROA	31,223	0.01	0.26	0	0.05	0.08
R2000	2,900	0.65	0.48	0	0	1
SGROWTH	30,910	1.37	21.47	1	1.09	1.23
SIZE	31,223	6.29	1.78	5.02	6.2	7.43
SP500	31,223	0.21	0.41	0	0	0
STDEV	31,223	0.06	0.03	0.04	0.05	0.07

results are consistent with our expectations that transient institutional ownership intensifies the firm's competition culture, while dedicated institutional ownership diminishes it.

4.4 Empirical Results

In this section, we report our multivariate results based on the empirical approaches adopted to deal with the practical challenges associated with our research design. In particular, based on the extant literature, we would expect to observe rather persistent levels of competition culture over time (Andreou et al., 2021; Cameron et al., 2014; Guiso et al., 2006, 2015a, 2015b; Hartnell et al., 2011). Hence, we adopt OLS and generalised least squares random effects (GLS-RE) regressions since, unlike fixed effects estimators, OLS and GLS-RE are able to provide valid estimates of parameters where the variable in interests appears to change slowly over time.

Table 4.3 Pearson correlation matrix

	COMP	*TRA*	*DED*	*AGE*	*DTURN*	*DYIELD*	*FLOAT*	*HHI*
TRA	**0.0958**							
DED	**−0.0621**	−0.0114						
AGE	**−0.1571**	**−0.1061**	**0.0644**					
DTURN	**−0.0259**	**0.1298**	−0.0062	0.0112				
DYIELD	**−0.0286**	**−0.0468**	0.0052	**0.0831**	0.0039			
FLOAT	0.0124	**0.1529**	**−0.0713**	**−0.2818**	**0.1225**	**−0.0747**		
HHI	**−0.0776**	**−0.0928**	**−0.0228**	**0.1830**	0.0026	**0.0466**	−0.0369	
LEV	**−0.0876**	−0.0055	**0.0588**	**0.1012**	**0.0261**	**0.0409**	**−0.0665**	**0.0779**
MKTCAP	−0.0238	**−0.1210**	0.0323	**0.2523**	−0.0163	0.0152	**−0.1697**	**0.0826**
MTB	0.0019	0.0071	0.0039	0.0032	0.0006	0.0011	−0.0177	−0.0040
PCTCOMP	**0.1389**	0.0012	**0.0651**	**−0.1616**	**−0.0315**	**−0.0575**	**0.0705**	**−0.0745**
RANK	**0.0532**	−0.0177	**−0.1236**	**−0.4013**	0.0181	0.0034	**0.5787**	**−0.0897**
RET	**−0.1054**	**−0.0803**	**0.0322**	**0.2821**	**−0.1528**	**0.0776**	**−0.2513**	**0.1216**
ROA	**−0.0239**	**0.0465**	**0.0243**	**0.1305**	**0.0498**	**0.0451**	**−0.0707**	**0.0702**
R2000	**0.0538**	**0.1221**	**−0.1499**	**−0.3297**	**0.0778**	−0.0121	**0.4682**	**−0.0903**
SGROWTH	**0.0278**	−0.0028	−0.0046	−0.0109	0.0115	−0.0037	0.0040	−0.0075
SIZE	**−0.0512**	**0.2368**	**0.0241**	**0.2867**	**0.0792**	**0.0151**	**−0.4069**	0.0122
SP500	**−0.1022**	**0.0626**	**0.0881**	**0.4053**	**0.0245**	**0.0330**	**−0.3701**	**0.0565**
STDEV	**0.1141**	**0.1165**	**−0.0271**	−0.3387	**0.1427**	**−0.0965**	**0.2944**	**−0.1413**

	LEV	*MKTCAP*	*MTB*	*RET*	*ROA*	*R2000*	*SGROWTH*	*SIZE*	*SP500*
MKTCAP	**0.0460**								
MTB	0.0035	0.0153							
RANK	**−0.1815**	**−0.3372**	**−0.0445**						
RET	**0.0512**	**0.1404**	−0.0085						
ROA	**−0.3109**	**0.0986**	−0.0032	**0.2943**					
R2000	**−0.1415**	**−0.2984**	**−0.0461**	**−0.3223**	**−0.1942**				
SGROWTH	0.0004	−0.0025	0.0000	−0.0045	−0.0057	−0.0230			
SIZE	**0.0994**	**0.4559**	**0.0205**	**0.3559**	**0.2017**	**−0.7712**	0.0068		
SP500	**0.1399**	**0.3268**	0.0046	**0.2191**	**0.1060**	**−0.6470**	0.0078	**0.6406**	
STDEV	**−0.0691**	**−0.1973**	0.0045	**−0.9629**	**−0.2903**	**0.4077**	0.0055	**−0.4243**	**−0.2758**

This table presents Pearson correlation coefficients for the variables used in the empirical analyses. The bold figures indicate significance at the 10% level or better

Next, we test H1 and H2 by investigating whether transient and dedicated institutional ownership are related to firms' competition culture. We expect that since transient institutional owners emphasize short-term performance, these investors should propel a firm towards adopting a competition culture. Meanwhile, since dedicated institutional investors are more likely to stress long-term performance, we expect that these investors will dampen a firm's competition culture. To test empirically whether transient (dedicated) institutional ownership is positively (negatively) related to competition culture, we estimate the following regression model:

$$\begin{aligned}\mathrm{COMP}_{t+1} = {} & \alpha_1 + \alpha_2\mathrm{TRA}_t(or\,\mathrm{DED}_t) + \alpha_3\mathrm{AGE}_t + \alpha_4\mathrm{DTURN}_t \\ & + \alpha_5\mathrm{LEV}_t + \alpha_6\mathrm{MTB}_t + \alpha_7\mathrm{RET}_t + \alpha_8\mathrm{ROA}_t \\ & + \alpha_9\mathrm{SIZE}_t + \alpha_{10}\mathrm{STDEV}_t + \varepsilon_t \end{aligned} \tag{4.2}$$

where COMP represents the level of firm's competition culture. The variables of interests TRA (DED) represent firm's level of transient (dedicated) institutional ownership. We include control variables that capture firm-specific characteristics. We adopt these control variables to ensure that the impact of our institutional ownership variables on the competition culture is not driven by other factors. Also, we include year dummies in all regressions to control for unobserved time-invariant year effects. In addition, the estimates include dummies based on Fama and French's (1997) 48 industry classifications to control for fixed industry effects. The standard errors are corrected for firm clustering to control for potential bias in the estimates that occur when the residuals are correlated across firms.

Further, we explore whether changes in a firm's competition culture are related to its composition of institutional ownership. For this, we rank firms into deciles based on their competition culture at time t and test whether institutional ownership structure can explain the t to $t + 1$ changes in a firm's decile rank of competition culture. Given the premise that transient institutional owners pressure a firm's management to adopt greater competition culture, we test empirically whether transient institutional ownership is significantly related to an *increase* in the firm's decile rank of competition culture by estimating the following regression model:

$$\begin{aligned}\Delta\text{COMP\_INC}_{t+1} = {} & \alpha_1 + \alpha_2\text{TRA}_t + \alpha_3\text{AGE}_t + \alpha_4\text{DTURN}_t \\ & + \alpha_5\text{LEV}_t + \alpha_6\text{MTB}_t + \alpha_7\text{RET}_t + \alpha_8\text{ROA}_t \\ & + \alpha_9\text{SIZE}_t + \alpha_{10}\text{STDEV}_t + \varepsilon_t \end{aligned} \tag{4.3}$$

where ΔCOMP_INC is an indicator variable that is set equal to one if the firm experiences an increase in the decile rank of COMP from last year and is zero otherwise. In this model, TRA represents our variable of interest, while the control variables are used to capture firm-specific characteristics. As before, we include year dummies to control for unobserved time-invariant year effects. In addition, we include dummies based on Fama and French's (1997) 48 industry classifications to control for fixed industry effects. The standard errors are clustered by firm.

Furthermore, since dedicated institutional investors are argued in H2 to be more likely to dampen a firm's competition culture, we investigate whether a firm's composition of dedicated institutional ownership is significantly related to a *decrease* in the firm's decile rank of competition culture. We test this empirically by estimating the following model:

$$\begin{aligned}\Delta\text{COMP\_DEC}_{t+1} = {} & \alpha_1 + \alpha_2\text{DED}_t + \alpha_3\text{AGE}_t + \alpha_4\text{DTURN}_t \\ & + \alpha_5\text{LEV}_t + \alpha_6\text{MTB}_t + \alpha_7\text{RET}_t + \alpha_8\text{ROA}_t \\ & + \alpha_9\text{SIZE}_t + \alpha_{10}\text{STDEV}_t + \varepsilon_t \end{aligned} \tag{4.4}$$

where ΔCOMP_DEC is an indicator variable set equal to one if the firm experiences a decrease in the decile rank of COMP from the past year and is zero otherwise. The variable of interests DED represents a firm's level of dedicated institutional ownership, and as before we include control variables that capture firm-specific characteristics. Also, year and industry dummies are included to control for unobserved time-invariant year and industry effects. The standard errors are corrected for firm clustering to control for potential bias in the estimates that occur when the residuals are correlated across firms.

The estimates of Eqs. (4.2–4.4) are provided in Table 4.4. The coefficient of interest is α_2, which is expected to be positive (negative) in the case of the relationship between transient (dedicated) institutional ownership and COMP. Consistent with H1 (H2), in Table 4.4 column (1) of

Panel A (Panel B) we find that the coefficient term on the TRA_t (DED_t) is 0.053 (−0.021) and significant at the 1% (10%) level with a t-value of 5.01 (1.89). Not only are these results statistically significant, but they are also economically significant. In particular, the coefficient value 0.053 on the TRA_t variable implies that a one standard deviation increase in transient institutional ownership leads to an approximate 0.106 (= [0.053 × 0.12]/ 0.06) increase in a firm's competition culture than would otherwise be the case, and given a mean for competition culture of 0.49, this represents an approximate 22% increase in its value.

Furthermore, our GLS-RE estimates of Eq. (4.2), as shown in column (4) of Panel A (Panel B), provide additional empirical support that transient (dedicated) institutional ownership increases (decreases) a firm's competition culture. Besides this, our logistic regression estimates of Eqs (4.3) and (4.4) are presented in column (7) of Panel A (Panel B). These estimates present further evidence consistent with H1 (H2) of the causal relationship between transient (dedicated) institutional ownership and increases (decreases) in a firm's competition culture. These results provide compelling evidence in support of our argument that transient institutional investors exert pressure on management to shift a firm's competition culture.

In further tests of the main hypotheses, we estimate models to examine the relationship between lagged values and differences in our institutional ownership variables and competition culture. These tests examine whether and how institutional ownership impacts a firm's competition culture at spans greater than one year. Regressions that examine the long-run relationship can help to further mitigate potential simultaneity issues and shed light on the direction of the relationship between institutional ownership and competition culture. If transient (dedicated) institutional ownership is positively (negatively) related to levels of competition culture and increases (decreases) in a firm's decile rank of competition culture in two- and three-years' time, it is more likely that transient (dedicated) institutional ownership alters a firm's competition culture than the inverse. In particular, we estimate the following empirical models:

$$\begin{aligned} \text{COMP}_{t+1} = & \alpha_1 + \alpha_2 \Delta \text{TRA}_t (or\, \Delta \text{DED}_t) + \alpha_3 \text{TRA}_{t-1} (or\, \text{DED}_{t-1}) \\ & + \alpha_4 \text{AGE}_t + \alpha_5 \text{DTURN}_t + \alpha_6 \text{LEV}_t + \alpha_7 \text{MTB}_t \\ & + \alpha_8 \text{RET}_t + \alpha_9 \text{ROA}_t + \alpha_{10} \text{SIZE}_t + \alpha_{11} \text{STDEV}_t + \varepsilon_t \end{aligned} \quad (4.5)$$

Table 4.4 OLS, random effects and logistic regressions of institutional ownership on competition culture

Panel A. The effect of transient institutional ownership on competition culture

	$COMP_{t+1}$						$\Delta COMP\_INC_{t+1}$		
	(1)	(2)	(3)	(4)	(5)	(6)	(7)	(8)	(9)
TRA_t	0.053***			0.022***			0.066***		
	(5.01)			(3.10)			(3.03)		
ΔTRA_t		0.031***	0.030***		0.011**	0.009*		0.056**	0.058**
		(4.37)	(4.30)		(2.02)	(1.79)		(2.26)	(2.33)
TRA_{t-1}		0.064***			0.034***			0.074***	
		(4.93)			(3.67)			(2.92)	
ΔTRA_{t-1}			0.048***			0.023***			0.083***
			(5.29)			(3.22)			(2.84)
TRA_{t-2}			0.066***			0.035***			0.069**
			(4.53)			(3.25)			(2.49)
AGE_t	−0.087***	−0.085***	−0.085***	−0.143***	−0.141***	−0.141***	0.049**	0.050**	0.049**
	(6.06)	(5.97)	(5.97)	(9.47)	(9.34)	(9.34)	(2.34)	(2.35)	(2.32)
$DTURN_t$	−0.019***	−0.019***	−0.018***	−0.004	−0.004	−0.003	0.015	0.015	0.01
	(4.26)	(4.27)	(4.07)	(1.22)	(1.32)	(0.98)	(0.69)	(0.70)	(0.44)
LEV_t	−0.057***	−0.057***	−0.057***	−0.01	−0.009	−0.009	−0.023	−0.023	−0.023
	(4.85)	(4.81)	(4.81)	(1.08)	(1.00)	(1.00)	(0.94)	(0.93)	(0.94)
MTB_t	−0.012	−0.011	−0.011	−0.009*	−0.009*	−0.009	−0.023	−0.023	−0.024
	(1.32)	(1.22)	(1.19)	(1.78)	(1.67)	(1.62)	(1.45)	(1.46)	(1.45)
RET_t	−0.065**	−0.070**	−0.069**	−0.054***	−0.059***	−0.058***	−0.223***	−0.226***	−0.227***
	(2.26)	(2.44)	(2.41)	(2.80)	(3.03)	(2.97)	(3.13)	(3.14)	(3.16)
ROA_t	−0.004	−0.004	−0.004	−0.017***	−0.017***	−0.017***	−0.006	−0.006	−0.006
	(0.35)	(0.35)	(0.34)	(2.69)	(2.72)	(2.69)	(0.27)	(0.28)	(0.30)
$SIZE_t$	−0.013	−0.017	−0.017	0.039***	0.034**	0.034**	−0.027	−0.027	−0.025

(continued)

Table 4.4 (continued)

Panel A. The effect of transient institutional ownership on competition culture

	$COMP_{t+1}$						$\Delta COMP\_INC_{t+1}$		
	(1)	*(2)*	*(3)*	*(4)*	*(5)*	*(6)*	*(7)*	*(8)*	*(9)*
	(0.83)	(1.06)	(1.05)	(2.81)	(2.41)	(2.40)	(1.13)	(1.16)	(1.07)
$STDEV_t$	−0.043	−0.049	−0.048	−0.054**	−0.059***	−0.058***	−0.227***	−0.230***	−0.230***
	(1.27)	(1.43)	(1.40)	(2.42)	(2.63)	(2.59)	(2.88)	(2.89)	(2.89)
R^2	0.18	0.18	0.18	0.05	0.05	0.05	0.02	0.02	0.02
N	31,223	31,223	31,223	31,223	31,223	31,223	13,034	13,034	13,034

Panel B. The effect of dedicated institutional ownership on competition culture

	$COMP_{t+1}$						$\Delta COMP\_DEC_{t+1}$		
	(1)	*(2)*	*(3)*	*(4)*	*(5)*	*(6)*	*(7)*	*(8)*	*(9)*
DED_t	−0.021*			−0.022***			−0.036		
	(1.89)			(2.68)			(1.64)		
ΔDED_t		−0.014*	−0.012		−0.016***	−0.016***		−0.074***	−0.075***
		(1.74)	(1.55)		(2.67)	(2.64)		(2.62)	(2.66)
DED_{t-1}		−0.023*			−0.025**			−0.01	
		(1.75)			(2.44)			(0.36)	
ΔDED_{t-1}			−0.006			−0.014*			−0.021
			(0.59)			(1.78)			(0.75)
DED_{t-2}			−0.029**			−0.032***			−0.004
			(1.96)			(2.69)			(0.13)

Panel B. The effect of dedicated institutional ownership on competition culture

	$COMP_{t+1}$						$\Delta COMP\_DEC_{t+1}$		
	(1)	(2)	(3)	(4)	(5)	(6)	(7)	(8)	(9)
AGE_t	−0.094***	−0.094***	−0.094***	−0.147***	−0.147***	−0.146***	−0.02	−0.019	−0.02
	(6.58)	(6.58)	(6.57)	(9.75)	(9.74)	(9.71)	(0.95)	(0.91)	(0.92)
$DTURN_t$	−0.014***	−0.014***	−0.013***	−0.002	−0.002	−0.002	0.040*	0.039*	0.039*
	(3.15)	(3.14)	(3.09)	(0.69)	(0.68)	(0.64)	(1.90)	(1.87)	(1.86)
LEV_t	−0.056***	−0.056***	−0.056***	−0.009	−0.009	−0.009	−0.013	−0.015	−0.015
	(4.76)	(4.75)	(4.71)	(1.02)	(1.01)	(0.98)	(0.65)	(0.75)	(0.78)
MTB_t	−0.013	−0.013	−0.013	−0.009*	−0.009*	−0.009*	−0.063	−0.061	−0.061
	(1.37)	(1.38)	(1.44)	(1.67)	(1.68)	(1.73)	(1.30)	(1.28)	(1.28)
RET_t	−0.031	−0.031	−0.031	−0.044**	−0.044**	−0.044**	−0.052	−0.052	−0.052
	(1.08)	(1.09)	(1.09)	(2.26)	(2.27)	(2.28)	(0.70)	(0.70)	(0.70)
ROA_t	−0.001	−0.001	−0.001	−0.016**	−0.016**	−0.016**	−0.005	−0.005	−0.005
	(0.13)	(0.13)	(0.13)	(2.49)	(2.50)	(2.48)	(0.26)	(0.25)	(0.25)
$SIZE_t$	0.01	0.01	0.011	0.050***	0.050***	0.051***	0.041*	0.039*	0.039
	(0.65)	(0.66)	(0.72)	(3.75)	(3.76)	(3.79)	(1.75)	(1.66)	(1.63)
$STDEV_t$	−0.005	−0.006	−0.006	−0.044*	−0.044**	−0.045**	−0.026	−0.024	−0.024
	(0.15)	(0.17)	(0.18)	(1.95)	(1.97)	(1.98)	(0.32)	(0.30)	(0.30)
R^2	0.17	0.17	0.17	0.05	0.05	0.05	0.02	0.02	0.02
N	31,223	31,223	31,223	31,223	31,223	31,223	13,037	13,037	13,037

$^*p < 0.1$; $^{**}p < 0.05$; $^{***}p < 0.01$

This table presents OLS (columns 1–3), GLS-RE (columns 4–6) and logistic regression (columns 7–9) estimates used to investigate the impact of transient (TRA) [Panel A] and dedicated (DED) [Panel B] institutional ownership on the level of firms' competition culture (COMP) (columns 1–6) and increases (ΔCOMP_INC) or decreases (ΔCOMP_DEC) in the decile rank of firm's competition culture (columns 7–9). All regressions include year fixed effects, while the OLS and logistic regression estimates also include industry fixed effects. The standard errors are all clustered at the firm-level. The *t*-values are given in parentheses

$$\Delta COMP\_INC_{t+1} = \alpha_1 + \alpha_2 \Delta TRA_t + \alpha_3 TRA_{t-1} + \alpha_4 AGE_t + \alpha_5 DTURN_t + \alpha_6 LEV_t + \alpha_7 MTB_t + \alpha_8 RET_t + \alpha_9 ROA_t + \alpha_{10} SIZE_t + \alpha_{11} STDEV_t + \varepsilon_t \quad (4.6)$$

$$\Delta \mathrm{COMP\_DEC}_{t+1} = \alpha_1 + \alpha_2 \Delta \mathrm{DED}_t + \alpha_3 \mathrm{DED}_{t-1} + \alpha_4 \mathrm{AGE}_t + \alpha_5 \mathrm{DTURN}_t + \alpha_6 \mathrm{LEV}_t + \alpha_7 \mathrm{MTB}_t + \alpha_8 \mathrm{RET}_t + \alpha_9 \mathrm{ROA}_t + \alpha_{10} \mathrm{SIZE}_t + \alpha_{11} \mathrm{STDEV}_t + \varepsilon_t \quad (4.7)$$

$$\mathrm{COMP}_{t+1} = \alpha_1 + \alpha_2 \Delta \mathrm{TRA}_t (or\, \Delta \mathrm{DED}_t) + \alpha_3 \Delta \mathrm{TRA}_{t-1} (or\, \Delta \mathrm{DED}_{t-1}) + \alpha_4 \mathrm{TRA}_{t-2} (or\, \mathrm{DED}_{t-2}) + \alpha_5 \mathrm{AGE}_t + \alpha_6 \mathrm{DTURN}_t + \alpha_7 \mathrm{LEV}_t + \alpha_8 \mathrm{MTB}_t + \alpha_9 \mathrm{RET}_t + \alpha_{10} \mathrm{ROA}_t + \alpha_{11} \mathrm{SIZE}_t + \alpha_{12} \mathrm{STDEV}_t + \varepsilon_t \quad (4.8)$$

$$\Delta \mathrm{COMP\_INC}_{t+1} = \alpha_1 + \alpha_2 \Delta \mathrm{TRA}_t + \alpha_3 \Delta \mathrm{TRA}_{t-1} + \alpha_4 \mathrm{TRA}_{t-2} + \alpha_5 \mathrm{AGE}_t + \alpha_6 \mathrm{DTURN}_t + \alpha_7 \mathrm{LEV}_t + \alpha_8 \mathrm{MTB}_t + \alpha_9 \mathrm{RET}_t + \alpha_{10} \mathrm{ROA}_t + \alpha_{11} \mathrm{SIZE}_t + \alpha_{12} \mathrm{STDEV}_t + \varepsilon_t \quad (4.9)$$

and,

$$\Delta \mathrm{COMP\_DEC}_{t+1} = \alpha_1 + \alpha_2 \Delta \mathrm{DED}_t + \alpha_3 \Delta \mathrm{DED}_{t-1} + \alpha_4 \mathrm{DED}_{t-2} + \alpha_5 \mathrm{AGE}_t + \alpha_6 \mathrm{DTURN}_t + \alpha_7 \mathrm{LEV}_t + \alpha_8 \mathrm{MTB}_t + \alpha_9 \mathrm{RET}_t + \alpha_{10} \mathrm{ROA}_t + \alpha_{11} \mathrm{SIZE}_t + \alpha_{12} \mathrm{STDEV}_t + \varepsilon_t \quad (4.10)$$

The estimates for the above specifications are reported in Table 4.4. We find for Eq. (4.5) that the coefficient term 0.064 (−0.023) for TRA_{t-1} (DED_{t-1}), which is provided in Table 4.5 column (2) in Panel A (Panel B), is significantly positive (negative) at the 1% (10%) level with a t-value of 4.93 (1.75); similar results hold for $\Delta\mathrm{TRA}_t$ ($\Delta\mathrm{DED}_t$), where the coefficient and t-value are 0.031 (−0.014) and 4.37 (1.74), thereby indicating a significantly positive (negative) relationship between the change in transient (dedicated) institutional ownership and competition culture at the

1% (10%) level. Besides this, based on Eq. (4.8), in column (3) the coefficient is 0.066 (−0.029) on the TRA_{t-2} (DED_{t-2}) variable, suggesting a positive (negative) and significant relationship between transient (dedicated) institutional ownership and firms' disposition to compete three years into the future at the 1% (5%) level given a t-value of 4.53 (1.96). Further, the coefficients of ΔTRA_t and ΔTRA_{t-1} are positive and significant at the 1% level in column (3) with coefficients terms of 0.030 and 0.048, and t-values of 4.30 and 5.29, respectively. The fact that first and second differences in transient institutional ownership help to predict future competition culture suggests that not only the level but also the change in transient institutional ownership propels a firm's competition culture. Similar long-run estimates of Eqs. (4.5) and (4.8) are produced using the GLS-RE estimator. These results are provided in Table 4.4 columns (5) and (6) and are consistent with the pooled OLS estimates of these equations. Moreover, the long-run estimates for the impact of transient (dedicated) institutional ownership on increases (decreases) in a firm's decile rank of competition culture, as specified in Eqs. (4.6, 4.7, 4.9, and 4.10) are consistent with the prior estimates. These results are given in Table 4.4 columns (8) and (9) of Panels A and B and offer further evidence in support of our argument that transient institutional investors are able to pressurize management to increase a firm's competition culture, while dedicated institutional investors lessen it. In addition, for completeness, fixed effects estimates of Eqs. (4.2, 4.5, and 4.8) are provided in Appendix A. These results are consistent with our previous findings.

As a further test of H1 (H2), we adopt an instrumental variables (IV) approach to identify the causal effect of transient (dedicated) institutional ownership on firms' competition culture based on the composition of the popular Russell indexes. To do this, we note that each May 31st, Russell 1000/2000 indexes are formed based on firms' market capitalization rankings, where the largest thousand firms constitute the Russell 1000, while the next two thousand firms comprise the Russell 2000. Since firms are unable to control small variations in their market capitalization, and thus Russell rankings at the cutoff point, assignment to Russell 1000 or Russell 2000 is practically random. This random assignment to Russell 1000 or Russell 2000 near the threshold leads to large differences in index weights for firms around the Russell 1000/2000 cutoff point. Prior literature has noted that the discontinuity in the Russell 1000/2000 indexes

Table 4.5 Instrumental variable regressions of institutional ownership on competition culture

	1st stage: TRA_t	*$COMP_t$*	*1st stage: DED_t*	*$COMP_t$*
	(1)	*(2)*	*(3)*	*(4)*
TRA_t		0.039**		
		(2.41)		
DED_t				−0.064**
				(2.13)
$R2000_t$	0.263***		−0.161***	
	(6.91)		(3.78)	
$R2000_t \times RANK_t$	−0.350***	0.012**	−0.641**	−0.006
	(10.09)	(2.16)	(2.04)	(1.31)
$MRKCAP_t$	−0.068***	0.001	−0.007	−0.002
	(5.73)	(0.48)	(0.86)	(1.03)
$FLOAT_t$	0.957***	−0.005**	−0.039	−0.001
	(5.38)	(2.05)	(0.23)	(0.79)
R^2	0.18		0.08	
N	2,440	2,440	2,440	2,440

*$p < 0.1$; **$p < 0.05$; ***$p < 0.01$

This table presents instrumental variable (IV) regressions of the relationships between transient (TRA) and dedicated (DED) institutional ownership and competition culture (COMP). The regressions include year and industry fixed effects and the standard errors are clustered by firm. The *t*-values are given in parentheses

drives a substantial difference in institutional ownership, since institutional investors are known to benchmark against the Russell 1000/2000 indexes, and hence are more likely to hold big positions in components that are assigned the largest index weights in order to reduce index-tracking error. Further, these differences in institutional ownership are likely to be unrelated to firm characteristics, since near the cutoff point observed differences in market capitalization are a small proportion of return variance (Appel et al., 2016; Crane et al., 2015).

Thus, our identification strategy is to use inclusion in the Russell 1000 or Russell 2000 as a source of exogenous variation in the institutional ownership structure of the firm. Consistent with prior literature, we posit that our instrument is correlated with variations observed in the transient and dedicated institutional ownership structures and that it meets the exclusion requirement, in that it should only affect the level of firms' competition culture via changes in transient and dedicated institutional ownership. We take advantage of this exogenous variation to test whether transient (dedicated) institutional investors have a positive (negative) influence on a firm's competition culture. To do this, we estimate the following:

$$\begin{aligned} \text{COMP}_t = {} & \alpha_1 + \alpha_2 \widehat{\text{TRA}}\left(or\,\widehat{\text{DED}}_t\right) + \alpha_3 \text{R2000}_t \times \text{RANK}_t \\ & + \alpha_4 \text{MRKCAP}_t + \alpha_5 \text{FLOAT}_t + \varepsilon_t \end{aligned} \tag{4.11a}$$

$$\begin{aligned} \text{TRA}_t(or\,\text{DED}_t) = {} & \gamma_1 + \delta_1 \text{R2000}_t + \beta_1 \text{R2000}_t \times \text{RANK}_t \\ & + \beta_2 \text{MRKCAP}_t + \beta_3 \text{FLOAT}_t + \mu_t \end{aligned} \tag{4.11b}$$

where *R2000* is a dummy variable equal to one if the firm is assigned to the Russell 2000 index and is zero if the firm is assigned to the Russell 1000 index, RANK is the firm's ranking order within the Russell index, measuring the distance from the index cutoff each year, which is based on firm's market capitalization, MRKCAP is firms' market capitalization on May 31st each year, and FLOAT is the difference between rank implied by the observed market capitalization and the rank assigned by Russell in June.

The results of Stock and Yogo's (2005) test for weak instruments indicate that *R2000* is a valid instrument and thus we adopt *R2000* as an instrument for transient (dedicated) institutional ownership. Table 4.5 reports the IV estimates, and the sign and significance of the fitted values of TRA (DED) are consistent with a causal relationship between transient (dedicated) institutional ownership and firms' competition culture in the direction that we postulate in H1 (H2).

In further support of our IV approach, we estimate a second IV model, which investigates the relationship between one-year-ahead COMP and institutional ownership as measured in year *t*:

$$\begin{aligned} \text{COMP}_{t+1} = {} & \alpha_1 + \alpha_2 \widehat{\text{TRA}}(\text{or}\widehat{\text{DED}}_t) + \alpha_3 \text{AGE}_t \\ & + \alpha_4 \text{DTURN}_t + \alpha_5 \text{LEV}_t + \alpha_6 \text{MTB}_t + \alpha_7 \text{ROA}_t \\ & + \alpha_8 \text{SIZE}_t + \alpha_9 \text{STDEV}_t + \varepsilon_t \end{aligned} \tag{4.12a}$$

$$\begin{aligned} \text{TRA}_t(\text{orDED}_t) = {} & \gamma_1 + \delta_1 \text{DYIELD}_t + \delta_2 \text{RET}_t + \delta_3 \text{SGROWTH}_t \\ & + \delta_4 \text{SP500}_t + \beta_1 \text{AGE}_t + \beta_2 \text{DTURN}_t + \beta_3 \text{LEV}_t \\ & + \beta_4 \text{MTB}_t + \beta_5 \text{ROA}_t + \beta_6 \text{SIZE}_t + \beta_7 \text{STDEV}_t + \mu_t \end{aligned} \tag{4.12b}$$

where consistent with prior work in this area (see, for example, Bushee, 2001; Callen & Fang, 2013), we adopt DYIELD, RET, SGROWTH, and *SP500* as instruments for dedicated and transient institutional ownership (refer to Table 4.1 for variable definitions). Compared to our prior instrumental variable estimation found in Table 4.5, where we instrument institutional ownership using inclusion in the Russell 2000 index, this approach allows us to conserve more of the main sample data and thereby increase the power of the analysis.

These estimates are provided in Table 4.6, where sign and significance of the fitted values of TRA (DED) are consistent with H1 (H2) and are in keeping with those presented in our previous analysis, according to which we find a positive (negative) relationship between competition culture and transient (dedicated) institutional ownership. Indeed, these instrumental variable results provide even stronger evidence in support of the relationship between competition culture and our measures of institutional ownership, as we are also able to take into account the possibility that endogeneity affects the results. The results of Stock and Yogo's (2005) test for weak instruments indicate that the instruments used are appropriate.

Finally, we estimate a dynamic panel GMM model, since it is plausible that the relationship between COMP and TRA (DED) is in fact dynamically endogenous. Thus, it is possible that causation runs both ways and that current levels of competition culture could affect both future institutional ownership and competition culture. Hence, to control for potential dynamic endogeneity, unobserved heterogeneity, and simultaneity, we follow Wintoki et al. (2012) by adopting the dynamic panel GMM model as proposed by Arellano and Bover (1995) and Blundell and Bond (1998). This approach allows us to explicitly control for lagged values of COMP. What is more, we are able to use the firms' information within our dataset as instruments. We estimate the following empirical model:

$$\begin{aligned}\text{COMP}_t = \alpha_1 + \alpha_2\text{TRA}_t(\text{orDED}_t) + \gamma_1\text{COMP}_{t-1} + \gamma_2\text{COMP}_{t-2} \\ + \beta_1\text{AGE}_t + \beta_2\text{DTURN}_t + \beta_3\text{LEV}_t + \beta_4\text{MTB}_t \\ +\beta_5\text{RET}_t + \beta_6\text{ROA}_t + \beta_7\text{SIZE}_t + \beta_8\text{STDEV}_t + \eta_t + \varepsilon_t\end{aligned} \tag{4.13}$$

Table 4.6 Instrumental variable regressions of institutional ownership on competition culture

	1st stage: TRA_t	*$COMP_{t+1}$*	*1st stage: DED_t*	*$COMP_{t+1}$*
	(1)	*(2)*	*(3)*	*(4)*
TRA_t		0.197***		
		(4.14)		
DED_t				−0.296*
				(1.79)
$DYIELD_t$	−0.106***		−0.029***	
	(12.57)		(3.78)	
$SGROWTH_t$	0.026***		−0.021***	
	(4.18)		(3.77)	
$SP500_t$	−0.252***		0.036	
	(7.27)		(1.24)	
RET_t	0.527***		0.152***	
	(21.12)		(6.64)	
AGE_t	−0.090***	−0.062***	−0.025**	−0.102***
	(7.94)	(3.77)	(2.31)	(6.45)
$DTURN_t$	0.090***	−0.031***	0.003	−0.013***
	(16.61)	(4.84)	(0.81)	(2.93)
LEV_t	0.016	−0.059***	0.035***	−0.047***
	(1.62)	(4.87)	(3.85)	(3.53)
MTB_t	0.002	−0.012	−0.026***	−0.020*
	(0.24)	(1.22)	(3.79)	(1.80)
ROA_t	0.041***	−0.019*	−0.007	−0.008
	(4.65)	(1.75)	(1.00)	(0.72)
$SIZE_t$	0.429***	−0.058***	0.105***	0.039*
	(29.24)	(2.59)	(9.23)	(1.78)
$STDEV_t$	0.599***	0.009	0.102***	0.012
	(22.03)	(0.71)	(3.85)	(0.76)
R^2	0.33		0.38	
N	30,910	30,910	30,910	30,910

$p < 0.1$; $^{**}p < 0.05$; $^{***}p < 0.01$

This table presents instrumental variable (IV) regressions used to investigate the relationship between transient (TRA) and dedicated (DED) ownership and competition culture (COMP). The regressions include year and industry fixed effects and the standard errors are clustered by firm. The t-values are given in parentheses where we first-difference Eq. (4.13) to eliminate unobserved heterogeneity and potential omitted variable bias. Next, we estimate the first-differenced model by GMM using lagged values (and differences) of competition culture and other firm characteristics as instruments. By using lagged variables as instruments, we control for potential simultaneity and reverse causality.

The results of the system GMM estimates are presented in Table 4.7. Consistent with the previously mentioned results, we evince a positive (negative) relationship between competition culture and transient (dedicated) institutional ownership. Further to the previous analyses, the GMM approach allows us to treat all independent and control variables as endogenous. In fact, in our empirical analysis, we assume that only firm age and the year dummies are exogenous. The $AR(1)$ and $AR(2)$ serial correlation tests results suggest that we cannot reject the null hypothesis of no serial correlation. Further, we apply Hansen's (1982) test for overidentification, as in Arellano and Bond (1991) to assess the validity of our instruments and based on the results we do not reject the null hypothesis that our instruments are valid. In addition, we conduct the difference-in-Hansen test of exogeneity in a manner like Bond et al. (2001) to determine whether the subset of instruments used in the level equation is exogenous. Again, we do not reject the null hypothesis that our instruments are exogenous. All told, the results of these specification tests lead us to conclude that our dynamic GMM regressions are valid and lend further credence to our arguments.

In summary, we provide robust evidence that transient ownership positively influences a firm's competition culture. This finding suggests that transient institutional owners pressurize managers to propel their firms' corporate culture towards the competition culture possibly in the pursuit of short-term financial objectives that may be harmful to the long-term value of the firm. Furthermore, we demonstrate that dedicated ownership lessens a firm's competition culture, and this is suggestive of dedicated institutional investors acting as effective monitors of management, thereby pushing managers to adopt a less intensive competition culture.

Table 4.7 Dynamic system GMM regressions of institutional ownership on competition culture

	*COMP*t	
	(1)	*(2)*
TRA_t	0.098**	
	(1.99)	
DED_t		−0.100*
		(1.68)
AGE_t	−0.031	−0.071**
	(1.62)	(2.53)
$DTURN_t$	−0.035	−0.014
	(0.96)	(0.42)
LEV_t	−0.096**	−0.064
	(2.18)	(0.96)
MTB_t	−0.038	0.025
	(0.93)	(0.51)
RET_t	−0.063	0.071
	(0.43)	(0.45)
ROA_t	−0.029	0.028
	(0.59)	(0.49)
$SIZE_t$	0.124**	0.063
	(2.54)	(0.79)
$STDEV_t$	−0.025	0.063
	(0.16)	(0.38)
$COMP_{t-1}$	0.580***	0.428***
	(6.22)	(4.18)
$COMP_{t-2}$	0.152**	0.121
	(1.98)	(1.61)
AR(1) test *p*-value	0.00	0.00
AR(2) test *p*-value	0.46	0.44
Hansen test for over-identification *p*-value	0.71	0.27
Diff-in-Hansen tests of exogeneity *p*-value	0.81	0.34
N	15,993	15,993

$p < 0.1$; $^{**}p < 0.05$; $^{***}p < 0.01$

This table presents dynamic panel GMM estimates of the relationship between transient (TRA) and dedicated (DED) ownership and competition culture (COMP). *AR*(1) and *AR*(2) are tests for first-order and second-order serial correlation in the first-differenced residuals, under the null of no serial correlation. The Hansen test of over-identification is under the null that all instruments are valid. The Diff-in-Hansen test exogeneity is under the null that instruments used for the equations in levels are exogenous. The *t*-values are given in parentheses

4.5 Summary

This chapter investigates the important role institutional ownership plays in determining firms' corporate culture. More specifically, we investigate how a firm's competition culture is influenced by institutional investors. Using a text-based measure of firms' competition culture, we document robust evidence that transient institutional ownership increases a firm's competition culture, while dedicated institutional ownership diminishes it. These results suggest that transient institutional ownership reinforces managements' competition culture, while dedicated institutional ownership helps to soothe it.

Our results have important implications of interest to academics and the wider business community. This is because the effect of institutional ownership on competition culture has implications for the manner in which firms are governed and managed. Our main findings should be of interest to boards of directors, who have a responsibility to eliminate any pressures on managers from outside investors to increase their competition culture in order to achieve short-term financial objectives. At the same time, boards should be savvy in designing strategies to attract institutional investors, since we observe that their investment horizons can have an impact on firms' corporate culture, which in turn has implications for firms' economic outcomes.

In the next chapter, we consider the relationship between competition culture and performance. We are motivated to consider this aspect of firm behaviour since we have argued in this chapter that competition culture focus managers to achieve superior financial performance in order to cater to capital market expectations.

References

Andreou, P. C., Antoniou, C., Horton, J., & Louca, C. (2016). Corporate Governance and Firm-Specific Stock Price Crashes. *European Financial Management, 22*, 916–956.

Andreou, P. C., Fiordelisi, F., Harris, T., & Philip, D. (2021). Institutional Ownership and Firms' Thrust to Compete. *British Journal of Management, 33*, 1346–1370.

Andreou, P. C., Harris, T., & Philip, D. (2020). Measuring Firms' Market Orientation using Textual Analysis of 10-K filings. *British Journal of Management, 31*, 872–895.

Andreou, P. C., Louca, C., & Petrou, A. P. (2017). CEO Age and Stock-price Crash Risk. *Review of Finance, 21*, 1287–1325.

Appel, I. R., Gormley, T. A., & Keim, D. B. (2016). Passive Investors not Passive Owners. *Journal of Financial Econometrics, 121*, 111–141.

Arellano, M., & Bond, S. (1991). Some Tests of Specification for Panel Data: Monte Carlo Evidence and an Application to Employment Equations. *The Review of Economic Studies, 58*, 277–297.

Arellano, M., & Bover, O. (1995). Another Look at the Instrumental Variable Estimation of Error-Components Models. *Journal of Econometrics, 68*, 29–51.

Audi, R., Loughran, T., & McDonald, B. (2016). Trust, but Verify: MD&A Language and the Role of Trust in Corporate Culture. *Journal of Business Ethics, 139*, 551–561.

Bebchuk, L., Brav, A., & Jian, W. (2015). The Long-term Effects of Hedge Fund Activism. *Columbia Law Review, 115*, 1085–1155.

Bernardo, A. E., & Welch, I. (2004). Liquidity and Financial Market Runs. *The Quarterly Journal of Economics, 119*, 135–158.

Bhandari, A., Mammadov, B., Thevenot, M., & Vakilzadeh, S. H. (2017). *The Invisible Hand: Corporate Culture and Its Implications for Earnings Management* (Working Paper). Warrington College of Business.

Blundell, R., & Bond, S. (1998). Initial Conditions and Moment Restrictions in Dynamic Panel Data Models. *Journal of Econometrics, 87*, 115–143.

Bond, S. R., Hoeffler, A., & Temple, J. R. W. (2001). *GMM Estimation of Empirical Growth Models*. Center for Economic Policy Research.

Brav, A., Jiang, W., & Kim, H. (2015). The Real Effects of Hedge Fund Activism: Productivity, Asset Allocation, and Labor Outcomes. *Review of Financial Studies, 28*, 2723–2769.

Bushee, B. J. (1998). The Influence of Institutional Investors on Myopic R&D Investment Behavior. *Accounting Review, 73*, 305–333.

Bushee, B. J. (2001). Do Institutional Investors Prefer Near-Term Earnings Over Long-Run Value? *Contemporary Accounting Research, 18*, 207–246.

Bushman, R. M., Hendricks, B. E., & Williams, C. D. (2016). Bank Competition: Measurement, Decision-Making, and Risk-Taking. *Journal of Accounting Research, 54*, 777–826.

Cai, F., & Zheng, L. (2004). Institutional Trading and Stock Returns. *Finance Research Letters, 1*, 178–189.

Callen, J. L., & Fang, X. (2013). Institutional Investor Stability and Crash Risk: Monitoring Versus Short-Termism? *Journal of Banking and Finance, 37*, 3047–3063.

Callen, J. L., & Fang, X. (2015). Religion and Stock Price Crash Risk. *Journal of Financial and Quantitative Analysis, 50*, 169–195.

Cella, C., Ellul, A., & Giannetti, M. (2013). Investors' Horizons and the Amplification of Market Shocks. *Review of Financial Studies, 26*, 1607–1648.

Cameron, K. S., & Quinn, R. E. (2011). *Diagnosing and Changing Organizational Culture: Based on the Competing Values Framework*. Wiley.
Cameron, K., Quinn, R., DeGraff, J., & Thakor, A. (2014). *Competing Values Leadership*. Edward Elgar Publishing.
Chen, J., Hong, H., & Stein, J. C. (2001). Forecasting Crashes: Trading Volume, Past Returns, and Conditional Skewness in Stock Prices. *Journal of Financial Economics, 61*, 345–381.
Chen, X., Harford, J., & Li, K. (2007). Monitoring: Which Institutions Matter? *Journal of Financial Economics, 86*, 279–305.
Crane, A. D., Michenaud, S., & Weston, J. P. (2015). The Effect of Institutional Ownership on Payout Policy: Evidence from Index Thresholds. *Review of Financial Studies, 29*, 1377–1408.
Cronqvist, H., Low, A., & Nilsson, M. (2007). *Does Corporate Culture Matter for Firm Policies?* (Working Paper). Fisher College of Business.
Deal, T. E., & Kennedy, A. A. (1982). *Corporate Cultures: The Rites and Rituals of Organizational Life*. Addison-Wesley.
Denison, D. R. (1990). *Corporate Culture and Organizational Effectiveness*. Wiley.
Dikolli, S. S., Kulp, S. L., & Sedatole, K. L. (2009). Transient Institutional Ownership and CEO Contracting. *The Accounting Review, 84*, 737–770.
Edmans, A. (2014). Blockholders and Corporate Governance. *Annual Review of Financial Economics, 6*, 23–50.
Elyasiani, E., & Jia, J. (2010). Distribution of Institutional Ownership and Corporate Firm Performance. *Journal of Banking and Finance, 34*, 606–620.
Elyasiani, E., Jia, J. J., & Mao, C. X. (2010). Institutional Ownership Stability and the Cost of Debt. *Journal of Financial Markets, 13*, 475–500.
Erhard, W., Jensen, M., & Zaffron, S. (2017). *Integrity: A Positive Model that Incorporates the Normative Phenomena of Morality, Ethics and Legality*. Available at SSRN 1542759.
Fama, E. F., & French, K. R. (1997). Industry Costs of Equity. *Journal of Financial Economics, 43*, 153–193.
Fiordelisi, F., & Ricci, O. (2014). Corporate Culture and CEO Turnover. *Journal of Corporate Finance, 28*, 66–82.
Fiordelisi, F., & Ricci, O. (2021). Corrigendum to "Corporate Culture and CEO Turnover." *Journal of Corporate Finance, 70*, 102064.
Fiordelisi, F., Renneboog, L., Ricci, O., & Lopes, S. S. (2019). Creative Corporate Culture and Innovation. *Journal of International Financial Markets, Institutions and Money, 63*, 101137.
Fos, V., & Kahn, C. (2015). *Governance through Threat of Intervention and Threat of Exit* (Working Paper). University of Illinois at Urbana–Champaign.

Gaspar, J. M., Massa, M., & Matos, P. (2005). Shareholder Investment Horizons and the Market for Corporate Control. *Journal of Financial Economics, 76*, 135–165.

Giannetti, M., & Yu, X. (2016). *The Corporate Finance Benefits of Short Horizon Investors*. Available at SSRN 2723357.

Gompers, P. A., & Metrick, A. (1998). *Institutional Investors and Equity Prices*. National Bureau of Economic Research.

Graham, J. R., Harvey, C. R., Grennen, J., & Rajgopal, S. (2022). Corporate Culture: Evidence from the Field. *Journal of Financial Economics, 146*, 552–593.

Graham, J. R., Harvey, C. R., & Rajgopal, S. (2005). The Economic Implications of Corporate Financial Reporting. *Journal of Accounting and Economics, 40*, 3–73.

Grennan, J. (2019). *A Corporate Culture Channel: How Increased Shareholder Governance Reduces Firm Value*. Available at SSRN 2345384.

Grieser, W. D., Kapadia, N., Li, R., & Simonov, A. (2016). *Fifty Shades of Corporate Culture*. Available at SSRN 2843776.

Guiso, L., Sapienza, P., & Zingales, L. (2006). Does Culture Affect Economic Outcomes? *The Journal of Economic Perspectives, 20*, 23–48.

Guiso, L., Sapienza, P., & Zingales, L. (2015a). Corporate Culture, Societal Culture, and Institutions. *American Economic Review, 105*, 336–339.

Guiso, L., Sapienza, P., & Zingales, L. (2015b). The Value of Corporate Culture. *Journal of Financial Economics, 117*, 60–76.

Handy, C. B. (1976). *Understanding Organizations*. Oxford University Press.

Hansen, L. P. (1982). Large Sample Properties of Generalized Method of Moments Estimators. *Econometrica: Journal of the Econometric Society, 50*, 1029–1054.

Harford, J., Kecskes, A., & Mansi, S. (2018). Do Long-term Investors Improve Corporate Decision Making? *Journal of Corporate Finance, 50*, 424–452.

Harris, L. C., & Ogbonna, E. (2001). Strategic Human Resource Management, Market Orientation, and Organizational Performance. *Journal of Business Research, 51*, 157–166.

Hartnell, C. A., Ou, A. Y., & Kinicki, A. (2011). Organizational Culture and Organizational Effectiveness: A Meta-Analytic Investigation of the Competing Values Framework's Theoretical Suppositions. *Journal of Applied Psychology, 96*, 677.

Hoberg, G., & Phillips, G. (2010). Product Market Synergies and Competition in Mergers and Acquisitions: A Text-Based Analysis. *Review of Financial Studies, 23*, 3773–3811.

Hoberg, G., & Phillips, G. (2016). Text-based Network Industries and Endogenous Product Differentiation. *Journal of Political Economy, 124*, 1423–1465.

Hoberg, G., Phillips, G., & Prabhala, N. (2014). Product Market Threats, Payouts, and Financial Flexibility. *The Journal of Finance, 69*, 293–324.

Hofstede, G. (1980). Culture and Organizations. *International Studies of Management and Organization, 10*, 15–41.

Hofstede, G. (2001). *Cultural Consequences*. Sage.

Hofstede, G. (2011). Dimensionalizing Cultures: The Hofstede Model in Context. *Online Readings in Psychology and Culture*. Available at https://doi.org/10.9707/2307-0919.1014

Hong, H., & Stein, J. C. (2003). Differences of Opinion, Short-Sales Constraints, and Market Crashes. *Review of Financial Studies, 16*, 487–525.

Jaworski, B. J., & Kohli, A. K. (1993). Competition Culture: Antecedents and Consequences. *The Journal of Marketing, 57*, 53–70.

Johnson, G. (1988). Rethinking Incrementalism. *Strategic Management Journal, 9*, 75–91.

Kearney, C., & Liu, S. (2014). Textual Sentiment in Finance: A Survey of Methods and Models. *International Review of Financial Analysis, 33*, 171–185.

Kohli, A. K., & Jaworski, B. J. (1990). Competition Culture: The Construct, Research Propositions, and Managerial Implications. *The Journal of Marketing, 54*, 1–18.

Li, F. (2010a). Textual Analysis of Corporate Disclosures: A Survey of the Literature. *Journal of Accounting Literature, 29*, 143.

Li, F. (2010b). The Information Content of Forward-Looking Statements in Corporate Filings: A Naive Bayesian Machine Learning Approach. *Journal of Accounting Research, 48*, 1049–1102.

Li, F., Lundholm, R., & Minnis, M. (2013a). A Measure of Competition Based on 10-K Filings. *Journal of Accounting Research, 51*, 399–436.

Li, K., Griffin, D., Yue, H., & Zhao, L. (2013b). How does Culture Influence Corporate Risk-Taking? *Journal of Corporate Finance, 23*, 1–22.

Li, X. (2010c). The Impacts of Product Market Competition on the Quantity and Quality of Voluntary Disclosures. *Review of Accounting Studies, 15*, 663–711.

Loughran, T., McDonald, B., & Yun, H. (2009). A Wolf in Sheep's Clothing: The Use of Ethics-Related Terms in 10-K Reports. *Journal of Business Ethics, 89*, 39–49.

Loughran, T., & McDonald, B. (2011). When Is a Liability not a Liability? Textual Analysis, Dictionaries, and 10-Ks. *The Journal of Finance, 66*, 35–65.

Loughran, T., & McDonald, B. (2016). Textual Analysis in Accounting and Finance: A survey. *Journal of Accounting Research, 54*, 1187–1230.

Luu, H., Nguyen, L., & Wilson, J. O. S. (2022). *Organizational Culture, Competition and Bank Loan Loss Provisions*. Available at SSRN 3921043.

McCahery, J. A., Sautner, Z., & Starks, L. T. (2016). Behind the Scenes: The Corporate Governance Preferences of Institutional Investors. *The Journal of Finance, 63*, 1729–1775.

Narver, J. C., & Slater, S. F. (1990). The Effect of a Competition Culture on Business Profitability. *The Journal of Marketing, 54*, 20–35.

Nofsinger, J. R., & Sias, R. W. (1999). Herding and Feedback Trading by Institutional and Individual Investors. *The Journal of Finance, 54*, 2263–2295.

O'Reilly, C. A., Chatman, J., & Caldwell, D. F. (1991). People and Organizational Culture: A Profile Comparison Approach to Assessing Person-organization Fit. *Academy of Management Journal, 34*, 487–516.

O'Reilly, C. A. I., Chatman, J., & Caldwell, D. F. (1996). People and Organizational Culture: A Profile Comparison Approach to Assessing Person-Organization Fit. *Academy of Management Journal, 34*, 487–516.

Quinn, R. E., & Cameron, K. (1983). Organizational Life Cycles and Shifting Criteria of Effectiveness: Some Preliminary Evidence. *Management Science, 29*, 33–51.

Quinn, R. E., & Rohrbaugh, J. (1983). A Spatial Model of Effectiveness Criteria: Towards a Competing Values Approach to Organizational Analysis. *Management Science, 29*, 363–377.

Reynolds, P. D. (1986). Organizational Culture as Related to Industry, Position and Performance: A Preliminary Report. *Journal of Management Studies, 23*, 333–345.

Schein, E. H. (1990). Organizational Culture: What It Is and How to Change it. In *Human Resource Management in International Firms*. Palgrave Macmillan.

Schein, E. H. (1992). *Organizational Culture and Leadership: A Dynamic View*. Jossey-Bass.

Schneider, B., Ehrhart, M. G., & Macey, W. H. (2013). Organizational Climate and Culture. *Annual Review of Psychology, 64*, 361–388.

Shleifer, A., & Vishny, R. W. (1986). Large Shareholders and Corporate Control. *The Journal of Political Economy, 94*, 461–488.

Stock, J. H., & Yogo, M. (2005). Testing for Weak Instruments in Linear IV Regression. In *Identification and Inference for Econometric Models. Essays in Honor of Thomas Rothenberg*. Cambridge University Press.

Ten Have, S., Ten Have, W., & Stevens, F. (2003). *Key Management Models: The Management Tools and Practices That Will Improve Your Business*. Pearson Education.

Tetlock, P. C. (2007). Giving Content to Investor Sentiment: The Role of Media in the Stock Market. *The Journal of Finance, 62*, 1139–1168.

Wang, Y., Farag, H., & Ahmad, W. (2021). Corporate Culture and Innovation: A Tale from an Emerging Market. *British Journal of Management, 32*, 1121–1140.

Wintoki, M. B., Linck, J. S., & Netter, J. M. (2012). Endogeneity and the Dynamics of Internal Corporate Governance. *Journal of Financial Economics, 105*, 581–606.

Yan, X. S., & Zhang, Z. (2009). Institutional Investors and Equity Returns: Are Short-Term Institutions Better Informed? *Review of Financial Studies, 22*, 893–924.

Zingales, L. (2015). The 'Cultural Revolution' in Finance. *Journal of Financial Economics, 117*, 1–4.

CHAPTER 5

Competition Culture and Performance

5.1 Introduction

In this chapter, we investigate whether and how competition culture impacts firms' stock return performance. We have argued in Chapter 4 that competition culture leads to increased performance, particularly in the short term, as managers in such firms are (i) better able to assimilate external market information in order to adapt more rapidly to dynamic market conditions, and (ii) more heavily pressured by transient (i.e., short-term) institutional investors to cater to their market expectations by delivering immediate results. If these ideas are true, then a positive and significant relationship between competition culture and firms' stock return performance particularly in the short term is plausible albeit possibly at the expense of increased firm-specific risk.

Thus, we seek to address the question: *what is the effect of competition culture on firms' stock return performance?* This question is important for a number of reasons. Firstly, the seminal studies related to our cultural framework i.e., the Competing Values Framework (CVF) posit that competition culture relates to the vigorous pursuit of performance through the processes of market relevant information in an efficient and proactive fashion (Cameron et al., 2014; Harris & Ogbonna, 2001; Hartnell et al., 2011; Jaworski & Kohli, 1993; Kohli & Jaworski, 1990; Kotter & Heskett, 1992; O'Reilly et al., 2014; Quinn & Cameron, 1983; Quinn & Rohrbaugh, 1983; Reynolds, 1986; Sørensen, 2002).

T. Harris, *Competition Culture and Corporate Finance*,
https://doi.org/10.1007/978-3-031-30156-8_5

Thus, competition culture enhances the firm's ability to adapt to dynamic market developments in a robust, timely, and efficient manner. Furthermore, managers at high competition culture firms should face enhanced career and other incentives to cater to investors' market expectations. Given these arguments and other extensive works in this area, we take the strong view that competition culture is positively related to a firm's performance (Andreou et al., 2020, 2021; Bhandari et al., 2017; Callen & Fang, 2015; Cronqvist et al., 2007; Erhard et al., 2017; Fiordelisi & Ricci, 2014, 2021; Graham et al., 2022; Grennan, 2019; Grieser et al., 2016; Guiso et al., 2006, 2009, 2015a, 2015b; Luu et al., 2022; Nguyen et al., 2019; Wang et al., 2021; Zingales, 2015).

To undertake our empirical work into the nature of the link between competition culture and firms' one-year-ahead buy-and-hold stock return performance (henceforth "short-term performance"), we first perform a textual analysis of 10-K filings to measure firms' *competition culture* using the CVF. In doing so, we follow a growing body of literature that applies textual analysis of firms' 10-K filings in finance-related research (see, for instance, Andreou et al., 2020, 2021; Bushman et al., 2016; Fiordelisi & Ricci, 2014, 2021; Fiordelisi et al., 2019; Graham et al., 2022; Loughran & McDonald, 2016; Loughran et al., 2009; Luu et al., 2022; Nguyen et al., 2019; Tetlock, 2007; Wang et al., 2021). Hence, as described in Chapter 4 and consistent with past works (see e.g.,Andreou et al., 2021; Fiordelisi & Ricci, 2014, 2021; Luu et al., 2022), we operationalize our measure of competition culture by parsing 10-K filings to identify a set of lexical items relating to attributes that shape firms.

This study makes the following important contribution to the extant literature. In particular, by utilizing a large body of publicly available firm data, our analysis provides panel data derived evidence of a strong and positive relationship between competition culture and a firm's short-term performance, thus supplementing the evidence in prior important studies in this area (for example, Andreou et al., 2020, 2021).

The remainder of this chapter is presented as follows: Sect. 5.2 developed the main hypotheses; details of the data and summary statistics are presented in Sect. 5.3; Sect. 5.4 present the empirical results; and Sect. 5.5 concludes.

5.2 Hypotheses

In this chapter, we explore the effect of competition culture on firms' short-term performance Conventionally, the leading perspective is that competition culture has a positive relationship with a firm's performance. This is in part because competition culture generates superior customer and competitive awareness advantages for firms. We argue that this in turn leads to more germane and better products, and an improved ability to tackle dynamic market developments in a more timely, effective, and efficient manner (Cameron et al., 2014; Harris & Ogbonna, 2001; Hartnell et al., 2011; Jaworski & Kohli, 1993; Kohli & Jaworski, 1990; Kotter & Heskett, 1992; O'Reilly et al., 2014; Quinn & Cameron, 1983; Quinn & Rohrbaugh, 1983; Reynolds, 1986; Sørensen, 2002). Furthermore, it could also be argued that increased competition culture serves to incentivize managers to achieve superior performance levels expected by institutional investors in order to reduce the threats of adverse investor action, dismissal, takeover bids, financing constraints, etc. Therefore, for these reasons we can reasonably presume that competition culture leads firms to achieve enhanced levels of performance. Thus, we hypothesize that a firm's competition culture should be positively related to short-term performance:

H1: Competition culture is positively associated with short-term performance.

5.3 Data, Variables, and Sample

5.3.1 Data

We build a unique sample in this study by merging data from multiple sources. Firstly, we obtain annual firm-level financial accounting data of US publicly traded firms for the period 1994 to 2017 from Compustat. Next, we acquire firms' stock returns information from CRSP database. To produce our measures of corporate culture we conduct a textual analysis of firms' 10-K filings obtained from the Securities Exchange Commission's (SEC's) Edgar database.

We perform analysis on all firms included in the Compustat database excluding financials (SIC 6000–6999) and utilities (SIC 4900–4999). In addition, to limit survivorship bias, firms that are inactive and/or acquired by another firm during the period of study are retained in the sample. Also, we attempt to mitigate the effects of outliers by winsorizing all

Table 5.1 Definition of variables

	Symbol		*Definitions*
Competition culture			
	COMP	=	firm's competition culture estimated for each fiscal year using the text-analysis approach
Performance			
	RETURNS	=	firm's buy-and-hold stock return
Other variables			
	AGE	=	firm's age as measured by the natural log of number of years since incorporation
	DIV_YIELD	=	annual dividend yield computed as cash dividend per divided by stock price
	LEV	=	leverage as measured by total debt divided by total assets
	MTB	=	the market-to-book value at the end of each fiscal year;
	RSALES	=	firm's revenue divided by those of its largest competitor in its industry, based on Fama and French's 48 industry classification
	SCON	=	percentage of total sales accounted for by the firm's four largest competitors in the same industry, based on Fama and French's 48 industry classification;
	SGROWTH	=	sales for the fiscal year divided by sales for the prior fiscal year
	STDEV	=	the volatility of firm-specific returns; and
	SIZE	=	firm's size as measured by the natural logarithm of total assets

continuous variables at the 1 and 99% levels. Finally, we delete from our sample all firm-year observations with missing data on the main variables of interest (listwise deletion). This results in a final main sample consisting of 55,680 firm-year observations. Table 5.1 reports the definitions of all variables.

5.3.2 *Measuring Competition Culture*

As in Chapter 4, we measure a firm's competition culture (*COMP*) by counting the number of times that the lexical items included in the bag of words describing corporate attributes for the competition culture are found in the 10-K filings and scale our measure by counts of the lexical items that describe the other cultural orientations as follows[1]:

$$\text{COMP} = \frac{\text{Number of lexical items describing the Competition Culture}}{\text{Total number of lexical items for all types of cultures}}. \tag{5.1}$$

5.3.3 *Measuring Short-Term Performance*

To study the relationship between competition culture and short-term performance measured using a firm's market adjusted buy-and-hold stock returns, we estimate firm's market adjusted buy-and-hold returns using the formula below:

$$\text{RETURNS}_{i,t} = \prod_{w=1}^{t}(1 + \text{RET}_{i,w}) - \prod_{w=1}^{t}(1 + \text{MKT}_{w}), \tag{5.2}$$

where $\text{RETURNS}_{i,t}$ is the return on stock i over the fiscal year, while $\text{RET}_{i,w}$ is the firm i's week w stock price return and MKT_w represents the equally weighted average weekly return of the market.

5.3.4 *Control Variables*

All empirical models include controls that capture firm-specific characteristics. In particular, we include the following: the number of fiscal years since the firm has joined the CRSP/Compustat merged database, AGE; dividend yield, DIV_YIELD, calculated as cash dividend divided by current share price; financial leverage as indicated by total liabilities scaled by total assets, LEV; the market value of equity by book value of equity, MTB; the size of a firm's total sales revenues in its principal

[1] While conducting our count we exclude negation of the lexical items by ignoring occasions when the word is preceded by "no", "non", "not", "less", "few", or "limited" by three or fewer words.

Table 5.2 Descriptive statistics for the variables used in the empirical analyses

Variable	*Obs*	*Mean*	*Std. dev*	*25th Pctl*	*Median*	*75th Pctl*
COMP	55,680	0.462	0.082	0.401	0.45	0.51
RETURNS	55,680	0.174	0.75	−0.238	0.04	0.371
AGE	55,680	23.892	14.601	13	21	32
DIV_YIELD	55,680	0.008	0.018	0	0	0.008
LEV	55,680	0.201	0.202	0.01	0.158	0.323
MTB	55,680	3.044	4.731	1.215	2.063	3.612
RSALES	55,680	0.01	0.022	0	0.001	0.007
SCON	55,680	0.634	0.131	0.583	0.673	0.726
SGROWTH	55,680	1.181	0.563	0.976	1.082	1.234
STDEV	55,680	0.249	0.139	0.148	0.215	0.312
SIZE	55,680	5.762	1.973	4.315	5.769	7.141

This table presents the mean, median, 25th percentile, 75th percentile, and the number of observations for the variables used in the study for the period 1994 to 2017

market segment relative to those of its largest competitor, RSALES; and the proportions of total sales accounted for by the four competitors with the largest sales, SCON.; sales growth computed as the percentage change between fiscal years t and $t-1$, SGROWTH; the volatility of weekly returns, STDEV, over the fiscal year (Bushman et al., 2016; Hong & Stein, 2003) and the natural logarithm of market value of equity, SIZE.

5.3.5 *Descriptive Statistics and Correlations*

Table 5.2 presents descriptive statistics of the variables used in our empirical analysis.[2] The mean value of our competition culture variable, COMP, is 0.462, and the mean value of the short-term performance variable, RETURNS, 0.174. We observe that the summary statistics on the variables are largely comparable to the values reported in previous studies using these data (see e.g., Andreou et al., 2020, 2021; Fiordelisi & Ricci, 2014, 2021).

[2] To mitigate the effects of outliers, all continuous variables are winsorized at the 1 and 99% levels.

We compute Pearson correlation coefficients for the variables used in our empirical analysis and report these in Table 5.3. Consistent with our expectations we find the relationship between COMP and our short-term performance variable, RETURNS to be positive and significant (correlation = 0.0163).

5.4 Empirical Results

Following the extant literature, we expect rather persistent levels of competition culture over time (Andreou et al., 2021; Cameron et al., 2014; Guiso et al., 2006, 2015a, 2015b; Hartnell et al., 2011; Nguyen et al., 2018). As a result, we adopt the OLS estimator as the primary regression tool for our empirical analysis. In addition, we provide generalized least square random effects (GLS-RE) regression estimates as supplementary results.

5.4.1 Competition Culture and Firm's Short-Term Performance

Next, we conduct multivariate regression analysis to explore the relationship between COMP and the firm's short-term performance. We consider this relationship since it is plausible that managers at firms with a strong competition culture are more driven to achieve superior financial performance for multiple reasons. Thus, we investigate whether competition culture is positively related to one-year-ahead buy and hold returns by estimating the following regression models:

$$\begin{aligned}\text{RETURNS}_{t+1} =& \alpha_1 + \alpha_2\text{COMP}_t + \alpha_3\text{AGE}_t + \alpha_4\text{DIV\_YIELD}_t \\ &+ \alpha_5\text{LEV}_t + \alpha_6\text{MTB}_t + \alpha_7\text{RSALES}_t + \alpha_8\text{SCON}_t \\ &+ \alpha_9\text{SGROWTH}_t + \alpha_{10}\text{STDEV}_t + \alpha_{11}\text{SIZE}_t + \varepsilon_t \end{aligned} \quad (5.3a)$$

$$\begin{aligned}\text{RETURNS}_{t+1} =& \alpha_1 + \alpha_2\Delta\text{COMP}_t + \alpha_3\text{COMP}_{t-1} + \alpha_4\text{AGE}_t \\ &+ \alpha_5\text{DIV\_YIELD}_t + \alpha_6\text{LEV}_t + \alpha_7\text{MTB}_t + \alpha_8\text{RSALES}_t \\ &+ \alpha_9\text{SCON}_t + \alpha_{10}\text{SGROWTH}_t + \alpha_{11}\text{STDEV}_t \\ &+ \alpha_{12}\text{SIZE}_t + \varepsilon_t \end{aligned} \quad (5.3b)$$

Table 5.3 Pearson correlation matrix

	COMP	*RETURNS*	*AGE*	*DIV_YIELD*	*LEV*	*MTB*	*RSALES*	*SCON*	*SGROWTH*	*STDEV*
RETURNS	**0.0163**									
AGE	**−0.2102**	**−0.0115**								
DIV_YIELD	**−0.1210**	**−0.0207**	**0.2297**							
LEV	**−0.2479**	0.0025	**0.0347**	**0.0939**						
MTB	**0.0927**	**−0.0561**	**−0.0465**	**−0.0377**	**−0.0718**					
RSALES	**−0.1397**	**−0.0275**	**0.2964**	**0.1636**	**0.1546**	0.0019				
SCON	**0.0627**	0.0076	**−0.0909**	**−0.0644**	**−0.0217**	**0.0374**	**−0.3170**			
SGROWTH	**0.0616**	**−0.0451**	**−0.1391**	**−0.0875**	**−0.0125**	**0.1141**	**−0.0642**	**0.0469**		
STDEV	**0.1224**	**0.1438**	**−0.3237**	**−0.2253**	**−0.0431**	−0.0006	**−0.2361**	**0.0599**	**0.0800**	
SIZE	**−0.0162**	**−0.1489**	**0.2912**	**0.1464**	**0.0512**	**0.1955**	**0.3959**	**0.0270**	**0.0214**	**−0.5125**

This table presents Pearson correlation coefficients for the variables used in the empirical analyses. The bold figures indicate significance at the 10% level and above and,

$$\begin{aligned}\text{RETURNS}_{t+1} = {} & \alpha_1 + \alpha_2 \Delta\text{COMP}_t + \alpha_3 \Delta\text{COMP}_{t-1} + \alpha_4 \text{COMP}_{t-2} \\ & + \alpha_5 \text{AGE}_t + \alpha_6 \text{DIV\_YIELD}_t + \alpha_7 \text{LEV}_t + \alpha_8 \text{MTB}_t \\ & + \alpha_9 \text{RSALES}_t + \alpha_{10} \text{SCON}_t + \alpha_{11} \text{SGROWTH}_t \\ & + \alpha_{12} \text{STDEV}_t + \alpha_{13} \text{SIZE}_t + \varepsilon_t . \end{aligned} \tag{5.3c}$$

To ensure that the impact of competition culture on firms' short-term performance is not a result of other factors, we include control variables that capture firm-specific characteristics. In addition, the regression models include year and industry dummies to control for an unobserved year and industry factors; further, the standard errors are clustered at the firm level. Our coefficient of interest is α_2, and we expect this to be positive and significant.

The results of Eq.'s (5.3a–5.3c) are presented in Table 5.4, where the dependent variable RETURNS_{t+1} is the one-period-ahead buy-and-hold stock return. We find the coefficient term 0.020 for COMP_t, which is provided in column (1) in Panel A, is significantly positive at the 1% level with a t-value of 4.06; similar results hold for ΔCOMP_t, , in column (2) where the coefficient and t-value are 0.017 and 3.08, thereby indicating a significantly positive relationship between the change in competition culture and short-term performance at the 1% 1 level. In addition, the coefficient is 0.025 on the COMP_{t-2} variable column (3), suggests a positive and significant relationship between competition culture and firms' short-term performance as measured by adjusted buy-and-hold returns to compete three years into the future at the 1% level given a t-value of 3.64. Similar long-run estimates of Eqs. (5.3a–5.3c) are produced using the GLS RE estimator and these results are provided in Table 5.4 Panel B and are consistent with the OLS estimates previously reported.

5.5 Summary

In this chapter, we explore the relationship between firms' competition culture and short-term performance as captured by one year ahead adjusted buy-and-hold returns. Using a text-based measure of firms' competition culture first developed in Chapter 4, we find strong evidence that firms with greater competition culture achieve superior short-term performance.

Table 5.4 Regressions of competition culture on stock returns

	RETURNS$_{t+1}$		
	(1)	*(2)*	*(3)*
$COMP_t$	0.020***		
	(4.06)		
$\Delta COMP_t$		0.017***	0.007
		(3.08)	(1.18)
$COMP_{t-1}$		0.026***	
		(4.08)	
$\Delta COMP_{t-1}$			0.011
			(1.50)
$COMP_{t-2}$			0.025***
			(3.64)
AGE_t	0.043***	0.039***	0.030***
	(10.84)	(9.22)	(6.55)
DIV_YIELD_t	−0.008*	−0.008*	−0.008
	(1.94)	(1.85)	(1.61)
LEV_t	0.015***	0.014***	0.019***
	(3.29)	(2.88)	(3.72)
MTB_t	−0.015***	−0.015***	−0.013**
	(3.42)	(3.16)	(2.49)
$RSALES_t$	0.061***	0.066***	0.066***
	(12.20)	(12.37)	(12.47)
$SCON_t$	−0.022**	−0.031***	−0.046***
	(2.54)	(3.28)	(4.35)
$SGROWTH_t$	−0.031***	−0.035***	−0.039***
	(5.86)	(5.91)	(5.19)
$STDEV_t$	0.062***	0.066***	0.076***
	(8.56)	(8.50)	(8.87)
$SIZE_t$	−0.138***	−0.142***	−0.142***
	(20.33)	(20.04)	(18.95)
R^2	0.13	0.14	0.14
N	55,680	50,784	43,963

(continued)

Table 5.4 (continued)

Panel B. GLS estimates for competition culture on short-term performance

	$RETURNS_{t+1}$ (1)	(2)	(3)
$COMP_t$	0.021***		
	(3.73)		
$\Delta COMP_t$		0.018***	0.009
		(3.08)	(1.41)
$COMP_{t-1}$		0.028***	
		(3.67)	
$\Delta COMP_{t-1}$			0.014*
			(1.74)
$COMP_{t-2}$			0.031***
			(3.39)
AGE_t	0.085***	0.093***	0.106***
	(15.26)	(14.31)	(12.87)
DIV_YIELD_t	0.001	0.001	0.001
	(0.12)	(0.14)	(0.17)
LEV_t	0.014***	0.012**	0.014**
	(2.65)	(2.09)	(2.01)
MTB_t	−0.019***	−0.018***	−0.014**
	(3.84)	(3.61)	(2.51)
$RSALES_t$	0.098***	0.117***	0.134***
	(14.33)	(14.29)	(13.75)
$SCON_t$	−0.001	−0.002	−0.001
	(0.13)	(0.16)	(0.07)
$SGROWTH_t$	−0.031***	− 0.034***	−0.040***
	(5.65)	(5.56)	(5.02)
$STDEV_t$	0.045***	0.044***	0.047***
	(5.85)	(5.26)	(4.91)
$SIZE_t$	−0.288***	−0.347***	−0.436***
	(32.25)	(31.03)	(34.69)
R^2	0.12	0.12	0.12
N	55,680	50,784	43,963

$^*p < 0.1$; $^{**}p < 0.05$; $^{***}p < 0.01$

This table presents OLS (Panel A) and GLS (Panel B) estimates to investigate the impact of competition culture on firms' short-term performance as measured by stock returns. All regressions include year and industry fixed effects, and the standard errors are clustered at the firm level. The t values are given in parentheses

Panel A. OLS estimates for competition culture on short-term performance

Our results are consistent with a firm's competition culture leading to greater customer and/or competitive advantages, which in turn results in superior performance as indicated by a firm's buy and hold stock returns. Equally, it could also be argued that our results provide evidence that increased competition culture serves to incentivize managers to achieve superior performance to cater to the peculiar expectations of primarily transient (i.e., short-term) institutional investors who prioritize immediate results perhaps at the costs of firm's risk and long-term stability.

Consequently, in the next chapter, we explore this darker aspect of the role of competition culture in firms by considering whether and how competition culture leads to increased idiosyncratic stock price crash risk.

References

Andreou, P. C., Fiordelisi, F., Harris, T., & Philip, D. (2021). Institutional Ownership and Firms' Thrust to Compete. *British Journal of Management, 33*, 1346–1370.

Andreou, P. C., Harris, T., & Philip, D. (2020). Measuring Firms' Market Orientation using Textual Analysis of 10-K filings. *British Journal of Management, 31*, 872–895.

Bhandari, A., Mammadov, B., Thevenot, M., Vakilzadeh, S. H. (2017). *The Invisible Hand: Corporate Culture and Its Implications for Earnings Management* (Working Paper). Warrington College of Business.

Bushman, R. M., Hendricks, B. E., & Williams, C. D. (2016). Bank Competition: Measurement, Decision-Making, and Risk-Taking. *Journal of Accounting Research, 54*, 777–826.

Callen, J. L., & Fang, X. (2015). Religion and Stock Price Crash Risk. *Journal of Financial and Quantitative Analysis, 50*, 169–195.

Cameron, K., Quinn, R., DeGraff, J., & Thakor, A. (2014). *Competing Values Leadership*. Edward Elgar Publishing.

Cronqvist, H., Low, A., & Nilsson, M. (2007). *Does Corporate Culture Matter for Firm Policies?* (Working Paper). Fisher College of Business.

Erhard, W., Jensen, M., & Zaffron, S. (2017). *Integrity: A Positive Model that Incorporates the Normative Phenomena of Morality, Ethics and Legality*. Available at SSRN 1542759.

Fiordelisi, F., & Ricci, O. (2014). Corporate Culture and CEO Turnover. *Journal of Corporate Finance, 28*, 66–82.

Fiordelisi, F., & Ricci, O. (2021). Corrigendum to "Corporate Culture and CEO Turnover." *Journal of Corporate Finance, 70*, 102064.

Fiordelisi, F., Renneboog, L., Ricci, O., & Lopes, S. S. (2019). Creative Corporate Culture and Innovation. *Journal of International Financial Markets, Institutions and Money, 63*, 101137.

Graham, J. R., Harvey, C. R., Grennen, J., & Rajgopal, S. (2022). Corporate Culture: Evidence from the Field. *Journal of Financial Economics, 146*, 552–593.

Grennan, J. (2019). *A Corporate Culture Channel: How Increased Shareholder Governance Reduces Firm Value*. Available at SSRN 2345384.

Grieser, W. D., Kapadia, N., Li, R., & Simonov, A. (2016). *Fifty Shades of Corporate Culture*. Available at SSRN 2843776.

Guiso, L., Sapienza, P., & Zingales, L. (2006). Does Culture Affect Economic Outcomes? *The Journal of Economic Perspectives, 20*, 23–48.

Guiso, L., Sapienza, P., & Zingales, L. (2009). Cultural Biases in Economic Exchange? *The Quarterly Journal of Economics, 124*, 1095–1131.

Guiso, L., Sapienza, P., & Zingales, L. (2015a). Corporate Culture, Societal Culture, and Institutions. *American Economic Review, 105*, 336–339.

Guiso, L., Sapienza, P., & Zingales, L. (2015b). The Value of Corporate Culture. *Journal of Financial Economics, 117*, 60–76.

Harris, L. C., & Ogbonna, E. (2001). Strategic Human Resource Management, Market Orientation, and Organizational Performance. *Journal of Business Research, 51*, 157–166.

Hartnell, C. A., Ou, A. Y., & Kinicki, A. (2011). Organizational Culture and Organizational Effectiveness: A Meta-Analytic Investigation of the Competing Values Framework's Theoretical Suppositions. *Journal of Applied Psychology, 96*, 677.

Hong, H., & Stein, J. C. (2003). Differences of Opinion, Short-Sales Constraints, and Market Crashes. *Review of Financial Studies, 16*, 487–525.

Jaworski, B. J., & Kohli, A. K. (1993). Competition Culture: Antecedents and Consequences. *The Journal of Marketing, 57*, 53–70.

Kohli, A. K., & Jaworski, B. J. (1990). Competition Culture: The Construct, Research Propositions, and Managerial Implications. *The Journal of Marketing, 54*, 1–18.

Kotter, J. P., & Heskett, J. (1992). *Corporate Culture and Performance*. The Free Press.

Loughran, T., & McDonald, B. (2016). Textual Analysis in Accounting and Finance: A Survey. *Journal of Accounting Research, 54*, 1187–1230.

Luu, H., Nguyen, L., & Wilson, J. O. S. (2022). *Organizational Culture, Competition and Bank Loan Loss Provisions*. Available at SSRN 3921043.

Nguyen, D. D., Hagendorff, J., & Eshraghi, A. (2018). Does a CEO's Cultural Heritage affect Performance under Competitive Pressure? *The Review of Financial Studies, 31*, 97–141.

Nguyen, D. D., Nguyen, L., & Sila, V. (2019). Does Corporate Culture affect Bank Risk-Taking? Evidence from Loan-Level data. *British Journal of Management, 30*, 106–133.

O'Reilly, C. A., III., Caldwell, D. F., Chatman, J. A., & Doerr, B. (2014). The Promise and Problems of Organizational Culture: CEO Personality, Culture, and Firm Performance. *Group and Organization Management, 39*, 595–625.

Quinn, R. E., & Cameron, K. (1983). Organizational Life Cycles and Shifting Criteria of Effectiveness: Some Preliminary Evidence. *Management Science, 29*, 33–51.

Quinn, R. E., & Rohrbaugh, J. (1983). A Spatial Model of Effectiveness Criteria: Towards a Competing Values Approach to Organizational Analysis. *Management Science, 29*, 363–377.

Reynolds, P. D. (1986). Organizational Culture as Related to Industry, Position and Performance: A Preliminary Report. *Journal of Management Studies, 23*, 333–345.

Sørensen, J. B. (2002). The Strength of Corporate Culture and the Reliability of Firm Performance. *Administrative Science Quarterly, 47*, 70–91.

Tetlock, P. C. (2007). Giving Content to Investor Sentiment: The Role of Media in the Stock Market. *The Journal of Finance, 62*, 1139–1168.

Wang, Y., Farag, H., & Ahmad, W. (2021). Corporate Culture and Innovation: A Tale from an Emerging Market. *British Journal of Management, 32*, 1121–1140.

Zingales, L. (2015). The 'Cultural Revolution' in Finance. *Journal of Financial Economics, 117*, 1–4.

CHAPTER 6

Competition Culture and Crash Risk

6.1 Introduction

We now investigate whether and how firms' competition culture influences firm-specific stock price crash risk. Furthermore, we explore whether firm's competition culture is a channel through which institutional investors are able to affect firm's crash risk.

As in prior chapters, we perform a textual analysis of 10-K filings to measure firms' *competition culture* based on the competing values framework (CVF) (e.g., Cameron et al., 2014; Quinn & Cameron, 1983; Quinn & Rohrbaugh, 1983). Past literature suggests that this approach provides an efficient way to measure latent corporate values which reflect competition culture, and to do so for a large number of US publicly listed firms (please see Andreou et al., 2021; Fiordelisi & Ricci, 2014, 2021). Henceforth, as described in Chapter 4 and consistent with past works, we operationalize our measure of competition culture by analysing 10-K filings to identify a set of words that reflect the firm's corporate culture.

As we have mentioned, Cameron et al. (2014) define the competition culture as a type of corporate value that focuses the firm on achieving superior financial performance by assimilating and responding to external environmental information. Further recall that the competing values framework postulates competition culture as an important corporate value that impacts corporate decision-making. Thus, within this framework, the competition culture of a firm is said to encapsulate those value-creating

T. Harris, *Competition Culture and Corporate Finance*,
https://doi.org/10.1007/978-3-031-30156-8_6

activities that are empowered by the vigorous pursuit of profitability and financial performance. However, when a firm's competition culture is excessive, it could be argued that the management can become highly susceptible to engaging in "bad" news hoarding and/or making suboptimal investment decisions that can potentially harm shareholder value creation.

Thus, having established the influential role of institutional investors on a firm's competition culture in Chapter 4 and that competition culture is positively related to short-term performance in Chapter 5, we contend that firms with a greater competition culture are more secretive and are more prone to firm-specific stock price crashes. Given this, we investigate the relationship between competition culture and a firm's proclivity to engage in "bad" news hoarding that results in stock price crashes. In general, managers have financial incentives and other career motives to overstate performance by opportunistically suppressing "bad" news while accelerating the release of "good" news in the hope that a firm's current poor performance will be masked by better future performance (Kim & Zhang, 2011a, 2011b, 2016). However, such practices make firms vulnerable to adverse economic outcomes in the form of large idiosyncratic stock price declines, known as crash risk (Andreou et al., 2017, 2021; Callen & Fang, 2013, 2015; Hutton et al., 2009). For firms with an intense competition culture, managerial incentives to conceal negative information would be naturally heightened, since such firms need to consistently deliver superior results as they inherently have the inclination to assimilate and cater to external market expectations. Hence, after controlling for known crash risk determinants, we empirically test this proposition and show a strong positive relationship between competition culture and one-year-ahead crash risk. As crash risk is associated with large stock price drops, this evidence corroborates that on average competition culture appears to be harmful to firms' shareholder value creation.

Combining the result that transient (dedicated) institutional ownership intensifies (lessens) firms' competition culture (please see Chapter 4) with the evidence that such behaviour leads to an increased propensity for crash risk, we suspect that competition culture is a channel through which institutional ownership can indirectly influence a firm's policies and outcomes. To further investigate this, we conduct subsample and mediation analyses, and the results are consistent with our expectations. For instance, we find that the positive relationship between competition culture and the one-year-ahead crash risk is present only within the subsample of firms that is dominated by high levels of transient institutional ownership and low levels of dedicated institutional ownership. This analysis shows that competition culture is in and of itself not value destroying; rather, the striking result is that the competition culture becomes harmful only when it is associated with a high proportion of transient and a low proportion of dedicated ownership. Thus, taken altogether, we conclude that institutional investors constitute a key corporate governance mechanism which can (either curb or) exacerbate a firm's competition culture, that can then give rise to the opportunistic behaviour of managers to strategically withhold and accumulate negative information pertaining to their firms' poor performance which impacts its policies and outcomes.

To safeguard against the possibility that our analyses are negatively affected by simultaneous causality issues, all of our baseline regression models rely on a one-year time lag between the independent and dependent variables. Thus, our models are less susceptible to the presence of a contemporaneous feedback mechanism (i.e., reverse causality) between the key variables. Further, to mitigate other endogeneity concerns, we re-estimate all of our empirical models using an instrumental variable (IV) analysis and we reach similar, and in certain cases even stronger results.

Our study contributes to the recent literature by revealing a dark side to competition culture: as greater competition culture results in increased firm-specific stock price crash risk, especially when a firm's investor base is represented by high (low) levels of transient (dedicated) institutional investors. In so doing, we contribute to the burgeoning literature that focuses on the impact of firms' organizational norms and principles on policies and economic outcomes (see, for example, Andreou et al., 2021; Callen & Fang, 2015; Erhard et al., 2017; Fiordelisi & Ricci, 2014, 2021; Grennan, 2019; Guiso et al., 2006, 2015a, 2015b; Loughran et al., 2009; Luu et al., 2022; Wang et al., 2021; Zingales, 2015) by introducing competition culture as another organizational effectiveness factor that links to shareholder value creation.

The remainder of this chapter is presented as follows: Sect. 6.2 developed the main hypotheses; details of the data and summary statistics are presented in Sect. 6.3; Sect. 6.4 present the empirical results; and Sect. 6.5 concludes.

6.2 Hypotheses

If managers at firms with high competition culture are more likely to cater to investors, then it is plausible that this is achieved, in part, by being more secretive and by concealing negative information about the firm (Andreou et al., 2017). If this is so, then, on average, we would also expect firms with greater competition culture to be more prone to experience firm-specific stock price crashes (e.g., Kim & Zhang, 2011a, 2011b, 2016) as "bad" news hoarding make firms vulnerable to adverse economic outcomes in the form of large idiosyncratic stock price declines, when such "bad" news is eventually revealed to the market (Andreou et al., 2016, 2017, 2021; Callen & Fang, 2013, 2015; Hutton et al., 2009). Consequently, we posit the following hypothesis in an alternative form;

H1: **Competition culture is positively associated with firm-specific stock price crash risk.**

6.3 Data, Variables and Sample

6.3.1 Data

Ours is a unique dataset built by merging information from a number of publicly available data sources. We obtain annual firm-level data of US publicly traded firms for the period 1994–2014 from Compustat. To measure the competition culture through textual analysis we obtain firms' 10-K reports from SEC's Edgar database. Finally, we obtain institutional ownership data from the Thomson Reuters Institutional Holdings Database.

We perform analysis on all firms included in the Compustat database excluding financials (SIC 6000–6999) and utilities (SIC 4900–4999). Also, to limit survivorship bias, firms that are inactive and/or acquired by another firm during the period of study are retained in the sample. In addition, we also delete from our sample all firm-year observations with missing data on the variables of interest. This results in a final main sample consisting of 31,223 firm-year observations. Table 6.1 reports the definition of all the variables used in the analysis.

Table 6.1 Definition of variables

	Symbol		*Definitions*
Competition culture			
	COMP	=	the firm's competition culture estimated for each fiscal year using the text-analysis approach;
Crash risk			
	DUVOL	=	for each firm over a fiscal year, all the weeks with firm-specific returns below the annual mean are separated from those firm-specific weekly returns which are above the annual mean; we categorize these weeks as "down weeks" and "up weeks", respectively. *DUVOL* is the log of the ratio of the standard deviations of the two subsamples, the one for the "down weeks" over the standard deviation of the "up weeks";
	ESIGMA	=	the negative of the worst deviation of firm-specific weekly returns from the average firm-specific weekly return divided by the standard deviation of firm-specific weekly returns;
	NCSKEW	=	the negative of the third moment of firm-specific weekly returns for each firm and year by the standard deviation of firm-specific weekly returns raised to the third power;
Institutional ownership			
	TRA	=	the percentage of stock ownership in the firm by transient institutional investors relative to total shares outstanding;
	DED	=	the percentage of stock ownership in the firm by dedicated institutional investors relative to total shares outstanding;
Other variables			
	AGE	=	number of years since the firm first appears in CRSP;
	DTURN	=	average monthly turnover for the current fiscal year, minus the average monthly share turnover for the previous year;

(continued)

Table 6.1 (continued)

Symbol		*Definitions*
HHI	=	the Herfindahl–Hirschman concentration ratio computed using total assets for each firm by FF 48 index and state;
LEV	=	long-term debt by total assets;
MTB	=	market to book value of equity at the end of the fiscal year;
RET	=	average weekly returns for the fiscal year;
ROA	=	return on assets defined as income before extraordinary items divided by total assets;
SIZE	=	natural logarithm of the market value of equity at the end of the fiscal year;
SP500	=	equal to 1 if the firm is included in the S&P 500 index, and is 0 otherwise;
STATE	=	equal to 1 if firms in the state have above median competition culture, and is 0 otherwise; and
STDEV	=	the volatility of firm-specific weekly returns

6.3.2 *Measuring Competition Culture*

As in our previous chapters in this book, we measure a firm's competition culture (COMP) by counting the number of times that the lexical items included in the bag of words describing corporate attributes for the competition culture are found in the 10-K filings and scale our measure by counts of the lexical items that describe the other cultural orientations as follows[1]:

$$\text{COMP} = \frac{\text{Number of lexical items describing the Competition Culture}}{\text{Total number of lexical items for all types of cultures}}. \tag{6.1}$$

[1] While conducting our count we exclude negation of the lexical items by ignoring occasions when the word is preceded by "no", "non", "not", "less", "few" or "limited" by three or fewer words.

6.3.3 Measuring Stock Price Crash Risk

We estimate the following three firm-specific measures of stock price crash risk, namely DUVOL, ESIGMA, and NCSKEW. Each of these measures reflects different aspects of the distribution of returns (Andreou et al., 2016, 2017, 2021; Callen & Fang, 2013; Chen et al., 2001; Hutton et al., 2009) and is computed by estimating firm-specific weekly returns using the following expanded index model regression:

$$\begin{aligned} r_{j,w} =& \alpha_j + \beta_{1,j} r_{m,w-2} + \beta_{2,j} r_{m,w-1} + \beta_{3,j} r_{m,w} \\ &+ \beta_{4,j} r_{m,w+1} + \beta_{5,j} r_{m,w+2} + \varepsilon_{j,w}, \end{aligned} \tag{6.2}$$

where $r_{j,w}$ is the return on the stock of firm j in the week w and $r_{m,w}$ is the CRSP value-weighted market index for the week w. We permit non-synchronous trading by including lead and lag terms for the market index as in Dimson (1979). Further, our regression removes market-wide return movements from firm returns, and thus the residual of our model is able to capture the weekly firm-specific returns. As the residuals from Eq. (6.2) are skewed, we compute the firm-specific weekly return for firm j in week w ($R_{j,w}$) as the natural logarithm of the residual plus one.

The DUVOL stock price crash risk measure is computed for each firm j over a fiscal year t, where all weeks with firm-specific returns that are below the annual mean are separated from those above the annual mean. DUVOL is the log of the ratio of the standard deviations of the weeks below the mean (DOWN) over the weeks above the mean (UP), and is computed as follows:

$$\text{DUVOL}_{j,t} = \log\{(n_u - 1) \sum_{\text{DOWN}} R_{j,w}^2 / (n_d - 1) \sum_{\text{UP}} R_{j,w}^2\}, \tag{6.3}$$

where n_u and n_d are the number of UP and DOWN weeks of the fiscal year t.

The ESIGMA stock price crash risk measure is the negative of the worst standard deviation of firm-specific weekly returns from the average firm-specific weekly return divided by the standard deviation of firm-specific weekly returns. We compute *ESIGMA* for a given firm in a fiscal year as follows:

$$\text{ESIGMA}_{j,t} = -\min \frac{R_{j,w} - \overline{R}_j}{\sigma_{R_j}}, \tag{6.4}$$

where $\overline{R}_j$ and σ_{R_j} are the mean and standard deviation of the firm-specific weekly returns $R_{j,w}$ for the firm j over the fiscal year t.

The NCSKEW stock price crash risk measure is defined as the negative of the third moment of firm-specific weekly returns for each firm-year divided by the standard deviation of firm-specific weekly returns raised to the third power, and is computed as follows:

$$\text{NCSKEW}_{j,t} = -\frac{\left(n(n-1)^{\frac{3}{2}} \sum R_{j,w}^3\right)}{\left((n-1)(n-2)\left(\sum R_{j,w}^2\right)^{\frac{3}{2}}\right)}, \tag{6.5}$$

where n is the number of observations of firm-specific weekly returns during the fiscal year t. The denominator in Eq. (6.5) is a normalization factor.

Larger values of DUVOL, ESIGMA, and NCSKEW signify greater crash risk.

6.3.4 *Measuring Institutional Ownership*

In this study, we adopt two measures for firms' institutional ownership structure, namely transient and dedicated institutional ownership (Bushee, 1998). Transient institutional ownership, TRA, is the percentage of stock ownership in the firm by transient institutional investors relative to total shares outstanding. Transient investors focus on short-term performance and invest based on the likelihood of earning short-term trading profits (Bushee, 1998, 2001; Callen & Fang, 2013). Dedicated institutional ownership, *DED*, is defined as the percentage of stock ownership in the firm by dedicated institutional investors relative to total shares outstanding. Dedicated investors are defined as those that hold large stakes in a limited number of firms, invest in the long term, and therefore have strong incentives to monitor the long-term performance of management (Bushee, 1998, 2001; Chen et al., 2001).

6.3.5 *Control Variables*

We carefully select control variables for our empirical work based on the extant literature (Bushee, 1998, 2001; Callen & Fang, 2013; Chen et al., 2001; Cheng & Warfield, 2005). To begin with, we include in all specifications controls to capture firm-specific characteristics. In particular, we include the following: the number of years since the firm was first included in the CRSP database, AGE; financial leverage as indicated by total liabilities to total assets, LEV; market value of equity to book value of equity, MTB; return on total assets, ROA; and the natural logarithm of market value of equity, SIZE.

In addition, since our specifications include crash risk as a dependent variable, we control for investor heterogeneity as it is possible that it influences both our crash risk variables and our independent variable of interest; namely, competition culture. To do so, we include the detrended average weekly stock trading volume, DTURN, average weekly stock returns, RET, and the volatility of weekly stock returns, STDEV, over the fiscal year (Andreou et al., 2016, 2017).

6.3.6 *Descriptive Statistics and Correlations*

Table 6.2 provides the summary statistics of the variables used in the multivariate analysis.[2] Specifically, our mean value of the competition culture variable, COMP, is 0.49. In addition, the idiosyncratic crash risk variables DUVOL, ESIGMA, and NCSKEW have mean values of—0.04, 2.61, and 0.04, respectively. We observe that the descriptive statistics on the main variables of interests are analogous to those values reported in prior studies that have used similar data (please see e.g., Andreou et al., 2016, 2021; Bushee, 2001; Callen & Fang, 2013) (Table 6.3).

Pearson correlation results consistent with our expectations are also found for the relationship between COMP and the crash risk measures DUVOL, ESIGMA, and NCSKEW. Specifically, we find positive and significant correlations between COMP and the various measures of crash risk, with 0.0179 correlation coefficient for DUVOL, 0.0278 correlation coefficient for ESIGMA and 0.0250 correlation coefficient for NCSKEW, all indicating that higher levels of COMP induce higher crash risk.

6.4 Empirical Results

In this section, we report our multivariate results based on empirical approaches adopted to deal with the practical challenges associated with our research design. Specifically, based on the extant literature (and our

[2] To mitigate the effects of outliers, all continuous variables are winsorized at the 1 and 99% levels.

Table 6.2 Descriptive statistics for the variables used in the empirical analyses

Variable	*Obs*	*Mean*	*Std. Dev*	*25th Pctl*	*Median*	*75th Pctl*
COMP	31,223	0.49	0.06	0.45	0.49	0.54
DUVOL	31,223	−0.04	0.37	−0.29	−0.05	0.19
ESIGMA	31,223	2.61	0.76	2.08	2.44	2.97
NCSKEW	31,223	0.04	0.84	−0.41	−0.01	0.42
TRA	31,223	0.15	0.12	0.06	0.13	0.22
DED	31,223	0.06	0.09	0	0.01	0.09
AGE	31,223	23.64	12.98	14	20	32
DTURN	31,223	1.19	23.18	−5.97	0.4	7.76
HHI	31,223	0.43	0.29	0.2	0.35	0.6
LEV	31,223	0.47	0.29	0.28	0.46	0.62
MTB	31,223	3.38	55.44	1.32	2.13	3.58
RET	31,223	−0.2	0.21	−0.25	−0.12	−0.06
ROA	31,223	0.01	0.26	0	0.05	0.08
SIZE	31,223	6.29	1.78	5.02	6.2	7.43
SP500	31,223	0.21	0.41	0	0	0
STATE	30,478	0.51	0.5	0	1	1
STDEV	31,223	0.06	0.03	0.04	0.05	0.07

This table presents the mean, median, 25thpercentile, 75th percentile, and the number of observations for the variables used in the study for the period 1994–2014

past results in Chapter 4), we expect and observe rather persistent levels of competition culture over time (Andreou et al., 2021; Cameron et al., 2014; Guiso et al., 2006, 2015a, 2015b; Hartnell et al., 2011; Nguyen et al., 2018). As a result, we adopt OLS estimators as the primary regression tool for our empirical analysis. In addition, we provide generalized least square random effects (GLS-RE) regression estimates as supplementary results (provided in Appendix B), as they are well-suited to this type of analysis since they allow for the inclusion of slow-moving or sluggish covariates without destabilizing the estimates of the effect of these variables.

6.4.1 *Competition Culture and Stock Price Crash Risk*

Next, we consider the relationship between firms' competition culture and firm-specific stock price crash risk. Given that our prior results, it is also likely that firms with a strong competition culture are more prone to stock price crashes when "bad" news, which was once concealed, is

Table 6.3 Pearson correlation matrix

	COMP	*DUVOL*	*ESIGMA*	*NCSKEW*	*TRA*	*DED*	*AGE*	*DTURN*
DUVOL	**0.0179**							
ESIGMA	**0.0278**	**0.7837**						
NCSKEW	**0.0250**	**0.9531**	**0.8308**					
TRA	**0.0958**	**0.1261**	**0.0832**	**0.1232**				
DED	**−0.0621**	0.0026	**−0.0188**	0.0007	−0.0114			
AGE	**−0.1571**	−0.0006	**−0.0343**	**−0.0241**	**−0.1061**	**0.0644**		
DTURN	**−0.0259**	**0.0465**	**0.0307**	**0.0469**	**0.1298**	−0.0062	0.0112	
HHI	**−0.0776**	−0.0143	−0.0028	**−0.0235**	**−0.0928**	**−0.0228**	**0.1830**	0.0026
LEV	**−0.0876**	**−0.0268**	**−0.0214**	**−0.0297**	−0.0055	**0.0588**	**0.1012**	**0.0261**
MTB	0.0019	0.0120	0.0132	0.0129	0.0071	0.0039	0.0032	0.0006
RET	**−0.1054**	**0.0610**	**0.0288**	**0.0148**	**−0.0803**	**0.0322**	**0.2821**	**−0.1528**
ROA	**−0.0239**	**0.0827**	**0.0452**	**0.0539**	**0.0465**	**0.0243**	**0.1305**	**0.0498**
SIZE	**−0.0512**	**0.1751**	**0.0876**	**0.1370**	**0.2368**	**0.0241**	**0.2867**	**0.0792**
SP500	**−0.1022**	**0.0365**	−0.0119	**0.0156**	**0.0626**	**0.0881**	**0.4053**	**0.0245**
STATE	**0.1467**	0.0103	**0.0219**	**0.0191**	0.0141	**0.0393**	**−0.1119**	**−0.0322**
STDEV	**0.1141**	**−0.0593**	**−0.0240**	−0.0090	**0.1165**	**−0.0271**	−0.3387	**0.1427**
	HHI	***LEV***	***MTB***	***RET***	***ROA***	***SIZE***	***SP500***	***STATE***
LEV	**0.0779**							
MTB	−0.0040	**0.0035**						
RET	**0.1216**	**0.0512**	−0.0085					
ROA	**0.0702**	**−0.3109**	−0.0032	**0.2943**				

(continued)

Table 6.3 (continued)

	COMP	*DUVOL*	*ESIGMA*	*NCSKEW*	*TRA*	*DED*	*AGE*	*DTURN*
SIZE	0.0122	**0.0994**	**0.0205**	**0.3559**	**0.2017**			
SP500	**0.0565**	**0.1399**	0.0046	**0.2191**	**0.1060**	**0.6406**		
STATE	**−0.1998**	**−0.0973**	0.0136	**−0.0735**	**−0.0606**	**−0.0374**	**−0.0382**	
STDEV	**−0.1413**	**−0.0691**	0.0045	**−0.9629**	**−0.2903**	**−0.4243**	**−0.2758**	**0.0883**

This table presents Pearson correlation coefficients for the variables used in the empirical analyses. The bold figures indicate significance at the 10% level and above released to the market. Thus, to test H1 which states that competition culture is indeed positively related to firm-specific stock price crash risk, we estimate the following model:

$$
\begin{aligned}
\text{CRASH}_{t+1} = & \alpha_1 + \alpha_2 \text{COMP}_t + \alpha_3 \text{AGE}_t + \alpha_4 \text{DTURN}_t \\
& + \alpha_5 \text{LEV}_t + \alpha_6 \text{MTB}_t + \alpha_7 \text{RET}_t + \alpha_8 \text{ROA}_t \\
& + \alpha_9 \text{SIZE}_t + \alpha_{10} \text{STDEV}_t + \varepsilon_t
\end{aligned} \tag{6.6}
$$

where CRASH is used to denote the idiosyncratic crash risk measures, DUVOL, ESIGMA, and NCSKEW. Consistent with our prior analysis, we account for the effect of other factors that may confound our results by including controls that capture other relevant firm-specific characteristics reported to have an effect on stock price crash risk. In addition, we include in all empirical models year and industry dummies to control for an unobserved time-invariant year and industry effects. The coefficient of interest is, α_2, and this is predicted to be positive and significant.

Table 6.4 provides the empirical analysis to assess the relationship between competition culture and stock price crash risk, where the coefficient terms 0.015, 0.018, and 0.019 on the COMP variable in columns (1), (2) and (3) suggests the nature of the relationship between competition culture and firm-specific crash risk. In particular, we report evidence of a positive and significant relationship between competition culture and future crash risk at the 10% (column 1) and 5% levels (columns 2 and 3) with *t*-values equal to 1.82, 2.14, and 2.26, respectively. We also provide in Appendix B GLS-RE regression estimates of Eq. (6.6) and OLS re-estimates of the same where we also include controls for managers' short-term incentives. The nature of our results remains unchanged.

Further, we estimate instrumental variables models to allow for potential endogeneity in the r relationship between competition culture and stock price crash risk. Specifically, we estimate the following:

$$
\begin{aligned}
\text{CRASH}_{t+1} = & \alpha_1 + \alpha_2 \widehat{\text{COMP}}_t + \alpha_3 \text{AGE}_t + \alpha_4 \text{DTURN}_t \\
& + \alpha_5 \text{LEV}_t + \alpha_6 \text{MTB}_t + \alpha_7 \text{RET}_t + \alpha_8 \text{ROA}_t \\
& + \alpha_9 \text{SIZE}_t + \alpha_{10} \text{STDEV}_t + \varepsilon_t
\end{aligned} \tag{6.7a}
$$

$$
\begin{aligned}
\text{COMP}_t = & \gamma_1 + \delta_1 \text{HHI}_t + \delta_2 \text{STATE}_t + \delta_3 \text{SP500}_t + \beta_1 \text{AGE}_t \\
& + \beta_2 \text{DTURN}_t + \beta_3 \text{LEV}_t + \beta_4 \text{MTB}_t + \beta_5 \text{RET}_t \\
& + \beta_6 \text{ROA}_t + \beta_7 \text{SIZE}_t + \beta_8 \text{STDEV}_t + \mu_t
\end{aligned} \tag{6.7b}
$$

where CRASH denotes our stock price crash risk variables DUVOL, ESIGMA, and NCSKEW, while the variables HHI, STATE, and SP500 instrument for competition culture. The Hausman (1978) tests suggest that COMP is endogenous, and the results are consistent with those presented in the prior analysis, where we argued and found that competition culture increases firm-specific stock price crash risk.

Our empirical findings presented in Table 6.5 support the notion that firms with a more intensified corporate culture to compete tend to also be more prone to stock price crashes. Overall, the results are consistent with those presented in the previous analysis, where we argue and find that the competition culture increases firm-specific stock price crash risk.

Table 6.4 OLS regressions of competition culture on stock price crash risk

	$DUVOL_{t+1}$	$ESIGMA_{t+1}$	$NCSKEW_{t+1}$
	(1)	*(2)*	*(3)*
$COMP_t$	0.015*	0.018**	0.019**
	(1.82)	(2.14)	(2.26)
AGE_t	−0.036***	−0.031***	−0.040***
	(4.18)	(3.54)	(4.64)
$DTURN_t$	0.025***	0.022***	0.022***
	(3.26)	(2.78)	(2.87)
LEV_t	−0.023***	0.002	−0.015*
	(2.65)	(0.29)	(1.78)
MTB_t	0.003	−0.002	0.002
	(0.35)	(0.31)	(0.22)
RET_t	0.146***	0.092***	0.155***
	(5.33)	(3.37)	(5.70)
ROA_t	0.068***	0.055***	0.052***
	(7.85)	(5.94)	(5.77)
$SIZE_t$	0.177***	0.095***	0.164***
	(18.11)	(9.80)	(16.92)
$STDEV_t$	0.156***	0.102***	0.192***
	(5.08)	(3.34)	(6.28)
R^2	0.05	0.03	0.05
N	18,654	18,654	18,654

$^*p < 0.1$; $^{**}p < 0.05$; $^{***}p < 0.01$

This table presents OLS estimates used to investigate the relationship between competition culture and crash risk. All regressions include year and industry fixed effects and the standard errors are clustered at the firm level. The t-values are given in parentheses

Table 6.5 Instrumental variable regressions of competition culture on stock price crash risk

Panel A. IV regression first and second stage results

	1st stage: $COMP_t$	*$DUVOL_{t+1}$*	*$ESIGMA_{t+1}$*	*$NCSKEW_{t+1}$*
	(1)	*(2)*	*(3)*	*(4)*
$COMP_t$		0.167**	0.228***	0.187***
		(2.35)	(3.11)	(2.62)
HHI_t	0.028			
	(1.62)			
$STATE_t$	0.217***			
	(8.42)			
$SP500_t$	−0.108**			
	(2.18)			
AGE_t	−0.095***	−0.019	−0.008	−0.021*
	(5.58)	(1.61)	(0.64)	(1.77)
$DTURN_t$	−0.025***	0.029***	0.027***	0.027***
	(4.44)	(3.66)	(3.36)	(3.33)
LEV_t	−0.040***	−0.015	0.013	−0.007
	(2.79)	(1.57)	(1.36)	(0.71)
MTB_t	−0.019**	0.005	0.001	0.005
	(1.64)	(0.68)	(0.14)	(0.58)
RET_t	−0.010	0.145***	0.091***	0.154***
	(0.26)	(5.16)	(3.20)	(5.50)
ROA_t	0.001	0.069***	0.055***	0.052***
	(0.11)	(7.57)	(5.61)	(5.57)
$SIZE_t$	0.051**	0.173***	0.089***	0.160***
	(2.38)	(16.74)	(8.39)	(15.35)
$STDEV_t$	−0.001	0.153***	0.099***	0.189***
	(0.03)	(4.85)	(3.09)	(5.98)
R^2	0.19			
N	18,654	18,654	18,651	18,654

*$p < 0.1$; **$p < 0.05$; ***$p < 0.01$

This table presents estimates from instrument variable regressions used to investigate the relationship between competition culture and crash risk [Panel A], and the results of a Stock and Yogo (2005) weak instruments test [Panel B]. The regressions include year and industry fixed effects and the standard errors are clustered by firm. The t-values are given in parentheses

6.4.2 *Does Competition Culture Mediate the Relationship between Institutional Ownership and Stock Price Crash Risk?*

Finally, we investigate whether firms' competition culture is a channel through which institutional ownership affects crash risk. Our previous findings in Chapter 4 suggest that transient (dedicated) institutional ownership intensifies (diminishes) firms' competition culture and that such firms are more likely achieve superior performance and experience stock price crashes. Consistent with these observations and prior work in this area (Andreou et al., 2016, 2017, 2021; Bushee, 1998, 2001; Callen & Fang, 2013), we argue that since transient institutional owners exert pressures on the firm to achieve short-term performance objectives (at the expense of long-term value), this serves to enhance competition culture, which in turn increases firm-specific crash risk. Further, since dedicated institutional investors appear to serve as effective monitors of the firm, this scrutiny serves to dampen excessive orientation toward the competition culture and thereby firm-specific crash risk.

To explore this, we re-estimate Eq. (6.6) for subsamples of *TRA* and *DED* that are sorted into subsamples of HIGH and LOW transient and dedicated institutional ownership. We define a subsample group as HIGH (LOW) if it is above (below) the yearly median of our institutional ownership measures. Thus, if competition culture serves the purpose that we describe, we would expect to observe that the relationship between competition culture and crash risk is stronger for those firms with above yearly median *TRA* and below yearly median *DED* (i.e., HIGH *TRA* and LOW *DED*). We expect this because a significant presence of transient institutional owners is likely to pressurize managers to emphasize short-term performance objectives. This coupled with an absence of dedicated investors, who tend to focus on long-term firm value, creates a less-than-effective counter to managerial myopia in firms with greater competition culture, which in turn triggers higher instances of stock price crashes for such firms.

The results of this subsample analysis are presented in Table 6.6, where we find that competition culture increases future firm-specific crash risk only for those firm-years where transient institutional ownership is above, and dedicated institutional ownership below, the yearly median (i.e., first quadrant in Table 6.6 labelled "HIGH *TRA* & LOW *DED*"). This result is exactly as we expect and suggests a strong interrelationship between institutional ownership, competition culture, and stock price crash risk.

In addition to the OLS estimates presented in Table 6.6, we provide GLS-RE estimates of these relations in Appendix B. These estimates also suggest a statistically significant relationship between COMP and our measures of stock price crash risk only when transient institutional ownership is above and dedicated ownership below, the yearly median. We find these results indeed striking, as they show that competition culture in and of itself is not value destroying; rather, these results suggest that competition culture becomes harmful only when it is associated with a high proportion of transient and a low proportion of dedicated ownership.

Additionally, we conduct a further empirical analysis to examine whether competition culture does actually mediate the relationship between institutional ownership and stock price crash risk. In order to do this, we now estimate the following system of Seemingly Unrelated Regressions (SURs):

$$\begin{aligned}\text{CRASH}_{t+1} = & \alpha_1 + \alpha_2\text{COMP}_t + \alpha_3\text{TRA}(or\text{DED}_t) + \alpha_4\text{AGE}_t \\ & + \alpha_5\text{DTURN}_t + \alpha_6\text{LEV}_t + \alpha_7\text{MTB}_t + \alpha_8\text{RET}_t \\ & + \alpha_9\text{ROA}_t + \alpha_{10}\text{SIZE}_t + \alpha_{11}\text{STDEV}_t + \varepsilon_t \end{aligned} \tag{6.8a}$$

$$\begin{aligned}\text{COMP}_t = & \beta_1 + \beta_2\text{TRA}(or\text{DED}_t) + \beta_3\text{AGE}_t + \beta_4\text{DTURN}_t \\ & + \beta_5\text{LEV}_t + \beta_6\text{MTB}_t + \beta_7\text{RET}_t + \beta_8\text{ROA}_t \\ & + \beta_9\text{SIZE}_t + \beta_{10}\text{STDEV}_t + \varepsilon_t \end{aligned} \tag{6.8b}$$

where all variables are as previously defined, and we include in our SUR estimates year and industry dummies. To shed further light as to whether competition culture mediates the relationship between transient and dedicated institutional ownership and firm-specific crash risk, we compute the Sobel test (with delta-method standard errors).

Table 6.7 presents our SUR estimates and Sobel test results. We observe significant test results for the indirect relationship between transient institutional ownership and stock price crash risk as indicated by ESIGMA (p-value $= 0.09$) and NCSKEW (p-value $= 0.09$) in Panel A. These findings, coupled with our subsample analysis results, suggest that a firm's competition culture is a channel through which institutional ownership affects future firm-specific stock price crash risk.

Table 6.6 Subsample analyses of competition culture on stock price crash risk

Panel A. The effect of competition culture on crash risk for subsamples of high transient and low (or high) dedicated ownership firms

	HIGH TRA *&* *LOW* DED			*HIGH* TRA *&* *HIGH* DED		
	$DUVOL_{t+1}$ (1)	$ESIGMA_{t+1}$ (2)	$NCSKEW_{t+1}$ (3)	$DUVOL_{t+1}$ (4)	$ESIGMA_{t+1}$ (5)	$NCSKEW_{t+1}$ (6)
$COMP_t$	0.051***	0.058***	0.056***	0.008	0.002	0.011
	(2.80)	(3.06)	(3.05)	(0.42)	(0.11)	(0.56)
AGE_t	−0.023	−0.002	−0.029	−0.035*	−0.017	−0.038**
	(1.20)	(0.13)	(1.51)	(1.82)	(0.81)	(2.00)
$DTURN_t$	0.041***	0.036**	0.041***	0.041**	0.025	0.040**
	(2.71)	(2.26)	(2.65)	(2.40)	(1.46)	(2.41)
LEV_t	−0.043**	−0.025	−0.038**	−0.016	0.021	−0.008
	(2.31)	(1.25)	(2.00)	(0.79)	(0.98)	(0.41)
MTB_t	0.004	0.001	0.003	0.027*	0.005	0.024
	(0.19)	(0.06)	(0.13)	(1.81)	(0.31)	(1.51)
RET_t	0.063	−0.013	0.043	0.134*	0.137*	0.130*
	(0.95)	(0.18)	(0.65)	(1.74)	(1.72)	(1.71)
ROA_t	0.043**	0.047**	0.034	0.048**	0.038	0.029
	(2.15)	(2.14)	(1.55)	(2.00)	(1.41)	(1.11)
$SIZE_t$	0.159***	0.098***	0.132***	0.130***	0.063**	0.108***
	(5.55)	(3.38)	(4.56)	(4.93)	(2.25)	(4.07)
$STDEV_t$	0.09	0.033	0.102	0.170**	0.182**	0.181**
	(1.24)	(0.44)	(1.41)	(2.14)	(2.17)	(2.28)
R^2	0.05	0.04	0.04	0.06	0.04	0.05
N	4,011	4,011	4,011	3,575	3,575	3,575

Panel B. The effect of competition orientation on crash risk for subsamples of low transient and low (or high) dedicated ownership firms

	LOW TRA & *LOW* DED			*LOW* TRA & *HIGH* DED		
	$DUVOL_{t+1}$	$ESIGMA_{t+1}$	$NCSKEW_{t+1}$	$DUVOL_{t+1}$	$ESIGMA_{t+1}$	$NCSKEW_{t+1}$
	(1)	*(2)*	*(3)*	*(4)*	*(5)*	*(6)*
$COMP_t$	0.008	0.004	0.01	−0.002	0.005	−0.002
	(0.50)	(0.27)	(0.65)	(0.11)	(0.27)	(0.09)
AGE_t	−0.022	−0.021	−0.022	−0.037*	−0.050***	−0.041**
	(1.26)	(1.28)	(1.28)	(1.89)	(2.64)	(2.20)
$DTURN_t$	−0.006	−0.012	−0.02	−0.03	−0.027	−0.035
	(0.36)	(0.75)	(1.25)	(1.22)	(1.07)	(1.44)
LEV_t	−0.005	0.019	0.005	−0.011	−0.001	−0.01
	(0.28)	(1.18)	(0.29)	(0.55)	(0.03)	(0.49)
MTB_t	0.002	0	0.004	−0.001	0	−0.008
	(0.10)	(0.01)	(0.25)	(0.05)	(0.01)	(0.45)
RET_t	0.07	0.072	0.082*	0.160**	0.039	0.167**
	(1.39)	(1.49)	(1.68)	(2.15)	(0.53)	(2.33)
ROA_t	0.063***	0.048***	0.050***	0.076***	0.076***	0.057**
	(4.04)	(2.97)	(3.25)	(3.48)	(3.43)	(2.51)
$SIZE_t$	0.216***	0.131***	0.205***	0.107***	0.038*	0.107***
	(10.06)	(6.26)	(9.61)	(4.58)	(1.74)	(4.64)
$STDEV_t$	0.074	0.069	0.118**	0.129	0.017	0.175**
	(1.29)	(1.27)	(2.10)	(1.63)	(0.22)	(2.26)
R^2	0.08	0.05	0.06	0.05	0.04	0.04
R^2	0.08	0.05	0.06	0.05	0.04	0.04
N	4,505	4,505	4,505	3,088	3,088	3,088

$^*p < 0.1$; $^{**}p < 0.05$; $^{***}p < 0.01$

This table presents OLS estimates used to investigate the relationship between competition culture and crash risk for subsamples of firms. All regressions include year and industry fixed effects and the standard errors are clustered at the firm level. The *t*-values are given in parentheses

Table 6.7 Seemingly unrelated regressions of institutional ownership, competition culture, and stock price crash risk

Panel A. The indirect effect of transient institutional ownership on crash risk.

	$COMP_t$	$DUVOL_{t+1}$	$COMP_t$	$ESIGMA_{t+1}$	$COMP_t$	$NCSKEW_{t+1}$
	(1)	(2)	(3)	(4)	(5)	(6)
$COMP_t$		0.015*		0.017*		0.017**
		(1.75)		(1.95)		(2.00)
TRA_t	0.029***	0.080***	0.029***	0.057***	0.029***	0.079***
	(3.26)	(8.32)	(3.26)	(5.87)	(3.26)	(8.20)
AGE_t	−0.094***	−0.026***	−0.094***	−0.023**	−0.094***	−0.030***
	(10.74)	(2.84)	(10.74)	(2.37)	(10.74)	(3.16)
$DTURN_t$	−0.032***	0.019**	−0.032***	0.013	−0.032***	0.013
	(4.14)	(2.24)	(4.14)	(1.50)	(4.14)	(1.55)
LEV_t	−0.055***	−0.024***	−0.055***	0.001	−0.055***	−0.017*
	(6.67)	(2.71)	(6.67)	(0.08)	(6.67)	(1.87)
MTB_t	−0.018**	0.011	−0.018**	0.003	−0.018**	0.009
	(2.23)	(1.24)	(2.23)	(0.34)	(2.23)	(1.03)
RET_t	−0.006	0.116***	−0.006	0.083**	−0.006	0.118***
	(0.18)	(3.56)	(0.18)	(2.51)	(0.18)	(3.60)
ROA_t	0	0.060***	0	0.053***	0	0.045***
	(0.04)	(6.29)	(0.04)	(5.45)	(0.04)	(4.72)
$SIZE_t$	0.008	0.139***	0.008	0.068***	0.008	0.125***
	(0.80)	(12.51)	(0.80)	(5.99)	(0.80)	(11.23)
$STDEV_t$	0.01	0.120***	0.01	0.093***	0.01	0.153***
	(0.31)	(3.48)	(0.31)	(2.63)	(0.31)	(4.40)
Breusch–Pagan test chi^2		1.00		1.00		1.00
Breusch–Pagan test p-value		1.00		1.00		1.00
Sobel test statistic		1.54		1.67		1.70

Panel A The indirect effect of transient institutional ownership on crash risk.

	$COMP_t$	$DUVOL_{t+1}$	$COMP_t$	$ESIGMA_{t+1}$	$COMP_t$	$NCSKEW_{t+1}$
	(1)	(2)	(3)	(4)	(5)	(6)
Sobel test *p*-value		0.12		0.09		0.09
R^2	0.18	0.05	0.18	0.03	0.18	0.04
N	15,179	15,179	15,179	15,179	15,179	15,179

Panel B The indirect effect of dedicated institutional ownership on crash risk

	$COMP_t$	$DUVOL_{t+1}$	$COMP_t$	$ESIGMA_{t+1}$	$COMP_t$	$NCSKEW_{t+1}$
	(1)	(2)	(3)	(4)	(5)	(6)
$COMP_t$		0.017**		0.019**		0.019**
		(1.98)		(2.09)		(2.21)
DED_t	−0.028***	0.006	−0.028***	−0.007	−0.028***	−0.001
	(2.60)	(0.51)	(2.60)	(0.58)	(2.60)	(0.11)
AGE_t	−0.099***	−0.038***	−0.099***	−0.031***	−0.099***	−0.041***
	(11.39)	(4.14)	(11.39)	(3.30)	(11.39)	(4.45)
$DTURN_t$	−0.030***	0.025***	−0.030***	0.018**	−0.030***	0.020**
	(3.85)	(3.02)	(3.85)	(2.05)	(3.85)	(2.33)
LEV_t	−0.054***	−0.023**	−0.054***	0.002	−0.054***	−0.015*
	(6.51)	(2.55)	(6.51)	(0.22)	(6.51)	(1.69)
MTB_t	−0.018**	0.011	−0.018**	0.003	−0.018**	0.009
	(2.25)	(1.29)	(2.25)	(0.37)	(2.25)	(1.07)
RET_t	0.016	0.161***	0.016	0.118***	0.016	0.164***
	(0.53)	(5.01)	(0.53)	(3.59)	(0.53)	(5.06)
ROA_t	0.001	0.064***	0.001	0.056***	0.001	0.049***
	(0.06)	(6.70)	(0.06)	(5.72)	(0.06)	(5.10)
$SIZE_t$	0.021**	0.167***	0.021**	0.089***	0.021**	0.154***

(continued)

Table 6.7 (continued)

Panel B. The indirect effect of dedicated institutional ownership on crash risk

	$COMP_t$	$DUVOL_{t+1}$	$COMP_t$	$ESIGMA_{t+1}$	$COMP_t$	$NCSKEW_{t+1}$
	(1)	*(2)*	*(3)*	*(4)*	*(5)*	*(6)*
	(2.19)	(15.71)	(2.19)	(8.24)	(2.19)	(14.40)
$STDEV_t$	0.034	0.175***	0.034	0.134***	0.034	0.207***
	(1.06)	(5.13)	(1.06)	(3.85)	(1.06)	(6.07)
Breusch–Pagan test chi^2		0.00		0.00		0.00
Breusch–Pagan test p-value		1.00		0.99		1.00
Sobel test statistic		−1.57		−1.63		−1.68
Sobel test p-value		0.12		0.10		0.10
R^2	0.18	0.05	0.18	0.03	0.18	0.04
N	15,179	15,179	15,179	15,179	15,179	15,179

$^*p < 0.1$; $^{**}p < 0.05$; $^{***}p < 0.01$

This table presents seemingly unrelated regression estimates and Sobel test results used to investigate the indirect relationship between transient and dedicated institutional ownership and crash risk as mediated by competition culture. All regressions include year and industry fixed effects and the standard errors are clustered at the firm level. The t-values are given in parentheses

6.5 Summary

We explore the role that firms' competition culture plays in determining corporate policies and outcomes. In particular, we investigate whether and how firms' competition culture is associated with adverse outcomes such as an increase in future firm-specific crash risk. Using a text-based measure of firms' competition culture, we find that firms with greater competition culture are more prone to stock price crashes.

Overall, our results primarily suggest that the firm's competition culture increases stock price crash risk. Further, we find that although the competition culture can result in increased stock prices crashes, this behaviour is only observed for those firms with above median levels of transient and below median levels of dedicated institutional ownership. This result suggests that firms' competition culture is a channel through which institutional ownership affects crash risk; a finding that is supported by further mediation tests.

The results of this chapter have important implications of interest to academics and the wider business community. In particular, the influence of competition culture on stock price crash risk has repercussions for investor activity. In this vein, our results can be used by investors to screen firms, thereby reducing the potential that they will experience value-destroying stock price crashes, and by regulators forming policies regarding firms' governance systems.

In this chapter, we have argued that the relationship between competition culture and stock price crashes is underpinned by the hoarding of "bad" news, which once released results in stock price crashes. If this is so, then we would also expect high competition culture firms to consistently meet/beat analysts' earnings expectations and we consider this aspect of firm behaviour in the next chapter.

References

Andreou, P. C., Antoniou, C., Horton, J., & Louca, C. (2016). Corporate Governance and Firm-Specific Stock Price Crashes. *European Financial Management, 22*, 916–956.

Andreou, P. C., Fiordelisi, F., Harris, T., & Philip, D. (2021). Institutional Ownership and Firms' Thrust to Compete. *British Journal of Management, 33*, 1346–1370.

Andreou, P. C., Louca, C., & Petrou, A. P. (2017). CEO Age and Stock-Price Crash Risk. *Review of Finance, 21*, 1287–1325.

Bushee, B. J. (1998). The Influence of Institutional Investors on Myopic R&D Investment Behavior. *Accounting Review, 73*, 305–333.

Bushee, B. J. (2001). Do Institutional Investors Prefer Near-Term Earnings Over Long-Run Value? *Contemporary Accounting Research, 18*, 207–246.

Callen, J. L., & Fang, X. (2013). Institutional Investor Stability and Crash Risk: Monitoring Versus Short-Termism? *Journal of Banking and Finance, 37*, 3047–3063.

Callen, J. L., & Fang, X. (2015). Religion and Stock Price Crash Risk. *Journal of Financial and Quantitative Analysis, 50*, 169–195.

Cameron, K., Quinn, R., DeGraff, J., & Thakor, A. (2014). *Competing Values Leadership*. Edward Elgar Publishing.

Chen, J., Hong, H., & Stein, J. C. (2001). Forecasting Crashes: Trading Volume, Past Returns, and Conditional Skewness in Stock Prices. *Journal of Financial Economics, 61*, 345–381.

Cheng, Q., & Warfield, T. D. (2005). Equity Incentives and Earnings Management. *The Accounting Review, 80*, 441–476.

Dimson, E. (1979). Risk Measurement When Shares are Subject to Infrequent Trading. *Journal of Financial Economics, 7*, 197–226.

Erhard, W., Jensen, M., Zaffron, S. (2017). *Integrity: A Positive Model that Incorporates the Normative Phenomena of Morality, Ethics and Legality*. Available at SSRN 1542759.

Fiordelisi, F., & Ricci, O. (2014). Corporate Culture and CEO Turnover. *Journal of Corporate Finance, 28*, 66–82.

Fiordelisi, F., & Ricci, O. (2021). Corrigendum to "Corporate Culture and CEO Turnover." *Journal of Corporate Finance, 70*, 102064.

Grennan, J. (2019). *A Corporate Culture Channel: How Increased Shareholder Governance Reduces Firm Value*. Available at SSRN 2345384.

Guiso, L., Sapienza, P., & Zingales, L. (2006). Does Culture Affect Economic Outcomes? *The Journal of Economic Perspectives, 20*, 23–48.

Guiso, L., Sapienza, P., & Zingales, L. (2015a). Corporate Culture, Societal Culture, and Institutions. *American Economic Review, 105*, 336–339.

Guiso, L., Sapienza, P., & Zingales, L. (2015b). The Value of Corporate Culture. *Journal of Financial Economics, 117*, 60–76.

Hartnell, C. A., Ou, A. Y., & Kinicki, A. (2011). Organizational Culture and Organizational Effectiveness: A Meta-Analytic Investigation of the Competing Values Framework's Theoretical Suppositions. *Journal of Applied Psychology, 96*, 677.

Hausman, J. A. (1978). Specification Tests in Econometrics. *Econometrica: Journal of the Econometric Society, 46*, 1251–1271.

Hutton, A. P., Marcus, A. J., & Tehranian, H. (2009). Opaque Financial Reports, R2, and Crash Risk. *Journal of Financial Economics, 94*, 67–86.

Kim, J. B., Li, Y., & Zhang, L. (2011a). CFOs versus CEOs: Equity Incentives and Crashes. *Journal of Financial Economics, 101*, 713–730.

Kim, J. B., Li, Y., & Zhang, L. (2011b). Corporate Tax Avoidance and Stock Price Crash Risk: Firm-level Analysis. *Journal of Financial Economics, 100*, 639–662.

Kim, J. B., & Zhang, L. (2016). Accounting Conservatism and Stock Price Crash Risk: Firm-level Evidence. *Contemporary Accounting Research, 33*, 412–441.

Loughran, T., McDonald, B., & Yun, H. (2009). A Wolf in Sheep's Clothing: The Use of Ethics-Related Terms in 10-K Reports. *Journal of Business Ethics, 89*, 39–49.

Luu, H., Nguyen, L., & Wilson, J. O. S. (2022). *Organizational Culture, Competition and Bank Loan Loss Provisions*. Available at SSRN 3921043.

Nguyen, D. D., Hagendorff, J., & Eshraghi, A. (2018). Does a CEO's Cultural Heritage affect Performance under Competitive Pressure? *The Review of Financial Studies, 31*, 97–141.

Quinn, R. E., & Cameron, K. (1983). Organizational Life Cycles and Shifting Criteria of Effectiveness: Some Preliminary Evidence. *Management Science, 29*, 33–51.

Quinn, R. E., & Rohrbaugh, J. (1983). A Spatial Model of Effectiveness Criteria: Towards a Competing Values Approach to Organizational Analysis. *Management Science, 29*, 363–377.

Stock, J. H., & Yogo, M. (2005). Testing for Weak Instruments in Linear IV Regression. In *Identification and Inference for Econometric Models. Essays in Honor of Thomas Rothenberg*. Cambridge University Press.

Wang, Y., Farag, H., & Ahmad, W. (2021). Corporate Culture and Innovation: A Tale from an Emerging Market. *British Journal of Management, 32*, 1121–1140.

Zingales, L. (2015). The 'Cultural Revolution' in Finance. *Journal of Financial Economics, 117*, 1–4.

CHAPTER 7

Competition Culture and Meeting/Beating Analysts' Earnings Forecasts

7.1 Introduction

In this chapter, we investigate whether and how firms' competition culture influences their propensity to meet and/or beat analysts' earnings forecasts. We have argued that the mechanism underpinning the relationship between competition culture and stock price crashes is the hoarding of "bad" news, which once released results in sudden idiosyncratic stock price crashes. If high competition culture firms systematically withhold negative news from the market in order to meet the expectations of investors, then we expect to observe such firms being more likely to consistently meet/beat analysts' earnings forecasts.

As previously done, we perform a textual analysis of 10-K filings to measure firms' competition culture based on the competing values framework (CVF) (e.g., Cameron et al., 2014; Quinn & Cameron, 1983; Quinn & Rohrbaugh, 1983) and use this measure to explore the relationship between competition culture and firms' propensity to meet/beat analysts' expectations. We adopt this measurement approach for corporate culture because past literature suggests that it provides an efficient way of capturing firms' values related to the competition culture for a large sample of firms. Hence, as described in previous chapters and consistent with past works, we operationalize our measure of competition culture by parsing 10-K filings to identify a set of lexical items relating to attributes that shape firms' corporate culture.

T. Harris, *Competition Culture and Corporate Finance*,
https://doi.org/10.1007/978-3-031-30156-8_7

Utilizing this measure of competition culture, we argue and find evidence that firms with greater levels of competition culture are motivated to consistently meet and/or beat analysts' earnings expectations. In particular, we contend that the thrust towards being more aggressive in the pursuit of profitability as identified in Chapter 5, a theoretical core trait of firms with high levels of competition culture, increases the probability that such firms are able to meet and/or beat their earnings forecast. In this vein, we make use of our measure of competition culture to investigate whether firms, which place more emphasis on this cultural orientation, are indeed more likely to meet and/or beat analysts' forecasts. Consistent with our expectations, we find a significantly greater tendency to meet and/or beat analysts' forecasts for firms with greater competition culture.

To safeguard against the possibility that our analyses are negatively affected by simultaneous causality issues, all of our baseline regression models rely on a one-year time-lag between the independent and dependent variables. Thus, our models are less susceptible to the presence of a contemporaneous feedback mechanism (i.e., reverse causality) between the key variables. Further, to mitigate other endogeneity concerns, we re-estimate all of our empirical models using an instrumental variable (IV) analysis and we reach similar, and in certain cases even stronger results.

Our study contributes to the recent literature by first demonstrating that firms with a dominant competition culture are more inclined to achieve earnings expectations. In so doing, we contribute to the burgeoning literature that focuses on the impact of firms' organizational norms and principles on policies and economic outcomes (see, for example, Andreou et al., 2021; Callen & Fang, 2015; Fiordelisi & Ricci, 2014, 2021; Grennan, 2019; Guiso et al., 2006, 2015a, 2015b; Loughran et al., 2009; Luu et al., 2022; Wang et al., 2021; Zingales, 2015; etc.).

The remainder of this chapter is presented as follows: Sect. 7.2 developed the main hypotheses; details of the data and summary statistics are presented in Sect. 7.3; Sect. 7.4 present the empirical results; and Sect. 7.5 concludes.

7.2 Hypotheses

In this chapter, we first investigate the impact of competition culture on firms' propensity to meet and/or beat analysts' earnings expectations. Theory and prior empirical works suggest that managers at firms with greater levels of competition culture are more motivated towards the aggressive pursuit of superior financial results for investors (Cameron et al., 2014; Harris & Ogbonna, 2001; Hartnell et al., 2011; Jaworski & Kohli, 1993; Kohli & Jaworski, 1990; Nguyen et al., 2018; O'Reilly et al., 2014; Reynolds, 1986; Sørensen, 2002). Hence, consistent with this past literature and our own reasoning within the CVF, we argue that the pressure towards being more forceful in the quest for financial performance should result in such firms consistently meeting and/or beating analysts' forecasts expectations. Consequently, we posit the following hypothesis in an alternative form;

H1: Competition culture is positively associated with meeting/beating analysts' earnings forecast.

7.3 Data, Variables, and Sample

7.3.1 Data

We build a unique dataset built by merging information from a number of publicly available data sources. Firstly, we obtain annual firm-level data of US publicly traded firms for the period 1994–2014 from Compustat. To measure the competition culture through textual analysis we obtain firms' 10-K reports from SEC's Edgar database. We obtain analyst forecast data from the Institutional Brokers Estimate System (I/B/E/S) database provided by the Thomson Reuters Corporation.

We perform analysis on all firms included in the Compustat database excluding financials (SIC 6000-6999) and utilities (SIC 4900-4999). Also, to limit survivorship bias, firms that are inactive and/or acquired by another firm during the period of study are retained in the sample. Further, we also delete from our sample all firm-year observations with missing data on the variables of interest. This results in a final main sample consisting of 31,223 firm year observations. Table 7.1 reports the definition of all the variables used in the analysis.

Table 7.1 Definition of variables

	Symbol		Definitions
Competition culture			
	COMP	=	the firm's competition culture estimated for each fiscal year using the text-analysis approach;
Meeting/beating earnings forecasts			
	MEET	=	an indicator that is equal to 1 if earnings meet analysts' forecasts and is 0 otherwise;
	MB_1	=	an indicator that is equal to 1 if earnings meet or just beat by a maximum of 1 cent of analysts' forecasts and is 0 otherwise;
	MB_2	=	an indicator that is equal to 1 if earnings meet or just beat by a maximum of 2 cents of analysts' forecasts and is 0 otherwise;
Other variables			
	AGE	=	number of years since the firm first appears in CRSP;
	CVAF	=	the coefficient of variation (standard deviation scaled by the mean) of the consensus forecast;
	HHI	=	the Herfindahl-Hirschman concentration ratio computed using total assets for each firm by FF 48 index and state;
	ICLAIM	=	implicit claim proxied by labour intensity, calculated as 1 minus the ratio of gross property plant and equipment to total assets at the end of the fiscal year;
	LEV	=	long-term debt by total assets;
	MTB	=	market to book value of equity at the end of the fiscal year;
	NOA	=	net operating asset (i.e., shareholders' equity minus and marketable securities, plus total debt) at the end of the prior fiscal year, scaled by sales for the prior fiscal year;

(continued)

Table 7.1 (continued)

Symbol		Definitions
NUMEST	=	number of analysts whose forecast are included in the consensus forecast;
ROA	=	return on assets defined as income before extraordinary items divided by total assets;
SGROWTH	=	sales for the fiscal year divided by sales for the prior fiscal year;
SIZE	=	natural logarithm of the market value of equity at the end of the fiscal year;
SP500	=	equal to 1 if the firm is included in the S&P 500 index, and is 0 otherwise; and
STATE	=	equal to 1 if firms in the state have above median competition culture, and is 0 otherwise

7.3.2 Measuring Competition Culture

As done in previous chapters, we measure a firm's competition culture (COMP) by counting the number of times that the lexical items that describe competition culture are found in the 10-K filings and scaling by the count of the lexical items that describe all cultural orientations according to the CVF. In particular, we measure competition culture as follows[1]:

$$\text{COMP} = \frac{\text{Number of lexical items describing the Competition Culture}}{\text{Total number of lexical items for all types of cultures}} \tag{7.1}$$

7.3.3 Measuring Meeting/Beating Earnings Forecasts

We employ analysts'-forecast-based measures to capture firms' propensity to meet and/or beat analysts' earnings forecasts. In particular, we follow Cheng and Warfield (2005) to develop measures that are based

[1] While conducting our count we exclude negation of the lexical items by ignoring occasions when the word is preceded by "no", "non", "not", "less", "few", or "limited" by three or fewer words.

on meeting and beating analysts' consensus forecasts. Specifically, we compute these measures by taking the difference between actual earnings per share and the consensus of analysts' forecasts. If earnings meet analysts' forecasts, we assign the indicator variable, MEET, a value of one, and zero otherwise. If earnings meet or beat the consensus forecast by at most 1 cent, then the indicator variable MB_1 is assigned the value one, and zero otherwise. Finally, if the difference between analysts' forecasts and earnings is at most (positive) 2 cents we assign the indicator variable, MB_2, a value of one, and zero otherwise.

7.3.4 Control Variables

We carefully select control variables for our empirical work based on the extant literature (Bushee, 1998, 2001; Callen & Fang, 2013; Chen et al., 2001; Cheng & Warfield, 2005). To begin with, we include in all specifications controls to capture firm-specific characteristics. In particular, we include the following: the number of years since the firm was first included in the CRSP database, AGE; financial leverage as indicated by total liabilities to total assets, LEV; market value of equity to book value of equity, MTB; return on total assets, ROA; the natural logarithm of market value of equity, SIZE.

Further, since we investigate the relationship between competition culture and firms' proclivity to meet analysts' expectations, we include controls that are likely to be correlated with the indicators of meeting and/or beating analysts' forecasts that have been adopted in prior studies (Cheng & Warfield, 2005). In particular, we include implicit claims, ICLAIM, since according to Bowen et al. (1995) the implicit claims between the firm and shareholders can be negatively affected (due to adverse publicity) should the firm not meet analysts' forecasts. Additionally, we include net operating assets, NOA, as Barton and Simko (2002) find that firms with higher beginning-of-period net operating assets are less likely to meet analysts' forecasts. We also include controls for the number of analysts, NUMEST, and the dispersion of their forecast, CVAF. We include these variables because it has been argued that incentives to meet analysts forecast increase according to the number of analysts following the firm and the consensus of their estimates (Payne & Robb, 2000). Finally, we include sales growth, SGROWTH, since incentives to meet analysts' expectations are usually higher for growth firms (Skinner & Sloan, 2002).

Table 7.2 Descriptive statistics for the variables used in the empirical analyses

Variable	*Obs*	*Mean*	*Std. Dev*	*25th Pctl*	*Median*	*75th Pctl*
COMP	31,223	0.49	0.06	0.45	0.49	0.54
MEET	26,331	0.14	0.34	0	0	0
MB_1	26,331	0.28	0.45	0	0	1
MB_2	26,331	0.36	0.48	0	0	1
AGE	31,223	23.64	12.98	14	20	32
CVAF	22,863	0.06	0.92	0	0.04	0.1
HHI	31,223	0.43	0.29	0.2	0.35	0.6
ICLAIM	31,100	0.51	0.38	0.31	0.6	0.8
LEV	31,223	0.47	0.29	0.28	0.46	0.62
MTB	31,223	3.38	55.44	1.32	2.13	3.58
NOA	31,022	2.66	127.98	0.3	0.51	0.81
NUMEST	26,389	7.52	6.4	3	6	10
ROA	31,223	0.01	0.26	0	0.05	0.08
SGROWTH	30,910	1.37	21.47	1	1.09	1.23
SIZE	31,223	6.29	1.78	5.02	6.2	7.43
SP500	31,223	0.21	0.41	0	0	0
STATE	30,478	0.51	0.5	0	1	1

Source This table presents the mean, median, 25th percentile, 75th percentile, and the number of observations for the variables used in the study for the period 1994–2014

7.3.5 *Descriptive Statistics and Correlations*

Table 7.2 presents descriptive statistics of the variables used in our empirical analysis.[2] In particular, the mean value of our competition culture variable, COMP, is 0.49, and the mean values of the meeting and beating analysts' forecasts variables, MEET, MB_1, and MB_2 are 0.14, 0.28, and 0.36, respectively.

We compute Pearson correlation coefficients for the variables used in our empirical analysis and report these in Table 7.3. Some of the more interesting correlations include the relation between COMP and two of our meet and/or beat analysts' forecasts variables, MB_1 and MB_2. Principally, we observe a positive and significant correlation between COMP and MB_1 (correlation = 0.0277), and between COMP and MB_2 (correlation = 0.0365).

[2] To mitigate the effects of outliers, all continuous variables are winsorized at the 1 and 99% levels.

Table 7.3 Pearson correlation matrix

	COMP	*MEET*	*MB_1*	*MB_2*	*AGE*	*CVAF*
MEET	0.0048					
MB_1	**0.0277**	**0.6496**				
MB_2	**0.0365**	**0.5282**	**0.8132**			
AGE	**−0.1571**	**0.0319**	**0.0418**	**0.0374**		
CVAF	−0.0073	−0.0052	−0.0050	−0.0047	0.0091	
DTURN	**−0.0259**	−0.0092	−0.0099	−0.0131	0.0112	0.0072
HHI	**−0.0776**	−0.0020	−0.0147	**−0.0160**	**0.1830**	0.0005
ICLAIM	**0.2689**	**0.0265**	**0.0466**	**0.0579**	**−0.1770**	**−0.0189**
LEV	**−0.0876**	**−0.0381**	**−0.0612**	**−0.0681**	**0.1012**	−0.0040
MTB	0.0019	0.0033	0.0112	0.0099	0.0032	0.0043
NOA	−0.0137	−0.0057	−0.0089	−0.0097	**−0.0157**	−0.0037
NUMEST	**−0.0331**	**0.0445**	**0.0767**	**0.0920**	**0.1382**	−0.0019
RET	**−0.1054**	0.0146	0.0154	**0.0220**	**0.2821**	**0.0206**
ROA	**−0.0239**	**0.0552**	**0.0809**	**0.0890**	**0.1305**	**0.0465**
SGROWTH	−0.0055	−0.0034	−0.0053	−0.0065	−0.0109	0.0017
SIZE	**−0.0512**	**0.0469**	**0.0774**	**0.0925**	**0.2867**	0.0049
SP500	**−0.1022**	**0.0671**	**0.0907**	**0.0967**	**0.4053**	0.0037
STATE	**0.1467**	−0.0017	0.0150	**0.0249**	**−0.1119**	0.0010
STDEV	**0.1141**	−0.0139	**−0.0171**	**−0.0246**	−0.3387	**−0.0172**

	HHI	*ICLAIM*	*LEV*	*MTB*	*NOA*	*NUMEST*	*ROA*	*SGROWTH*	*SIZE*	*SP500*
ICLAIM	**−0.0642**									
LEV	**0.0779**	**−0.1759**								
MTB	−0.0040	0.0007	0.0035							
NOA	−0.0120	−0.0043	0.0088	−0.0004						
NUMEST	**−0.0757**	**−0.0242**	**0.0424**	0.0139	−0.0042					
ROA	**0.0702**	**−0.0424**	**−0.3109**	−0.0032	**−0.0280**	**0.1278**				
SGROWTH	−0.0075	0.0022	0.0004	0.0000	−0.0004	0.0057	−0.0057			
SIZE	0.0122	−0.0106	**0.0994**	**0.0205**	0.0034	**0.7334**	**0.2017**	0.0068		
SP500	**0.0565**	**−0.0591**	**0.1399**	0.0046	0.0003	**0.5407**	**0.1060**	0.0078	**0.6406**	
STATE	**−0.1998**	**0.1375**	**−0.0973**	0.0136	0.0047	**0.0256**	**−0.0606**	−0.0056	**−0.0374**	**−0.0382**

7.4 Empirical Results

In this section, we report our multivariate results based on empirical approaches adopted to deal with the practical challenges associated with our research design. Specifically, based on the extant literature we expect and observe rather persistent levels of competition culture over time (Andreou et al., 2021; Cameron et al., 2014; Guiso et al., 2006, 2015a, 2015b; Hartnell et al., 2011; Nguyen et al., 2018). As a result, we adopt OLS estimators as the primary regression tool for our empirical analysis. In addition, we provide generalized least square random effects (GLS-RE) regression estimates as supplementary results (provided in Appendix B), as they are well-suited to this type of analysis since they allow for the inclusion of slow-moving or sluggish covariates without destabilizing the estimates of the effect of these variables.

7.4.1 Competition Culture and Meeting/Beating Earnings Forecast

First, to test H1 we explore the relationship between COMP and firms' propensity to meet and/or beat firms' analysts' consensus forecasts. We consider this relationship since it is plausible that managers at firms with a strong competition culture are more driven to achieve superior financial performance and therefore should be more likely to meet if not beat analysts' expectations. Hence, we test whether competition culture is positively related to one-year-ahead analysts' consensus forecasts. To do this, we estimate the following regression models:

$$\begin{aligned} \mathrm{AF}_{t+1} = {} & \alpha_1 + \alpha_2\mathrm{COMP}_t + \alpha_3\mathrm{AGE}_t + \alpha_4\mathrm{CVAF}_t + \alpha_5\mathrm{ICLAIM}_t \\ & + \alpha_6\mathrm{LEV}_t + \alpha_7\mathrm{MTB}_t + \alpha_8\mathrm{NOA}_t + \alpha_9\mathrm{NUMEST}_t \\ & + \alpha_{10}\mathrm{ROA}_t + \alpha_{11}\mathrm{SGROWTH}_t + \alpha_{12}\mathrm{SIZE}_t + \varepsilon_t, \end{aligned} \tag{7.2}$$

where the variable AF is measured by one of MEET, MB_1, or MB_2. To ensure that the impact of competition culture on firms' inclination to meet and/or beat analysts' consensus forecasts is not a result of other factors, we include control variables that capture firm-specific characteristics. In addition, the regression models include year and industry dummies to control for an unobserved year and industry factors; further, the standard errors are clustered at the firm level. Our coefficient of interest is α_2, and we expect this to be positive.

The results are provided in Table 7.4, where the coefficients terms 0.060, 0.059, and 0.070 on the COMP variable in columns (1), (2), and (3) capture the effect of competition culture on the firm-level measures of meeting/beating analysts' forecasts. Consistent with our expectations, we find evidence that this relationship is positive and significant at the 10% (columns 1), 5% (column 2), and 1% (column 3) levels with *t*-values of 1.73, 2.10, and 2.62, respectively.

Table 7.4 Logistic regressions of competition culture on meet/beat earnings forecasts

	$MEET_{t+1}$	MB_1_{t+1}	MB_2_{t+1}
	(1)	*(2)*	*(3)*
$COMP_t$	0.060*	0.059**	0.070***
	(1.73)	(2.10)	(2.62)
AGE_t	0.024	0.009	0.005
	(0.69)	(0.27)	(0.17)
$CVAF_t$	−0.026	−0.028	−0.011
	(0.98)	(1.29)	(0.58)
$ICLAIM_t$	0.007	0.046	0.05
	(0.15)	(1.14)	(1.33)
LEV_t	−0.095***	−0.123***	−0.135***
	(2.65)	(4.09)	(4.78)
MTB_t	0.095***	0.073***	0.065***
	(2.99)	(2.86)	(2.67)
NOA_t	−0.003	−0.028	−0.008
	(0.10)	(0.92)	(0.27)
$NUMEST_t$	0.119***	0.119***	0.130***
	(2.86)	(3.26)	(3.63)
ROA_t	0.161***	0.178***	0.168***
	(4.29)	(5.81)	(5.91)
$SGROWTH_t$	−0.078***	−0.044*	−0.063***
	(2.60)	(1.79)	(2.71)
$SIZE_t$	0.007	0.079*	0.094**
	(0.14)	(1.81)	(2.21)
R^2/Pseudo R^2	0.05	0.06	0.07
N	13,068	13,141	13,141

*$p < 0.1$; **$p < 0.05$; ***$p < 0.01$

Source This table presents logistic regression estimates used to investigate the relationship between competition culture and meeting and/or beating analysts' forecasts. All regressions include year and industry fixed effects and the standard errors are clustered at the firm level. The *t*-values are given in parentheses.

The relationship between competition culture and meeting and/or beating analysts' forecasts could suffer from simultaneity bias. This is because it is plausible that in addition to competition culture driving firms to meet investor and capital market expectations, managements' disposition to the competition culture could also be affected by firms' past ability to meet and/or beat analysts' forecasts. As a result, we estimate the following instrumental variable model to allow for potential endogeneity:

$$\begin{aligned}\mathrm{AF}_{t+1} = {} & \alpha_1 + \alpha_2\widehat{\mathrm{COMP}}_t + \alpha_3\mathrm{AGE}_t + \alpha_4\mathrm{CVAF}_t + \alpha_5\mathrm{ICLAIM}_t \\ & + \alpha_6\mathrm{LEV}_t + \alpha_7\mathrm{MTB}_t + \alpha_8\mathrm{NOA}_t + \alpha_9\mathrm{NUMEST}_t \\ & + \alpha_{10}\mathrm{ROA}_t + \alpha_{11}\mathrm{SGROWTH}_t + \alpha_{12}\mathrm{SIZE}_t + \varepsilon_t, \end{aligned} \tag{7.3a}$$

$$\begin{aligned}\mathrm{COMP}_t = {} & \gamma_1 + \delta_1\mathrm{HHI}_t + \delta_2\mathrm{STATE}_t + \delta_3\mathrm{SP500}_t + \beta_1\mathrm{AGE}_t \\ & + \beta_2\mathrm{CVAF}_t + \beta_3\mathrm{ICLAIM}_t + \beta_4\mathrm{LEV}_t \\ & + \beta_5\mathrm{MTB}_t + \beta_6\mathrm{NOA}_t + \beta_7\mathrm{NUMEST}_t \\ & + \beta_8\mathrm{ROA}_t + \beta_9\mathrm{SGROWTH}_t + \beta_{10}\mathrm{SIZE}_t + \mu_t, \end{aligned} \tag{7.3b}$$

where AF represents MEET, MB_1, and MB_2. To estimate the above empirical models, we adopt HHI, STATE, and SP500 as instruments for competition culture. These instruments are consistent with the prior work of (Bushman et al., 2016), and the results of the Stock and Yogo (2005) test for weak instruments suggest that they are suitable.

The results of the Hausman (1978) tests for endogeneity suggest that we should reject the null hypothesis that COMP is exogenous. Table 7.5 provides estimates for the first and second stage regressions; the results are consistent with H1 and those in the main analysis, where we found that competition culture heightens managers' tendency to meet and/or beat analysts' earnings expectations.

7.5 Summary

In this chapter, we explore the role that firms' competition culture plays in determining corporate policies and outcomes. More specifically, we investigate whether and how firms' competition culture is related to firms' propensity to meet and/or beat analysts' forecasts. Using a text-based measure of firms' competition culture, we find that firms with greater competition culture exhibit a higher incidence of meeting and/or beating analysts' forecasts. Overall, our results primarily suggest that the

Table 7.5 Instrumental variables regressions of competition culture on meet/beat earnings forecasts

	1st stage: $COMP_t$	$MEET_{t+1}$	MB_1_{t+1}	MB_2_{t+1}
	(1)	(2)	(3)	(4)
$COMP_t$		0.036*	0.039**	0.045***
		(1.94)	(2.32)	(2.72)
HHI_t	0.021			
	(1.12)			
$STATE_t$	0.198***			
	(6.83)			
$SP500_t$	−0.118**			
	(2.21)			
AGE_t	−0.025	0.011	0.003	0.001
	(1.28)	(0.57)	(0.15)	(0.07)
$CVAF_t$	0.006	−0.013	−0.015	−0.006
	(0.81)	(0.93)	(1.22)	(0.51)
$ICLAIM_t$	0.221***	0.011	0.032	0.039*
	(9.94)	(0.45)	(1.41)	(1.76)
LEV_t	−0.018	−0.052***	−0.073***	−0.082***
	(1.10)	(2.74)	(4.26)	(4.87)
MTB_t	0.016	0.049***	0.041***	0.037**
	(1.31)	(2.77)	(2.69)	(2.51)
NOA_t	0.084***	−0.002	−0.016	−0.003
	(5.50)	(0.11)	(0.92)	(0.20)
$NUMEST_t$	−0.013	0.064***	0.072***	0.080***
	(0.64)	(2.79)	(3.29)	(3.63)
ROA_t	0.013	0.080***	0.098***	0.096***
	(0.91)	(4.07)	(5.69)	(5.85)
$SGROWTH_t$	0.016*	−0.041**	−0.025*	−0.036***
	(1.70)	(2.48)	(1.73)	(2.63)
$SIZE_t$	−0.011	0.003	0.044*	0.055**
	(0.39)	(0.10)	(1.70)	(2.12)
R^2	0.25			
N	13,141	13,068	13,141	13,141

$^*p < 0.1$; $^{**}p < 0.05$; $^{***}p < 0.01$

Source This table presents instrumental variable estimates used to investigate the relationship between competition culture and meeting/beating analysts' forecasts. The regressions include year and industry fixed effects and the standard errors are clustered by firm. The *t*-values are given in parentheses.

firm's competition culture can lead to incentives for managers to extend themselves in an endeavour to meet and/or beat the consensus earnings forecasts.

The results of this chapter have important implications of interest to academics and the wider business community. In particular, the influence of competition culture on firms' propensity to meet and/or beat analysts' forecasts has implications for regulators and those charged with corporate governance as it suggests that the corporate culture of firms should be considered when forming policies regarding firms' governance systems.

In the next chapter, we explore the relationship between competition culture and earnings management behaviour. We consider this aspect of the firm's activity in order to gain deeper insight into a possible mechanism behind high competition culture firm's ability to consistently meet and/or beat analysts' forecasts and experience stock price crashes.

References

Andreou, P. C., Fiordelisi, F., Harris, T., & Philip, D. (2021). Institutional Ownership and Firms' Thrust to Compete. *British Journal of Management, 33*, 1346–1370.

Barton, J., & Simko, P. J. (2002). The Balance Sheet as an Earnings Management Constraint. *The Accounting Review, 77*, 1–27.

Bowen, R. M., DuCharme, L., & Shores, D. (1995). Stakeholders' Implicit Claims and Accounting Method Choice. *Journal of Accounting and Economics, 20*, 255–295.

Bushee, B. J. (1998). The Influence of Institutional Investors on Myopic R&D Investment Behavior. *Accounting Review, 73*, 305–333.

Bushee, B. J. (2001). Do Institutional Investors Prefer Near-Term Earnings Over Long-Run Value? *Contemporary Accounting Research, 18*, 207–246.

Bushman, R. M., Hendricks, B. E., & Williams, C. D. (2016). Bank Competition: Measurement, Decision-Making, and Risk-Taking. *Journal of Accounting Research, 54*, 777–826.

Callen, J. L., & Fang, X. (2013). Institutional Investor Stability and Crash Risk: Monitoring Versus Short-Termism? *Journal of Banking and Finance, 37*, 3047–3063.

Callen, J. L., & Fang, X. (2015). Religion and Stock Price Crash Risk. *Journal of Financial and Quantitative Analysis, 50*, 169–195.

Cameron, K., Quinn, R., DeGraff, J., & Thakor, A. (2014). *Competing Values Leadership*. Edward Elgar Publishing.

Chen, J., Hong, H., & Stein, J. C. (2001). Forecasting Crashes: Trading Volume, Past Returns, and Conditional Skewness in Stock Prices. *Journal of Financial Economics, 61*, 345–381.

Cheng, Q., & Warfield, T. D. (2005). Equity Incentives and Earnings Management. *The Accounting Review, 80*, 441–476.

Fiordelisi, F., & Ricci, O. (2014). Corporate Culture and CEO Turnover. *Journal of Corporate Finance, 28*, 66–82.

Fiordelisi, F., & Ricci, O. (2021). Corrigendum to "Corporate Culture and CEO Turnover". *Journal of Corporate Finance, 70*, 102064.

Grennan, J. (2019). *A Corporate Culture Channel: How Increased Shareholder Governance Reduces Firm Value*. Available at SSRN 2345384.

Guiso, L., Sapienza, P., & Zingales, L. (2006). Does Culture Affect Economic Outcomes? *The Journal of Economic Perspectives, 20*, 23–48.

Guiso, L., Sapienza, P., & Zingales, L. (2015a). Corporate Culture, Societal Culture, and Institutions. *American Economic Review, 105*, 336–339.

Guiso, L., Sapienza, P., & Zingales, L. (2015b). The Value of Corporate Culture. *Journal of Financial Economics, 117*, 60–76.

Harris, L. C., & Ogbonna, E. (2001). Strategic Human Resource Management, Market Orientation, and Organizational Performance. *Journal of Business Research, 51*, 157–166.

Hartnell, C. A., Ou, A. Y., & Kinicki, A. (2011). Organizational Culture and Organizational Effectiveness: A Meta-Analytic Investigation of the Competing Values Framework's Theoretical Suppositions. *Journal of Applied Psychology, 96*, 677.

Hausman, J. A. (1978). Specification Tests in Econometrics. *Econometrica: Journal of the Econometric Society, 46*, 1251–1271.

Jaworski, B. J., & Kohli, A. K. (1993). Competition Culture: Antecedents and Consequences. *The Journal of Marketing, 57*, 53–70.

Kohli, A. K., & Jaworski, B. J. (1990). Competition Culture: The Construct, Research Propositions, and Managerial Implications. *The Journal of Marketing, 54*, 1–18.

Loughran, T., McDonald, B., & Yun, H. (2009). A Wolf in Sheep's Clothing: The Use of Ethics-Related Terms in 10-K Reports. *Journal of Business Ethics, 89*, 39–49.

Luu, H., Nguyen, L., & Wilson, J. O. S. (2022). *Organizational Culture, Competition and Bank Loan Loss Provisions*. Available at SSRN 3921043.

Nguyen, D. D., Hagendorff, J., & Eshraghi, A. (2018). Does a CEO's Cultural Heritage Affect Performance Under Competitive Pressure? *The Review of Financial Studies, 31*, 97–141.

O'Reilly, C. A., III., Caldwell, D. F., Chatman, J. A., & Doerr, B. (2014). The Promise and Problems of Organizational Culture: CEO Personality, Culture, and Firm Performance. *Group and Organization Management, 39*, 595–625.

Payne, J. L., & Robb, S. W. G. (2000). Earnings Management: The Effect of Ex Ante Earnings Expectations. *Journal of Accounting, Auditing and Finance, 15*, 371–392.

Quinn, R. E., & Cameron, K. (1983). Organizational Life Cycles and Shifting Criteria of Effectiveness: Some Preliminary Evidence. *Management Science, 29*, 33–51.

Quinn, R. E., & Rohrbaugh, J. (1983). A Spatial Model of Effectiveness Criteria: Towards a Competing Values Approach to Organizational Analysis. *Management Science, 29*, 363–377.

Reynolds, P. D. (1986). Organizational Culture as Related to Industry, Position and Performance: A Preliminary Report. *Journal of Management Studies, 23*, 333–345.

Skinner, D. J., & Sloan, R. G. (2002). Earnings Surprises, Growth Expectations, and Stock Returns or Don't Let an Earnings Torpedo Sink Your Portfolio. *Review of Accounting Studies, 7*, 289–312.

Sørensen, J. B. (2002). The Strength of Corporate Culture and the Reliability of Firm Performance. *Administrative Science Quarterly, 47*, 70–91.

Stock, J. H., & Yogo, M. (2005). Testing for Weak Instruments in Linear IV Regression. In *Identification and Inference for Econometric Models. Essays in Honor of Thomas Rothenberg*. Cambridge University Press.

Wang, Y., Farag, H., & Ahmad, W. (2021). Corporate Culture and Innovation: A Tale from an Emerging Market. *British Journal of Management, 32*, 1121–1140.

Zingales, L. (2015). The 'Cultural Revolution' in Finance. *Journal of Financial Economics, 117*, 1–4.

CHAPTER 8

Competition Culture and Earnings Management

8.1 Introduction

In recent decades, earnings manipulation has attracted significant attention from researchers and regulators around the globe (see e.g., Bergstresser & Philippon, 2006; Bertomeu et al., 2021; Fan et al., 2019; Healy, 1985; Jiang et al., 2020; Kothari et al., 2005; Lara et al., 2020). This is in part due to the suggestion that the deliberate misrepresentation of reported financial performance results in earnings reflecting the desires of management as opposed to the financial performance of the firm and the danger this poses for the investing public. To be sure, when earnings are being managed, managers actively schedule the timing of revenues (gains) and expenses (losses) to smooth out bumps in earnings and this can lead to a misallocation of economic resources. Over time, much of the earnings management literature has suggested that the greatest cause of earnings manipulation is the self interest motivation of managers to achieve targets (Bergstresser & Philippon, 2006; Healy, 1985; Healy & Wahlen, 1999).

In this chapter, we examine whether competition culture serves to exacerbate managers proclivity to engage in earnings manipulation. Our prior results suggest that competition culture leads to elevated levels of performance and increased prevalence of stock price crashes, primarily due to the presence of transient (i.e., short-term) institutional investors (Andreou et al., 2021). In this vein, we have argued that increased

T. Harris, *Competition Culture and Corporate Finance*,
https://doi.org/10.1007/978-3-031-30156-8_8

competition culture has a darker side as it serves to induce managers propensity to withhold "bad" news. In this chapter, we further argue that managers at such firms are motivated to manipulate earnings to cater to the expectations of market participants, reduce the threats of dismissal, takeover bids, liquidation, and/or to reduce firms' contracting and financing constraints (e.g., Bergstresser & Philippon, 2006; Bhandari et al., 2017; DeBacker et al., 2015; Dechow et al., 1996; Grieser et al., 2016; Liu, 2016; Teoh et al., 1998a, 1998b). If this is so, then we would expect to observe a positive relationship between competition culture and earnings management.

However, it is possible that competition culture has a disciplinary effect on managers' behaviour and better aligns their interest with those of shareholders. Thus, if increased competition culture serves to discipline management, then an increase in the competition culture should result in a decrease in earnings manipulation. However, if competition culture does not drive managerial opportunism or management discipline, then increases in competition culture should not have a significant effect on earnings management behaviour (see, e.g., Healy & Wahlen, 1999).

We carefully design our empirical approach to test whether earnings management is indeed enhanced by competition culture. Firstly, we construct a firm-level measure of competition culture by conducting a textual analysis of firms' 10–K reports as first reported in Chapter 4. Using this measure, we investigate whether and how competition culture relates to well-documented measures of earnings management that capture firms' tendency to engage in accruals and real earnings management activity.

We provide robust evidence that competition culture is indeed positively related to accruals-based earnings management and negatively associated with real earnings management behaviour. These findings suggest that competition culture increases the risk of earnings manipulation via accruals as managers seek to cater to market expectations and reduce the threats of dismissal but serves to reduce managers real earnings management behaviour since such activity is not in the interest of managers. Additionally, based on analyses that control for firm-specific characteristics and other potential confounding factors, our results provide a clear picture wherein earnings management practices are largely prevalent among high competition culture firms. Hence, we conclude that when firms' have greater levels of competition culture, they exhibit a much higher proclivity to engage in opportunistic earnings manipulation via accruals but are less likely to engage in real earnings manipulation.

What is more, our empirical approach is carefully crafted to tackle econometric problems, which often cloud the interpretation of results. For instance, we implement two-stage least squares (2SLS) instrumental variable regressions using firms' industry-year average competition culture and state-year average competition culture as instruments to further control for potential reverse causality. In addition, to preclude the possibility that our results suffer from a self-selection bias, we utilize a Heckman two-stage self-selection model (Heckman, 1979). We find evidence consistent with our expectations.

The remainder of this paper is presented as follows: Sect. 8.2 presents the main hypotheses; details of the data and summary statistics are presented in Sect. 8.3; Sect. 8.4 presents the empirical results; and Sect. 8.5 concludes.

8.2 Hypotheses

We argue in this chapter that relative performance pressures propel managers to engage in discretionary accruals-based accounting manipulation when competition culture is high. We posit that managers are tempted to temporarily boost firm's earnings by employing more aggressive accounting practices to cater to market expectations. Specifically, we argue that the desire by managers to retain their positions entices them to engage in earnings management via accruals manipulation. Thus, we hypothesize that firm's competition culture should be positively related to accruals-based earnings manipulation:

H1: Competition culture is positively associated with accruals earnings management

Secondly, we argue that like with discretionary accruals, managers can introduce bias to real activities to influence reported earnings. For example, they can reduce the cost of goods sold through over-production and/or by cutting discretionary expenditures such as advertising expenses and research and development (R&D) expenses. Nevertheless, we posit that when competition culture is high, real earnings management can be very costly for the firm and risky for managers. In this situation, managers may have incentives to use their judgement to manipulate accounting numbers and misrepresent firm performance. However, such choices involve taking operational decisions that would adversely affect firms' competitive positions not simply reported earnings. For instance, in many industries discretionary advertising and R&D expenses can be important investments to attain and maintain firms' competitive positions. Similarly, over-production to decrease the cost of goods sold temporarily entails holding excessive levels of inventory which increases the risk of obsolescence. Hence, we hypothesize that competition culture should be negatively related to real earnings management:

H1: Competition culture is negatively associated with real earnings management

8.3 Data, Variables, and Sample

8.3.1 Data

To investigate the impact of competition culture on earnings management we build a unique sample by gathering information acquired from various data sources. Firstly, we obtain from Standard and Poor's COMPUSTAT database annual firm-level accounting and market data pertaining to US publicly listed nonfinancial firms for the period 1994–2017. Secondly, to measure competition culture, we obtain from the SEC's Edgar database firms' 10–K reports.

We perform analysis on all firms included in the Compustat database excluding financials (SIC 6000-6999) and utilities (SIC 4900-4999). In addition, to limit survivorship bias, firms that are inactive and/or acquired by another firm during the period of study are retained in the sample. Also, we attempt to mitigate the effects of outliers by winsorizing all continuous variables at the 1 and 99% levels. Finally, we delete from our sample all firm-year observations with missing data on the main variables of interest (listwise deletion). This results in a final main sample consisting of 52,818 firm-year observations. Table 8.1 reports the definitions of all variables.

8.3.2 Measuring Competition Culture

As in Chapter 4, (and prior studies e.g., Andreou et al., 2021; Fiordelisi & Ricci, 2014, 2021) we measure a firm's competition culture (COMP) by counting the number of times that the lexical items included in the bag of words describing corporate attributes for the competition culture are found in the 10-K filings and scale our measure by counts of the lexical

Table 8.1 Definition of variables

Symbol		*Definitions*
Competition culture		
COMP	=	firm's competition culture estimated for each fiscal year using the text-analysis approach;
Earnings management		
DWCA	=	Accrual earnings management measured as abnormal working capital accruals (Hribar & Collins, 2002) estimated using the modified cross–sectional Jones approach (Dechow et al., 1995) adjusted to control for the influence of firm performance and growth (Collins et al., 2017; Kothari et al., 2005);
REM	=	Real earnings management measured as the addition of APROD and ADEXP which are Roychowdhury's (2006) abnormal production cost and abnormal discretionary expenses by minus 1, respectively;
APROD	=	Roychowdhury's (2006) abnormal production cost;
ADEXP	=	Roychowdhury's (2006) abnormal discretionary expenses by minus 1;
Other variables		
AGE	=	firm's age as measured by the natural log of number of years since incorporation;
BIG4	=	indicator that is equal to 1 if the firm is audited by one of the Big 4 accounting firms (i.e., KPMG, PWC, Deloitte, E&Y) and is 0 otherwise;
MODIFIED	=	equal to 1 if firm's auditor issues a modified audit opinion (i.e. auop = 2, 4 or 5), and 0 otherwise;
LEV	=	leverage as measured by total debt divided by total assets;
MTB	=	the market-to-book value at the end of each fiscal year;
TENURE	=	number of years the firm has been audited by the same accounting firm;
CLAIM	=	implicit claim proxied by labour intensity, calculated as 1 minus the ratio of gross property plant and equipment to total assets at the end of the fiscal year;

(continued)

Table 8.1 (continued)

Symbol		*Definitions*
LIT	=	equals to 1 if firm is in one of the following industries: pharmaceutical/biotechnological (SIC 2833-2836, 8731-8734), computer (3570-3577, 7370-7374), electronics (3600-3674), or retail (5200-5961), and 0 otherwise;
SIZE	=	firm's size as measured by the natural logarithm of total assets; and
ZSCORE	=	Altman's (1968) bankruptcy score measure at the beginning of the year (= 1.2 × [(act − lct)/at] + 1.4 × [re/at] + 3.3 × [ebit/at] + 0.6 × [(csho*prcc_f)/lt] + 0.999 × [revt/at])

items that describe the other cultural orientations as follows[1]:

$$\text{COMP} = \frac{\text{Number of lexical items describing the Competition Culture}}{\text{Total number of lexical items for all types of cultures}}. \tag{8.1}$$

8.3.3 *Measuring Accrual Earnings Management*

For our empirical analyses we adopt a discretionary accruals-based measure of earnings management. This approach to measuring earnings management has been widely accepted in empirical finance (and accounting) related literature (see, e.g., Ali & Zhang, 2015; Dechow & Sloan, 1991; Dechow et al., 1995, 2012; Healy & Wahlen, 1999; Hribar & Collins, 2002; Jiang et al., 2020; Jones, 1991; Lara et al., 2020). It is well known that in financial reporting accounting accruals depend on the accounting choices of managers and are essentially the difference between cash flows and reported earnings. To measure earnings management via accruals, we follow Hribar and Collin's (2002) approach and capture working capital accruals from data contained in the statement

[1] While conducting our count we exclude negation of the lexical items by ignoring occasions when the word is preceded by "no", "non", "not", "less", "few", or "limited" by three or fewer words.

of cash flows. Following this, working capital accruals, WCA, are decomposed into abnormal (i.e., discretionary) working capital accruals, DWCA, and normal (i.e., nondiscretionary) working capital accruals, NWCA, where abnormal working capital accruals cannot be explained from normal activities, while normal working capital accruals are explained from the normal activities of the firm. As a result, managers can influence abnormal working capital accruals but are unable to influence normal working capital accruals. To estimate our measure of abnormal working capital accruals, we utilize the modified Jones model (Dechow et al., 1995), which we adjust to account for the influence of firm performance and growth (Collins et al., 2017; Kothari et al., 2005).

First, we compute WCA_t as:

$$\begin{aligned} WCA_t = (&RECCH_t + INVCH_t + APALCH_t \\ &+TXACH_t + AOLOCH_t)/TA_{t-1} \end{aligned} \quad (8.2)$$

The variable, $RECCT_t$ is firms' accounts receivable decrease (increase), $INVCH_t$ denotes changes in inventory, $APALCH_t$ represents increases (decreases) in accounts payable and accrued liabilities; $TXACH_t$ denotes changes in income taxes accrued, while $AOLOCH_t$ is net changes in firm's assets and liabilities. We estimate abnormal working capital accruals as the residuals from the following empirical model:

$$\begin{aligned} WCA_t = &a_0 + a_1\left(\frac{1}{TA_{t-1}}\right) + a_2\frac{(\Delta REV_t - \Delta AR_t)}{TA_{t-1}} + a_3\frac{(PPE_t)}{TA_{t-1}}, \\ &+ a_4(ROA_t) + a_5(SG_t) + \varepsilon_t. \end{aligned} \quad (8.3)$$

The variable, TA_{t-1}, is total assets at year $t-1$; ΔREV_t represents changes in revenue in year t; ΔAR_t is equal to changes in accounts receivables in year t, PPE_t firms' property, plant, and equipment in year t, ROA_t firms' net income scaled by total assets in year t, and SG_t the current growth in sales.

8.3.4 *Measuring Real Earnings Management*

We construct two independent measures of real earnings management: namely, discretionary expenditures, and over- or under-production. As in Roychowdhury (2006), we estimate abnormal production costs, APROD, and abnormal discretionary expenditures, ADEXP, as the residuals from the following models:

$$\text{PROD}_t = \text{b}_0 + \text{b}_1\left(\frac{1}{\text{TA}_{t-1}}\right) + \text{b}_2\frac{(\text{REV}_t)}{\text{TA}_{t-1}} + \text{b}_3\frac{(\Delta\text{REV}_t)}{\text{TA}_{t-1}} + \text{b}_4\frac{(\Delta\text{REV}_{t-1})}{\text{TA}_{t-1}} + \varepsilon_t, \tag{8.4}$$

and,

$$\text{DEXP}_t = \text{c}_0 + \text{c}_1\left(\frac{1}{\text{TA}_{t-1}}\right) + \text{c}_2\frac{(\text{REV}_t - 1)}{\text{TA}_{t-1}} + \varepsilon_t. \tag{8.5}$$

The variable, PROD_t, is expressed as the sum of costs of goods sold and the change in inventory scaled by total assets at year $t - 1$, while DEXP_t, is the sum of SG&A, R&D, and advertising scaled by total assets at year $t - 1$.

Finally, we also utilize the variable REM to capture overall real earnings management activity and define this measure as the sum of APROD and ADEXP.

8.3.5 Control Variables

We select control variables for our empirical work based on the extant literature to capture firm-specific characteristics. In particular, we include the following measures: AGE, the number of years since the firm first appears in COMPUSTAT; BIG4, an indicator that is equal to one if the firm is audited by one of the big4 accounting firms (i.e., Deloitte, PwC, Ernst & Young, and KPMG), and zero otherwise; MODIFIED, an indicator that is equal to one if the firm's auditor issues a modified audit opinion, and zero otherwise; financial leverage as indicated by total liabilities to total assets, LEV; the market value of equity to book value of equity MTB; the number of years the firm was audited by the same auditor TENURE; implicit claim, CLAIM, proxied by labour intensity, calculated as one minus the ratio of gross property plant and equipment to total assets at the end of the fiscal year (Bowen et al., 1995); a dummy variable that captures whether the firm is in a high litigation industry, LIT; the natural logarithm of the market value of equity, SIZE; and finally Altman's (1968) bankruptcy measure ZSCORE.

8.3.6 *Descriptive Statistics and Correlations*

Table 8.2 highlights descriptive statistics for all variables used in our empirical analyses, where the mean of our earnings management variables DWCA, REM, APROD, and ADEXP, are, 0.050, −0.028, −0.027, and −0.007, respectively. The mean value of our measure of competition culture, COMP is 0.461. These summary statistics are compared with those reported in previous studies that have used these data (Ali & Zhang, 2015; Barton & Simko, 2002; Bhandari et al., 2017; Bowen et al., 1995; Cheng & Warfield, 2005; Cheng et al., 2016; DeBacker et al., 2015; Dechow & Dichev, 2002; Fan et al., 2019; Grieser et al., 2016; Jiang et al., 2020; Lara et al., 2020; Liu, 2016; Roychowdhury, 2006; Skinner & Sloan, 2002).

Table 8.3 presents Pearson correlation coefficients for the main variables used in the empirical analysis. Some of the more interesting correlation results include the relationship between DWCA and COMP, where we find, consistent with expectations, a positive and significant correlation (correlation = 0.0518). Also, we find a negative and statistically significant correlation between REM and COMP (correlation =

Table 8.2 Descriptive statistics for the variables used in the empirical analyses

Variable	*Obs*	*Mean*	*Std. Dev*	*25th Pctl*	*Median*	*75th Pctl*
COMP	52,818	0.161	0.08	0.102	0.151	0.209
DWCA	52,818	0.05	0.057	0.014	0.032	0.065
REM	52,818	−0.028	0.459	−0.246	0.013	0.233
APROD	52,818	−0.027	0.212	−0.136	−0.013	0.091
ADEXP	52,818	0.007	0.282	−0.098	0.033	0.159
AGE	52,818	24.366	15.17	13	21	32
BIG4	52,818	0.723	0.448	0	1	1
MODIFIED	52,818	0.281	0.45	0	0	1
LEV	52,818	0.198	0.198	0.012	0.158	0.315
MTB	52,818	2.999	4.701	1.186	2.032	3.555
TENURE	52,818	15.077	10.113	7	13	20
CLAIM	52,818	0.513	0.374	0.32	0.61	0.799
LIT	52,818	0.382	0.486	0	0	1
SIZE	52,818	5.682	2.144	4.077	5.652	7.156
ZSCORE	52,818	4.646	6.59	2.044	3.47	5.73

Source This table presents the mean, median, 25th percentile, 75th percentile, and the number of observations for the variables used in the study for the period 1994–2017

−0.1578), a negative and statistically significant correlation between APROD and COMP (correlation = −0.1359), and a negative and statistically significant correlation between ADEXP and COMP (correlation = −0.1557). These results are consistent with our expectations that competition culture is positively related to accrual-based earnings management and negatively related to real earnings management activity.

8.4 Empirical Results

We follow past literature (please see Andreou et al., 2020, 2021) and our prior empirical approach (as in Chapters 4–7), in adopting OLS estimators as the primary regression tool for our empirical analysis as this estimator is able to handle slow moving variables such as competition culture.

8.4.1 Competition Culture and Earnings Management

We consider whether and how competition culture impacts upon earnings management as indicated by discretionary working capital accruals and real earnings management. We argue that culture in H1 that competition culture creates performance pressures which increase managers propensity to opportunistically engage in discretionary accruals-based accounting manipulation when competition culture increases. To empirically test this relationship, we estimate the following regression model:

$$\begin{aligned} \mathrm{DWCA}_t = {} & \alpha_1 + \alpha_2\mathrm{COMP}_t + \alpha_3\mathrm{AGE}_t + \alpha_4\mathrm{BIG4}_t + \alpha_5\mathrm{MODIFIED}_t \\ & + \alpha_6\mathrm{LEV}_t + \alpha_7\mathrm{MTB}_t + \alpha_8\mathrm{TENURE}_t + \alpha_9\mathrm{CLAIM}_t \\ & + \alpha_{10}\mathrm{LIT}_t + \alpha_{11}\mathrm{SIZE}_t + \alpha_{12}\mathrm{ZSCORE}_t + \varepsilon_t. \end{aligned} \tag{8.6}$$

We include control variables that capture firm-specific characteristics. These control variables are adopted to help ensure that the impact of our measure of competition culture, COMP, on earnings management, DWCA, is not driven by other factors. In addition, we include year (and industry) dummies to control for unobserved time–invariant year (and industry) factors. The industry dummies are based on Fama and French's (1997) 48 industry classifications. The standard errors are clustered at the firm level to control for potential bias that can occur when the residuals are correlated by the firm.

The coefficient of interest is α_2, and in the case of the relationship between competition culture and accruals earnings management, this

Table 8.3 Pearson correlation matrix

	COMP	*DWCA*	*REM*	*APROD*	*ADEXP*	*AGE*	*BIG4*
DWCA	0.0518						
REM	−0.1578	−0.0605					
APROD	−0.1359	−0.0453	0.8999				
ADEXP	−0.1557	−0.1358	0.7583	0.5242			
AGE	−0.2030	−0.1690	0.0777	0.0653	0.1298		
BIG4	0.0018	−0.1212	−0.0629	−0.0215	−0.0813	0.1019	
MODIFIED	−0.0614	−0.0355	0.0243	0.0244	−0.0016	0.0711	0.1002
LEV	−0.2364	−0.0703	0.1385	0.1081	0.1027	0.0439	0.0361
MTB	0.0780	0.0679	−0.1762	−0.1561	−0.1625	−0.0296	0.0193
TENURE	−0.1209	−0.1556	0.0203	0.0223	0.0719	0.6506	0.2291
CLAIM	0.2171	0.1190	−0.0504	−0.0542	−0.0576	−0.1782	−0.002
LIT	0.2557	0.0830	−0.1537	−0.1575	−0.1222	−0.1834	0.0346
SIZE	−0.0176	−0.2573	−0.0892	−0.0469	−0.0394	0.3574	0.3922
ZSCORE	0.1288	−0.0062	−0.1451	−0.1330	−0.0143	−0.0104	0.0243

(continued)

Table 8.3 (continued)

	MODIFIED	*LEV*	*MTB*	*TENURE*	*CLAIM*	*LIT*	*SIZE*
LEV	**0.0730**						
MTB	**−0.0247**	**−0.0595**					
TENURE	**0.0595**	**0.0172**	0.002				
CLAIM	**−0.0455**	**−0.2238**	**0.0803**	**−0.1245**			
LIT	**−0.0129**	**−0.1740**	**0.0841**	**−0.1287**	**0.1689**		
SIZE	**0.0960**	**0.0283**	**0.2002**	**0.3797**	**0.0064**	**0.0134**	
ZSCORE	**−0.1150**	**−0.3745**	**0.2590**	**0.0312**	**0.1758**	**0.0544**	**0.1955**

Source This table presents Pearson correlation coefficients for the variables used in the empirical analyses. The bold figures indicate significance at the 10% level and above coefficient is expected to be positive and significant in our empirical estimates. Results alternative to our expectations are possible; however, if α_2 is negative, or is positive but insignificant, the relationship between competition culture and earnings management is not as we predict. We find that the coefficient term 0.013 on the COMP variable, which is presented in Table 8.4 column (1), is significant at the 5% level with a t–value of 2.16.

Next, we consider whether and how competition culture relates to real earnings management activity. We argue in proposing H2 that when firms' competition culture is high, real earnings management can become increasingly costly for the firm. Hence, we posit that relative performance pressures brought about by higher levels of competition culture decrease managers' inclination to attempt to manipulate earnings by reducing the cost of goods sold through over-production and/or by cutting discretionary expenditures such as advertising expenses and research and development (R&D) expenses. Consequently, we argue that competition culture should be negatively related to real earnings management. To empirically test this relationship, we estimate the following regression models:

$$\begin{aligned} \text{REM}_t = {} & \alpha_1 + \alpha_2\text{COMP}_t + \alpha_3\text{AGE}_t + \alpha_4\text{BIG4}_t + \alpha_5\text{MODIFIED}_t \\ & + \alpha_6\text{LEV}_t + \alpha_7\text{MTB}_t + \alpha_8\text{TENURE}_t + \alpha_9\text{CLAIM}_t \\ & + \alpha_{10}\text{LIT}_t + \alpha_{11}\text{SIZE}_t + \alpha_{12}\text{ZSCORE}_t + \varepsilon_t, \end{aligned} \tag{8.7}$$

$$\begin{aligned} \text{APROD}_t = {} & \alpha_1 + \alpha_2\text{COMP}_t + \alpha_3\text{AGE}_t + \alpha_4\text{BIG4}_t + \alpha_5\text{MODIFIED}_t \\ & + \alpha_6\text{LEV}_t + \alpha_7\text{MTB}_t + \alpha_8\text{TENURE}_t + \alpha_9\text{CLAIM}_t \\ & + \alpha_{10}\text{LIT}_t + \alpha_{11}\text{SIZE}_t + \alpha_{12}\text{ZSCORE}_t + \varepsilon_t, \end{aligned} \tag{8.8}$$

and,

$$\begin{aligned} \text{ADEXP}_t = {} & \alpha_1 + \alpha_2\text{COMP}_t + \alpha_3\text{AGE}_t + \alpha_4\text{BIG4}_t + \alpha_5\text{MODIFIED}_t \\ & + \alpha_6\text{LEV}_t + \alpha_7\text{MTB}_t + \alpha_8\text{TENURE}_t + \alpha_9\text{CLAIM}_t \\ & + \alpha_{10}\text{LIT}_t + \alpha_{11}\text{SIZE}_t + \alpha_{12}\text{ZSCORE}_t + \varepsilon_t. \end{aligned} \tag{8.9}$$

In Eq.'s (8.7), (8.8), and (8.9) the α_2's are the coefficients of interest which capture the relationship between competition culture and our measures of real earnings management, REM, APROD, and ADEXP.

Table 8.4 OLS regressions of competition culture on earnings management

	$DWCA_t$	REM_t	$APROD_t$	$ADEXP_t$
	(1)	(2)	(3)	(4)
$COMP_t$	0.013**	−0.097***	−0.077***	−0.109***
	(2.16)	(10.86)	(8.64)	(11.98)
AGE_t	−0.050***	0.079***	0.047***	0.111***
	(6.73)	(5.30)	(3.06)	(8.25)
$BIG4_t$	−0.088***	−0.092***	−0.029	−0.181***
	(4.87)	(4.06)	(1.25)	(7.98)
$MODIFIED_t$	0.016	0.030**	0.017	-0.011
	(1.03)	(2.25)	(1.20)	(0.78)
LEV_t	0.007	0.094***	0.058***	0.107***
	(0.59)	(8.84)	(5.44)	(9.66)
MTB_t	0.016*	−0.120***	−0.098***	−0.158***
	(1.88)	(12.66)	(10.98)	(14.37)
$TENURE_t$	−0.018***	−0.018	−0.023	0.013
	(2.70)	(1.16)	(1.41)	(0.91)
$CLAIM_t$	0.016	0.050***	0.050***	−0.011
	(1.63)	(3.39)	(3.42)	(0.71)

	$DWCA_t$	REM_t	$APROD_t$	$ADEXP_t$
	(1)	(2)	(3)	(4)
LIT_t	0.051*	−0.348***	−0.331***	−0.313***
	(1.74)	(6.78)	(6.12)	(6.58)
$SIZE_t$	−0.136***	−0.081***	−0.033**	−0.053***
	(20.16)	(5.44)	(2.16)	(3.65)
$ZSCORE_t$	−0.025**	−0.044***	−0.060***	0.098***
	(2.05)	(4.15)	(5.63)	(8.05)
R^2	0.08	0.13	0.12	0.12
N	52,818	52,818	52,818	52,818

*$p < 0.1$; **$p < 0.05$; ***$p < 0.01$

Source This table presents estimates used to investigate the relationship between competition culture and earnings management as indicated by the discretionary working capital accruals (columns 1), real earnings management (columns 2), abnormal production costs (columns 3), and abnormal discretionary expenses (columns 4). All regressions include year and industry fixed effects and the standard errors are clustered at the firm level. The *t*-values are given in parentheses

These coefficients are expected to be negative and significant in our empirical estimates.

Table 8.4 columns (2), (3), and (4) present the results of our empirical estimation for the impact of competition culture on real earnings management. The results for our estimates of Eq. (8.7) for the effect of COMP on REM are presented in column (2). Here we find the coefficient term on the COMP variable −0.097 to be significant at the 1% level with a *t*–value of 10.86. Similarly, the empirical estimates of the model presented in Eq. (8.8) for the impact of COMP on APROD are shown in column (3). We find the coefficient term on the COMP variable −0.077 to be significant at the 1% level with a *t*–value of 8.64. In column (8), we report the empirical estimates of Eq. (8.9); the coefficient term of interests on the COMP variable is −0.109 and this is found to be significant at the 1% level with a *t*–value of 11.98.

8.4.2 *Instrumental Variable Regressions*

In addition to the relationship that we describe, it is possible that the level of competition culture is influenced by past instances of accruals and/or real earnings management behaviour; therefore, our measure of competition culture could be jointly determined with our measures of real and accruals-based earnings management and consequently the results of our analysis subject to potential bias. We attempt to correct for this bias by estimating the following two-stage models to allow for potential endogeneity:

$$\begin{aligned}\mathrm{COMP}_t = {} & \delta_1 + \gamma_1 \mathrm{COMP\_INDUST}_t + \gamma_2 \mathrm{COMP\_STATE} + \beta_1 \mathrm{AGE}_t \\ & + \beta_2 \mathrm{BIG4}_t + \beta_3 \mathrm{MODIFIED}_t + \beta_4 \mathrm{LEV}_t \\ & + \beta_5 \mathrm{MTB}_t + \beta_6 \mathrm{TENURE}_t + \beta_7 \mathrm{CLAIM}_t \\ & + \beta_8 \mathrm{LIT}_t + \beta_9 \mathrm{SIZE}_t + \beta_{10} \mathrm{ZSCORE}_t + \varepsilon_t, \qquad (8.10\mathrm{a})\end{aligned}$$

$$\begin{aligned}\mathrm{DWCA}_t = {} & \alpha_1 + \alpha_2 \widehat{\mathrm{COMP}}_t + \alpha_3 \mathrm{AGE}_t + \alpha_4 \mathrm{BIG4}_t + \alpha_5 \mathrm{MODIFIED}_t \\ & + \alpha_6 \mathrm{LEV}_t + \alpha_7 \mathrm{MTB}_t + \alpha_8 \mathrm{TENURE}_t + \alpha_9 \mathrm{CLAIM}_t \\ & + \alpha_{10} \mathrm{LIT}_t + \alpha_{11} \mathrm{SIZE}_t + \alpha_{12} \mathrm{ZSCORE}_t + \varepsilon_t, \qquad (8.10\mathrm{b})\end{aligned}$$

and,

$$\begin{aligned}\text{COMP}_t = \delta_1 + \gamma_1\text{COMP\_INDUST}_t + \gamma_2\text{COMP\_STATE} + \beta_1\text{AGE}_t \\ + \beta_2\text{BIG4}_t + \beta_3\text{MODIFIED}_t + \beta_4\text{LEV}_t \\ + \beta_5\text{MTB}_t + \beta_6\text{TENURE}_t + \beta_7\text{CLAIM}_t \\ + \beta_8\text{LIT}_t + \beta_9\text{SIZE}_t + \beta_{10}\text{ZSCORE}_t + \varepsilon_t,\end{aligned} \tag{8.11a}$$

$$\begin{aligned}\text{REM}_t = \alpha_1 + \alpha_2\hat{\text{COMP}}_t + \alpha_3\text{AGE}_t + \alpha_4\text{BIG4}_t + \alpha_5\text{MODIFIED}_t \\ + \alpha_6\text{LEV}_t + \alpha_7\text{MTB}_t + \alpha_8\text{TENURE}_t + \alpha_9\text{CLAIM}_t \\ + \alpha_{10}\text{LIT}_t + \alpha_{11}\text{SIZE}_t + \alpha_{12}\text{ZSCORE}_t + \varepsilon_t,\end{aligned} \tag{8.11b}$$

$$\begin{aligned}\text{APROD} = \alpha_1 + \alpha_2\hat{\text{COMP}}_t + \alpha_3\text{AGE}_t + \alpha_4\text{BIG4}_t + \alpha_5\text{MODIFIED}_t \\ + \alpha_6\text{LEV}_t + \alpha_7\text{MTB}_t + \alpha_8\text{TENURE}_t + \alpha_9\text{CLAIM}_t \\ + \alpha_{10}\text{LIT}_t + \alpha_{11}\text{SIZE}_t + \alpha_{12}\text{ZSCORE}_t + \varepsilon_t,\end{aligned} \tag{8.11c}$$

$$\begin{aligned}\text{ADEXP}_t = \alpha_1 + \alpha_2\hat{\text{COMP}}_t + \alpha_3\text{AGE}_t + \alpha_4\text{BIG4}_t + \alpha_5\text{MODIFIED}_t \\ + \alpha_6\text{LEV}_t + \alpha_7\text{MTB}_t + \alpha_8\text{TENURE}_t + \alpha_9\text{CLAIM}_t \\ + \alpha_{10}\text{LIT}_t + \alpha_{11}\text{SIZE}_t + \alpha_{12}\text{ZSCORE}_t + \varepsilon_t.\end{aligned} \tag{8.11d}$$

We adopt COMP_INDUST and COMP_STATE as instruments for competition culture. In particular, COMP_STATE is defined as the yearly average level of competition culture in the firm's state. Likewise, we define the variable COMP_INDUST as the yearly average level of competition culture in the firm's industry. The results of our 2SLS IV estimates are presented in Table 8.5. The sign and significance of the fitted value of COMP for all models are consistent with those presented in our main analysis.

To reassure that our 2SLS IV results are valid we conduct several diagnostic tests. We conduct Hausman's (1978) tests to assess the endogeneity of the first stage of our 2SLS IV estimates; our results suggest that we should reject the null hypotheses that our measures of earnings management and competition culture are exogenous. In addition, the Stock and Yogo's (2005) test for weak instruments suggests that our instruments are appropriate. Furthermore, the Hansen J-statistics indicate that the instruments used in our analyses are uncorrelated with the disturbance process of the models and this satisfies the exclusion principle.

Table 8.5 2SLS instrumental variable regressions of competition culture on earnings management

	$COMP_t$	$DWCA_t$	REM_t	$APROD_t$	$ADEXP_t$
	(1)	(2)	(3)	(4)	(5)
$COMP\_INDUST_t$	0.319***				
	(17.60)				
$COMP\_STATE_t$	0.180***				
	(16.44)				
$COMP_t$		0.252***	−0.431***	−0.341***	−0.497***
		(5.90)	(7.73)	(6.06)	(9.00)
AGE_t	−0.131***	−0.014	0.030*	0.009	0.055***
	(10.84)	(1.43)	(1.76)	(0.50)	(3.41)
$BIG4_t$	0.040**	−0.101***	−0.072***	−0.013	−0.158***
	(2.21)	(5.43)	(3.14)	(0.56)	(6.84)
$MODIFIED_t$	−0.050***	0.030*	0.011	0.001	−0.033**
	(4.15)	(1.86)	(0.81)	(0.10)	(2.21)
LEV_t	−0.110***	0.037***	0.051***	0.024*	0.058***
	(13.32)	(2.77)	(4.15)	(1.93)	(4.56)
MTB_t	0.015***	0.015*	−0.112***	−0.092***	−0.149***
	(2.80)	(1.79)	(11.75)	(10.20)	(13.51)
$TENURE_t$	0.024**	−0.022***	−0.012	−0.018	0.02
	(2.06)	(3.45)	(0.77)	(1.12)	(1.41)
$CLAIM_t$	0.032***	0.005	0.066***	0.063***	0.008
	(3.23)	(0.47)	(4.34)	(4.17)	(0.51)

	$COMP_t$	$DWCA_t$	REM_t	$APROD_t$	$ADEXP_t$
	(1)	(2)	(3)	(4)	(5)
LIT_t	0.288***	−0.02	−0.240***	−0.246***	−0.187***
	(7.80)	(0.55)	(4.40)	(4.30)	(3.62)
$SIZE_t$	−0.028**	−0.133***	−0.088***	−0.039**	−0.062***
	(2.48)	(19.63)	(5.91)	(2.52)	(4.25)
$ZSCORE_t$	0.049***	−0.034***	−0.028***	−0.048***	0.116***
	(5.49)	(2.59)	(2.58)	(4.33)	(9.21)
R^2	0.23	0.08	0.12	0.12	0.12
N	52,445	52,445	52,445	52,445	52,445

*$p < 0.1$; **$p < 0.05$; ***$p < 0.01$

Source This table presents estimates from 2SLS IV regressions used to investigate the relationship between competition culture and earnings management. Columns (1) present first stage results, while columns (2), (3) (4), and (5) highlight the second stage estimates. All regressions include year and industry fixed effects and the standard errors are clustered at the firm level. The t-values are given in parentheses

8.4.3 Heckman Two-Stage Self-Selection Model

We seek to establish further evidence of a causal relationship between our firm-level measure of competition culture and our measures of accruals and real earnings management practices. To do this we recognize that one problem with our main estimations is that they assume that the error term ε is uncorrelated with the explanatory variable of interest, COMP. A potential concern here is that a selection bias arises when an independent variable included in the model is potentially a choice variable and therefore could be correlated with an unobservable variable that is captured by the error term. As a result, the correlation between ε and COMP is potentially non-zero, thereby leading to inconsistent estimates.

To control for selection bias, Heckman (1979) proposes a two-stage estimation procedure, commonly known as a treatment effect model when the dependent variable is observed for all observations in the data (Heckman, 1979). In the first stage, a regression for observing an above median score on competition culture, COMP_HIGH is estimated using a Probit model where we use the same firm-specific control variables used in the prior analyses. The estimated parameters from this first stage are used to calculate the inverse Mill's ratio, LAMBDA, which is then included as an additional explanatory variable in the second stage. To be clear, we estimate the following empirical models:

$$\begin{aligned}\text{COMP\_HIGH}_t = {} & \alpha_1 + \alpha_2\text{AGE}_t + \alpha_3\text{BIG4}_t + \alpha_4\text{MODIFIES}_t + \alpha_5\text{LEV}_t \\ & + \alpha_6\text{MTB}_t + \alpha_7\text{TENURE}_t + \alpha_8\text{CLAIM}_t \\ & + \alpha_9\text{LIT}_t + \alpha_{10}\text{SIZE}_t + \alpha_{11}\text{LAMBDA}_t + \varepsilon_t, \quad (8.12\text{a})\end{aligned}$$

$$\begin{aligned}\text{DWCA}_t = {} & \alpha_1 + \alpha_2\text{COMP}_t + \alpha_3\text{AGE}_t + \alpha_4\text{BIG4}_t + \alpha_5\text{MODIFIED}_t \\ & + \alpha_6\text{LEV}_t + \alpha_7\text{MTB}_t + \alpha_8\text{TENURE}_t \\ & + \alpha_9\text{CLAIM}_t + \alpha_{10}\text{LIT}_t + \alpha_{11}\text{SIZE}_t \\ & + \alpha_{12}\text{ZSCORE}_t + \alpha_{13}LAMBDA + \varepsilon_t. \qquad (8.12\text{b})\end{aligned}$$

$$\begin{aligned}\text{REM}_t = {} & \alpha_1 + \alpha_2\text{COMP}_t + \alpha_3\text{AGE}_t + \alpha_4\text{BIG4}_t + \alpha_5\text{MODIFIED}_t \\ & + \alpha_6\text{LEV}_t + \alpha_7\text{MTB}_t + \alpha_8\text{TENURE}_t \\ & + \alpha_9\text{CLAIM}_t + \alpha_{10}\text{LIT}_t + \alpha_{11}\text{SIZE}_t \\ & + \alpha_{12}\text{ZSCORE}_t + \alpha_{13}\text{LAMBDA} + \varepsilon_t. \qquad (8.12\text{c})\end{aligned}$$

$$\begin{aligned}\text{APROD}_t = {} & \alpha_1 + \alpha_2\text{COMP}_t + \alpha_3\text{AGE}_t + \alpha_4\text{BIG4}_t + \alpha_5\text{MODIFIED}_t \\ & + \alpha_6\text{LEV}_t + \alpha_7\text{MTB}_t + \alpha_8\text{TENURE}_t \\ & + \alpha_9\text{CLAIM}_t + \alpha_{10}\text{LIT}_t + \alpha_{11}\text{SIZE}_t \\ & + \alpha_{12}\text{ZSCORE}_t + \alpha_{13}\text{LAMBDA} + \varepsilon_t. \end{aligned} \tag{8.12d}$$

and,

$$\begin{aligned}\text{ADEXP}_t = {} & \alpha_1 + \alpha_2\text{COMP}_t + \alpha_3\text{AGE}_t + \alpha_4\text{BIG4}_t + \alpha_5\text{MODIFIED}_t \\ & + \alpha_6\text{LEV}_t + \alpha_7\text{MTB}_t + \alpha_8\text{TENURE}_t \\ & + \alpha_9\text{CLAIM}_t + \alpha_{10}\text{LIT}_t + \alpha_{11}\text{SIZE}_t \\ & + \alpha_{12}\text{ZSCORE}_t + \alpha_{13}\text{LAMBDA} + \varepsilon_t. \end{aligned} \tag{8.12e}$$

The estimates from our empirical analysis are presented in Table 8.6. The coefficients of interest are the α_2's in Eq.'s (8.12b), (8.12c), (8.12d), and (8.12e). These coefficients capture the effect of competition culture on accruals (column 1) and real (columns 2–4) earnings management. Consistent with our expectations and our other results, we predict and find the coefficient of interest is positive and significant for the relationship between competition culture and accruals earnings management; meanwhile, the coefficients of interests are negative and significant as it relates to the effect of competition culture on our measures of real earnings management.

8.5 Summary

We examine the effect of competition culture on earnings management activity via accounting accruals, over production, and discretionary expenditure manipulation in this chapter. We argue that higher levels of competition culture should increase managers' incentives to manipulate accounting numbers via accrual. Furthermore, we argue that when firms' competition culture is high, real earnings management can be risky for managers as it will undermine the firm's future ability to compete and achieve superior performance. This should result in lower levels of real earnings management.

We find robust evidence that when competition culture is high managers engage in greater levels of accruals-based earnings management and lower levels of real earnings management behaviour. These findings suggest that competition culture can in fact lead to greater levels of

Table 8.6 Heckman self selection two stage regressions of competition culture on earnings management

	$DWCA_t$	REM_t	$APROD_t$	$ADEXP_t$
	(1)	*(2)*	*(3)*	*(4)*
$COMP_t$	0.010*	−0.090***	−0.072***	−0.097***
	(1.73)	(10.00)	(8.02)	(10.64)
AGE_t	0.144***	0.438***	0.310***	0.742***
	(3.42)	(7.97)	(5.57)	(13.40)
$BIG4_t$	−0.119***	−0.166***	−0.083***	−0.310***
	(6.03)	(6.66)	(3.27)	(12.34)
$MODIFIED_t$	0.086***	0.153***	0.106***	0.204***
	(4.03)	(6.92)	(4.72)	(9.08)
LEV_t	0.151***	0.384***	0.269***	0.615***
	(3.77)	(8.99)	(6.31)	(14.08)
MTB_t	0.01	−0.168***	−0.133***	−0.241***
	(1.34)	(13.82)	(11.45)	(17.80)
$TENURE_t$	−0.069***	−0.117***	−0.095***	−0.160***
	(5.70)	(5.44)	(4.35)	(7.67)
$CLAIM_t$	−0.044***	−0.068***	−0.036	−0.217***
	(2.72)	(3.00)	(1.60)	(9.19)
LIT_t	−0.249***	−0.913***	−0.743***	−1.305***
	(3.18)	(9.95)	(7.92)	(14.32)

	$DWCA_t$	REM_t	$APROD_t$	$ADEXP_t$
	(1)	*(2)*	*(3)*	*(4)*
$SIZE_t$	−0.107***	−0.011	0.018	0.070***
	(11.84)	(0.62)	(1.01)	(3.96)
$ZSCORE_t$	−0.044***	−0.079***	−0.085***	0.037***
	(3.06)	(6.90)	(7.51)	(2.86)
LAMBDA	−1.518***	−2.844***	−2.076***	−4.990***
	(4.58)	(7.04)	(5.07)	(12.26)
R^2	0.09	0.13	0.12	0.13
N	52,818	52,818	52,818	52,818

*$p < 0.1$; **$p < 0.05$; ***$p < 0.01$

Source This table presents estimates from Heckman's self-selection model used to investigate the relationship between managers' perception of competition culture and earnings management. The inverse Mills ratio (LAMBDA) is from the first stage Heckman Model. Columns (1)–(4) presents second stage results. All regressions include year and industry fixed effects and the standard errors are clustered at the firm-level. The *t*-values are given in parentheses accounting manipulation via accruals, due to the opportunistic behaviours of managers, but are also consistent with the notion that increased levels of competition culture diminish managements' propensity to take actions that undermine the future competitive position of the firm.

Our results have important implications that would be of interest to regulators, accounting standard-setters, academics, and the wider business community. This is because the effect of competition culture on earnings management behaviour has important implications for the manner in which firms are governed and managed. Particularly, our findings should be of interest to boards of directors, who have a responsibility to design corporate governance systems that help to achieve greater congruence between the objectives of managers and shareholders. In this vein, board members can use our results to inform the firm's corporate culture. Further, those charged with governance can use our findings to develop policies aimed at reducing the likelihood of earnings manipulation.

Thus far in this book, we have considered the role of competition culture in nonfinancial firms and have found that it is influenced by institutional investors and has implication for firms' stock return performance, idiosyncratic crash risk, and earnings manipulation. In the next chapter, we will explore the role of competition culture in financial firms (i.e., banks). Particularly we will consider the implications of competition culture for bank lending activity.

References

Ali, A., & Zhang, W. (2015). CEO Tenure and Earnings Management. *Journal of Accounting and Economics, 59*, 60–79.

Altman, E. I. (1968). Financial Ratios, Discriminant Analysis and the Prediction of Corporate Bankruptcy. *The Journal of Finance, 23*, 589–609.

Andreou, P. C., Fiordelisi, F., Harris, T., & Philip, D. (2021). Institutional Ownership and Firms' Thrust to Compete. *British Journal of Management, 33*, 1346–1370.

Andreou, P. C., Harris, T., & Philip, D. (2020). Measuring Firms' Market Orientation using Textual Analysis of 10-K Filings. *British Journal of Management, 31*, 872–895.

Barton, J., & Simko, P. J. (2002). The Balance Sheet as an Earnings Management Constraint. *The Accounting Review, 77*, 1–27.

Bergstresser, D., & Philippon, T. (2006). CEO Incentives and Earnings Management. *Journal of Financial Economics, 80*, 511–529.

Bertomeu, J., Cheynel, E., Li, E. X., & Liang, Y. (2021). How Pervasive is Earnings Management? Evidence from a Structural Model. *Management Science, 67*, 5145–5162.

Bhandari, A., Mammadov, B., Thevenot, M., & Vakilzadeh, S. H. (2017). *The Invisible Hand: Corporate Culture and Its Implications for Earnings Management* (Working Paper). Warrington College of Business, Gainesville, FL.

Bowen, R. M., DuCharme, L., & Shores, D. (1995). Stakeholders' Implicit Claims and Accounting Method Choice. *Journal of Accounting and Economics, 20*, 255–295.

Cheng, Q., Lee, J., & Shevlin, T. (2016). Internal Governance and Real Earnings Management. *The Accounting Review, 91*, 1051–1085.

Cheng, Q., & Warfield, T. D. (2005). Equity Incentives and Earnings Management. *The Accounting Review, 80*, 441–476.

Collins, D. W., Pungaliya, R. S., & Vijh, A. M. (2017). The Effects of Firm Growth and Model Specification Choices on Tests of Earnings Management in Quarterly Settings. *The Accounting Review, 92*, 69–100.

DeBacker, J., Heim, B. T., & Tran, A. (2015). Importing Corruption Culture from Overseas: Evidence from Corporate Tax Evasion in the United States. *Journal of Financial Economics, 117*, 122–138.

Dechow, P. M., & Dichev, I. D. (2002). The Quality of Accruals and Earnings: The Role of Accrual Estimation Errors. *The Accounting Review, 77*, 35–59.

Dechow, P. M., Hutton, A. P., Kim, J. H., & Sloan, R. G. (2012). Detecting Earnings Management: A New Approach. *Journal of Accounting Research, 50*, 275–334.

Dechow, P. M., & Sloan, R. G. (1991). Executive Incentives and the Horizon Problem: An Empirical Investigation. *Journal of Accounting and Economics, 14*, 51–89.

Dechow, P. M., Sloan, R. G., & Sweeney, A. P. (1995). Detecting Earnings Management. *The Accounting Review, 70*, 193–225.

Dechow, P. M., Sloan, R. G., & Sweeney, A. P. (1996). Causes and Consequences of Earnings Manipulation: An Analysis of Firms Subject to Enforcement Actions by the SEC. *Contemporary Accounting Research, 13*, 1–36.

Fama, E. F., & French, K. R. (1997). Industry Costs of Equity. *Journal of Financial Economics, 43*, 153–193.

Fan, Y., Jiang, Y., Zhang, X., & Zhou, Y. (2019). Women on Boards and Bank Earnings Management: From Zero to Hero. *Journal of Banking & Finance, 107*, 105607.

Fiordelisi, F., & Ricci, O. (2014). Corporate Culture and CEO Turnover. *Journal of Corporate Finance, 28*, 66–82.

Fiordelisi, F., & Ricci, O. (2021). Corrigendum to "Corporate Culture and CEO Turnover". *Journal of Corporate Finance, 70*, 102064.

Grieser, W. D., Kapadia, N., Li, R., & Simonov, A. (2016). *Fifty Shades of Corporate Culture*. Available at SSRN 2843776.

Hausman, J. A. (1978). Specification Tests in Econometrics. *Econometrica: Journal of the Econometric Society, 46*, 1251–1271.

Healy, P. M. (1985). The Effect of Bonus Schemes on Accounting Decisions. *Journal of Accounting and Economics, 7*, 85–107.

Healy, P., & Wahlen, J. (1999). A Review of the Earnings Management Literature and Its Implications for Standard Setting. *Accounting Horizons, 13*(4), 365–383.

Heckman, J. J. (1979). Sample Selection Bias as a Specification Error. *Econometrica: Journal of the Econometric Society, 47*, 153–161.

Hribar, P., & Collins, D. W. (2002). Errors in Estimating Accruals: Implications for Empirical Research. *Journal of Accounting Research, 40*, 105–134.

Jiang, F., Ma, Y., & Wang, X. (2020). Multiple Blockholders and Earnings Management. *Journal of Corporate Finance, 64*, 101689.

Jones, J. J. (1991). Earnings Management During Import Relief Investigations. *Journal of Accounting Research, 29*, 193–228.

Kothari, S. P., Leone, A. J., & Wasley, C. E. (2005). Performance Matched Discretionary Accrual Measures. *Journal of Accounting and Economics, 39*, 163–197.

Lara, J. M. G., Osma, B. G., & Penalva, F. (2020). Conditional Conservatism and the Limits to Earnings Management. *Journal of Accounting and Public Policy, 39*, 106738.

Liu, X. (2016). Corruption Culture and Corporate Misconduct. *Journal of Financial Economics, 122*, 307–327.

Roychowdhury, S. (2006). Earnings Management Through Real Activities Manipulation. *Journal of Accounting and Economics, 42*, 335–370.

Skinner, D. J., & Sloan, R. G. (2002). Earnings Surprises, Growth Expectations, and Stock Returns or Don't Let an Earnings Torpedo Sink Your Portfolio. *Review of Accounting Studies, 7*, 289–312.

Stock, J. H., & Yogo, M. (2005). Testing for Weak Instruments in Linear IV Regression. In *Identification and Inference for Econometric Models. Essays in Honor of Thomas Rothenberg*. Cambridge University Press.

Teoh, S. H., Welch, I., & Wong, T. J. (1998a). Earnings Management and the Long-Run Market Performance of Initial Public Offerings. *The Journal of Finance, 53*, 1935–1974.

Teoh, S. H., Welch, I., & Wong, T. J. (1998b). Earnings Management and the Underperformance of Seasoned Equity Offerings. *Journal of Financial Economics, 50*, 63–99.

CHAPTER 9

Competition Culture and Bank Lending

9.1 Introduction

In this final study chapter, we will explore whether competition culture has implications for lending behaviour. We focus our attention on the US banking industry as it has consistently grown in economic importance in recent decades (Antill et al., 2014). In fact, the entire financial services industry represented approximately 7.9% or $1.7 trillion of the gross domestic product as at the year ended 2012; at the time of writing this book a full decade later, this industry is estimated to increase its contribution to US GDP to $3.8 trillion by the end of 2023, a staggering $2.1 trillion increase! What's more, the banking industry's unique mode of financing, regulatory peculiarities, and heighten public scrutiny makes it an interesting area to study the effects of corporate culture. And, while prior studies have extensively explored the effect of culture on organizational outcomes in nonfinancial firms (see for example, Andreou et al., 2021; Callen & Fang, 2015; Cronqvist et al., 2007; Fiordelisi & Ricci, 2014, 2021; Graham et al., 2022; Guiso et al., 2006, 2009, 2015a, 2015b; Nguyen et al., 2018; Wang et al., 2021; Zingales, 2015, among others), US-based financial firms (from henceforth referred to as "banks") have not been given the same level of attention (Barth & Mansouri, 2021; Bushman et al., 2017; Fiordelisi et al., 2019; Luu et al., 2022; Nguyen et al., 2019; Song & Thakor, 2019, Thakor, 2015, 2020). In this chapter, we argue that banks' competition culture plays a particularly important

T. Harris, *Competition Culture and Corporate Finance*,
https://doi.org/10.1007/978-3-031-30156-8_9

role in explaining various corporate phenomenon associated with banks decision-making, thereby making the banking industry an interesting study in its own right. Without a doubt, banks play a central role in the sound functioning of the entire financial system, and of particular concern to bank regulators is whether and how excessive risk-taking by individual banks poses a threat to the financial system as a whole (see, e.g., Acharya et al., 2010; Hanson et al., 2011). In this vein, important undecided issues related to the extent to which banks' orientation towards the competition culture mitigates or exacerbates incentives for bank lending behaviour. As a result, we are motivated to consider the following research questions; "*what is the relationship between banks' competition culture and bank lending?*" and "*how does banks' pre-crisis competition culture relate to crisis period lending?*".

In keeping with our expectations, we find evidence in this chapter that banks with greater levels of competition culture are likely to engage in more lending. In addition, we find that banks' competition culture promotes more procyclic lending during the global financial crisis (GFC).

In conducting our analysis, we carefully design our approach to tackling econometric issues that may cloud the interpretation of the results. For instance, since banks' competition culture is reported to be a rather persistent variable over time, we utilize pooled cross-sectional models for our primary analyses where we include time fixed effects. We also conduct generalized least squares random effects (GLS-RE) estimates for the main relations, as this approach also allows us to capture the effects of slow-moving variables and permits an efficient estimation of model parameters. In addition, to safeguard against simultaneous causality issues, we supplement our main baseline regressions by estimating dynamic panel generalized method of moments (GMM) models for the relations between banks' competition culture and bank lending.

This study makes important contributions to the banking literature by offering an examination of the arguments regarding whether and how banks' corporate culture affects banks' lending practices. Recent studies on the effects of banks' corporate culture have suggested that corporate culture has significant economically meaningful effects on bank managers' propensity to engage in marginal lending and other risk-taking activities (see e.g., Bushman et al., 2017; Fiordelisi et al., 2019; Luu et al., 2022; Nguyen et al., 2019; Song & Thakor, 2019; Thakor, 2015, 2020). Furthermore, this stream of literature suggests that when prominent banks adopt corporate cultures that are overly aggressive, for instance by having higher levels of competition culture, this can lead to over-lending in the entire banking system as other banks follow suit (Nguyen et al., 2019). Nevertheless, to date, there is little convincing evidence concerning the effects of banks' corporate culture on banks' overall lending during times of financial crisis. Hence, this study seeks to bridge this gap.

This study also has important policy implications, and its findings would be of interest to bank regulators, bank managers, and the research community. This is because the effect of banks' competition culture on lending has implications for the manner in which banks and other financial firms are governed and managed. The insights provided here could be used to help reduce systematic risk, as banks manage the downside risk associated with the competition cultures, and thereby attract additional capital to such banks, especially during times of economic crisis when bank capital and financing are most under threat (Ahmed et al., 1999; Altamuro & Beatty, 2010; Beatty & Harris, 1999; Beatty & Liao, 2011, 2014; Ivashina & Scharfstein, 2010).

The following section presents the main hypotheses. Section 9.3 highlights the details of the data and summary statistics; Sect. 9.4 presents the preliminary empirical results; while Sect. 9.5 concludes.

9.2 Hypotheses

In this chapter, we use our measure of banks' competition culture to investigate whether and how it is related to bank lending activity. Consistent with past literature, (see e.g., Bushman et al., 2017; Luu et al., 2022; Nguyen et al., 2019; Song & Thakor, 2019; Thakor, 2015, 2020), we expect that banks which are more orientated towards the competition culture should engage in more lending activity. This proposition is reasonable since such banks are argued to engage in a more forceful and aggressive pursuit of performance objectives. In so doing, banks with a higher level of competition culture would likely be more willing to engage in greater lending activity as they reach for yield (e.g., Becker & Ivashina, 2015) even though this may mean accepting greater levels of risks (particularly credit risk) in exchange for interest revenues generated by extending such loans. Consequently, we posit the following hypothesis in the alternate form:

H1: Banks' competition culture is positively associated with banks' lending activity.

Further, we argue that high competition culture banks should exhibit procyclical lending behaviour. As a result, we expect that the positive relationships between banks' competition culture and bank lending should reverse during crisis periods. We argue that this is plausible since Ivashina and Scharfstein (2010) and Beatty and Liao (2011, 2014) noted that during periods of financial crisis bank lending is likely to be negatively affected since banks' financing and capital are more under threat. This is in part due to banks' inability to refinance during the crisis period as a result of severe financing frictions at these times (Myers & Majluf, 1984). We argue that this phenomenon is likely to be more pronounced for those banks that adopt a higher competition culture since such banks should be perceived as especially risky due to their more marginal pre-crisis period lending. Thus, we argue that banks with higher levels of pre-crisis competition culture will exhibit less crisis period lending.

H2: Banks' pre-crisis period competition culture is positively associated with banks' crisis period lending activity.

9.3 Data, Variables, and Sample

9.3.1 Data

To investigate relations between banks' competition culture and bank lending we compile a unique sample by gathering information assimilated from a number of data sources. First, we obtain US publicly listed bank (SIC 6000–6999) accounting and market data from the COMPUSTAT/CRSP merge database for the period 1994–2014. In addition, to measure competition culture, we obtain from the SEC's Edgar database banks' 10–K reports. Prior to the data analyses, we attempt to mitigate the effects of outliers by winsorizing all continuous variables at the 1 and 99% levels. Additionally, we attempt to limit survivorship bias by permitting banks that became inactive and/or that were acquired during the study period to remain in the study sample. Also, we delete all observations with missing data on the key variables of interest. Further, the National Bureau of Economic Research (NBER) recognizes the global financial crisis (GFC) as occurring between 2007 and 2009 and we adopted this period as the crisis period for our investigations. Definitions of the variables used in this chapter are presented in Table 9.1.

Table 9.1 Definition of variables

	Symbol		*Definitions*
Competition culture			
	COMP	=	the bank's competition culture estimated for each fiscal year using the text-analysis approach;
Bank lending			
	ΔLOAN	=	the change from the beginning of the fiscal year in the natural log of loans [Compustat item: lntal];
Other variables			
	CAP1	=	is the bank's tier 1 risk-adjusted capital ratio [Compustat item: capr1] at the beginning of the fiscal year, divided by 100;
	ΔUNEMP	=	the change in the US employment rate over the fiscal year;
	ΔCAP1	=	annual dividend yield;
	DEPOSITS	=	the lagged total deposits [Compustat item: dptc] divided by total assets [Compustat item: at], and
	SIZE	=	the natural logarithm of bank's total assets [Compustat item: at]

9.3.2 *Measuring Bank Competition Culture*

As in Chapter 4, we measure a bank's competition culture (COMP) by counting the number of times that the lexical items included in the bag of words describing corporate attributes for the competition culture are found in the 10-K filings and scale our measure by counts of the lexical items that describe the other cultural orientations as follows[1]:

$$\text{COMP} = \frac{\text{Number of lexical items describing the Competition Culture}}{\text{Total number of lexical items for all types of cultures}}. \tag{9.1}$$

[1] While conducting our count we exclude negation of the lexical items by ignoring occasions when the word is preceded by "no", "non", "not", "less", "few" or "limited" by three or fewer words.

9.3.3 *Measuring Bank Lending*

To capture the change in a bank's lending activity we make use of the following simple measure: ΔLOAN, which is the change from the beginning of the fiscal year in the natural log of loans [Compustat item: lntal].

9.3.4 *Control Variables*

Following past work in this area (see e.g., Beatty & Liao, 2014), we include the following control variables in order to statistically control for bank-specific characteristics. In particular, we include the following: CAP1 is the bank's tier 1 risk-adjusted capital ratio [Compustat item: capr1] at the beginning of the fiscal year, divided by 100. The variable ΔCAP1is the change in CAP1 of the fiscal year. The variable ΔUNEMP represents the change in the employment rate over the fiscal year. The variable DEPOSITS is the lagged total deposits [Compustat item: dptc] divided by total assets [Compustat item: at]. The variable SIZE is the natural logarithm of the bank's total assets [Compustat item: at].

9.3.5 *Descriptive Statistics and Correlations*

Table 9.2 provides descriptive statistics of the variables used in our empirical analysis.[2] In particular, the mean value of our banks' competition culture variable, COMP, is 0.45, and the mean for the change in lending variable, ΔLOAN, is 4.51. We observe that the summary statistics on the variables are largely comparable to the values reported in previous studies using these data (see, e.g., Beatty & Liao, 2014; Beatty et al., 1995; Bushman et al., 2016, 2017; Luu et al., 2022; Nguyen et al., 2019).

Further, we compute Pearson correlation coefficients for the variables used in our empirical analysis and report these in Table 9.3. One of the more interesting correlations includes the relationship between COMP and ΔLOAN, where we find a positive and significant correlation between COMP and ΔLOAN (correlation = 0.1601). These results are consistent with our expectations that banks' competition culture increases bank lending.

[2] To mitigate the effects of outliers, all continuous variables are winsorized at the 1 and 99% levels.

Table 9.2 Descriptive statistics

Variable	*Obs*	*Mean*	*Std. Dev*	*25th Pctl*	*Median*	*75th Pctl*
COMP	5,683	0.45	0.06	0.42	0.45	0.49
ΔLOAN	5,176	4.51	1.8	3.39	4.39	5.52
CAP1	5,683	0.12	0.04	0.09	0.11	0.13
ΔUNEMP	5,683	−0.08	1.04	−0.6	−0.4	0.1
ΔCAP1	5,683	0.00003	0.02	−0.01	0	0.01
DEPOSITS	5,683	0.75	0.1	0.69	0.77	0.82
SIZE	5,683	7.37	1.45	6.36	7.02	8.02

This table presents the mean, median, 25th percentile, 75th percentile, minimum value, maximum value, and the number of observations for all variables used in the study

Table 9.3 Pearson correlation matrix

	COMP	*ΔLOAN*	*CAP1*	*ΔUNEMP*	*ΔCAP1*	*DEPOSITS*
ΔLOAN	**0.1601**					
CAP1	0.0040	**−0.2212**				
ΔUNEMP	**0.0841**	**−0.0891**	**−0.0933**			
ΔCAP1	0.0007	−0.0062	**0.2778**	**−0.0342**		
DEPOSITS	**0.0692**	**−0.2495**	**0.0782**	**−0.1314**	−0.0248	
SIZE	**0.1878**	**0.7849**	**−0.2086**	**0.0353**	0.0236	**−0.3452**

This table presents the Pearson correlation coefficients for the main variables used in the empirical analyses. The bold figures indicate significance at the five percent level and above

9.4 Empirical Results

In this section, we report the results of the multivariate analysis pertaining to our examination of the relationship between banks' competition culture and lending.

9.4.1 Bank Competition Culture and Bank Lending Behaviour

First, we investigate whether banks' competition culture is related to bank lending activity. As proposed in H1, we expect that banks which are more orientated towards the competition culture should engage in more aggressive lending activity. To empirically test this, we estimate the following regression model:

$$\Delta \text{LOAN}_t = \alpha_1 + \alpha_2 \text{COMP}_t + \alpha_3 \text{CAP1}_t + \alpha_4 \Delta \text{UNEMP}_t + \alpha_5 \Delta \text{CAP1}_t + \alpha_6 \text{DEPOSITS}_{t-1} + \alpha_7 \text{SIZE}_{t-1} + \varepsilon_t \quad (9.2)$$

where all other variables are as previously defined. In addition, we include year dummies to control for unobserved time-invariant year factors in this and all subsequent models.

In further tests of H1, we estimate models to examine the relationship between lagged values and differences in our measure of competition culture and bank lending activity. These tests examine whether and how bank competition culture impacts changes in bank lending in future periods. Regressions that examine the long-run relationship can help to further mitigate potential simultaneity issues and shed light on the direction of the relationship between banks' competition culture and banks' lending activity. If banks' competition culture is positively related to changes in bank lending in future periods, it is more likely that banks' competition culture affects bank lending activity rather than the opposite. In particular, we estimate the following empirical models:

$$\Delta \text{LOAN}_t = \alpha_1 + \alpha_2 \Delta \text{COMP}_t + \alpha_3 \text{COMP}_{t-1} + \alpha_4 \text{CAP1}_t + \alpha_5 \Delta \text{UNEMP}_t + \alpha_6 \Delta \text{CAP1}_t + \alpha_7 \text{DEPOSITS}_{t-1} + \alpha_8 \text{SIZE}_{t-1} + \varepsilon_t \quad (9.3)$$

and,

$$\Delta \text{LOAN}_t = \alpha_1 + \alpha_2 \Delta \text{COMP}_t + \alpha_3 \Delta \text{COMP}_t + \alpha_4 \text{COMP}_{t-1} + \alpha_5 \text{CAP1}_t + \alpha_6 \Delta \text{UNEMP}_t + \alpha_7 \Delta \text{CAP1}_t + \alpha_8 \text{DEPOSITS}_{t-1} + \alpha_9 \text{SIZE}_{t-1} + \varepsilon_t \quad (9.4)$$

Table 9.4 presents the results where we find evidence consistent with high competition culture banks engaging in more lending activity. In particular, we report the coefficients term 0.045 on the COMP_t variable in column (1). This coefficient captures the effect of competition culture on the change in bank lending activity and consistent with our expectations and H1, we find evidence that this relationship is positive and significant at the 1% level (t-value = 4.13). Further, we find for Eq. (9.3) that the coefficient term 0.039 for COMP_{t-1}, in column (2) is significantly positive at the 1% level (t-value = 3.06). Besides this, estimates of Eq. (9.4), presented in column (3) document a coefficient of

0.037 on the $COMP_{t-2}$, variable, suggesting a positive and significant relationship between competition culture and changes in bank lending activity two years into the future at the 5% level given a t-value of 2.44. Furthermore, the coefficients of $\Delta COMP_t$ in column (2) and $\Delta COMP_t$ and $\Delta COMP_{t-1}$ in column (3) are positive and significant with coefficient terms of 0.023, 0.028, and 0.048, and t-values of 2.30, 2.50, and 3.70, respectively. The fact that first and second differences in competition culture help to predict future changes in banks' lending behaviour suggests that not only the level but also the change in banks' competition culture effects lending. Similar long-run estimates of Eqs. (9.2–9.4) are produced using the GLS-RE estimator. These results are provided in columns (4) to (6) and are consistent with the pooled OLS estimates of these equations. Furthermore, we re-estimate Eqs. (9.2–9.4) where we include controls for a bank's state of origin and find similar results. These results are presented in Appendix C.

Besides this, we estimate a dynamic panel GMM model to further examine the relationship between banks' competition culture and banks' lending activity. We adopt this estimation approach to control for the possibility that the relationship between COMP and ΔLOAN is dynamically endogenous. To be clear, if the relationship between COMP and ΔLOAN is in fact dynamically endogenous then this implies that the causal relationship between COMP and ΔLOAN runs in both directions, thereby biassing our previous estimates. Furthermore, in spite of the fact that we carefully select control variables to capture firm-specific effects, our prior results are open to the criticism that they are biassed due to omitted variables. Hence, to control for potential dynamic endogeneity, unobserved heterogeneity, and simultaneity, in the relationship between COMP and ΔLOAN we follow Wintoki et al. (2012) by adopting the dynamic panel GMM model as proposed by Arellano and Bover (1995) and Blundell and Bond (1998). This approach allows us to explicitly control for lagged values of ΔLOAN. In addition, we are able to use firm information within our dataset as instruments. We estimate the following empirical model:

$$\begin{aligned}\Delta LOAN_t = \alpha_1 &+ \alpha_2 COMP_t + \gamma_1 \Delta LOAN_{t-1} + \beta_1 CAP1_t \\ &+ \beta_2 \Delta UNEMP_t + \beta_3 \Delta CAP_t + \beta_4 DEPOSITS_{t-1} \\ &+ \beta_5 SIZE_{t-1} + \eta_t + \varepsilon_t \qquad (9.5)\end{aligned}$$

Table 9.4 OLS and random effects estimates of banks' competition culture and Lending

	$\Delta LOAN_t$ (1)	(2)	(3)	(4)	(5)	(6)
$COMP_t$	0.045***			0.027***		
	(4.13)			(2.66)		
$\Delta COMP_t$		0.023**	0.028**		0.012	0.020*
		(2.30)	(2.5)		(1.27)	(1.87)
$COMP_{t-1}$		0.039***			0.022*	
		(3.06)			(1.79)	
$\Delta COMP_{t-1}$			0.048***			0.036**
			(3.34)			(2.49)
$COMP_{t-2}$			0.037**			0.027*
			(2.44)			(1.88)
$CAP1_t$	−0.017	−0.053***	−0.060***	0.02	−0.009	−0.012
	(1.26)	(3.83)	(3.7)	(1.38)	(0.56)	(0.61)
$\Delta UNEMP_t$	0.330**	0.444**	0.356***	0.298*	0.400**	0.337**
	(2.12)	(2.34)	(2.66)	(1.91)	(2.07)	(2.55)
$\Delta CAP1_t$	−0.008	0.00	0.012	−0.01	−0.003	0.005
	(0.73)	(0.00)	(0.88)	(1.02)	(0.23)	(0.33)
$DEPOSITS_{t-1}$	0.024*	0.026**	0.036**	0.024*	0.021	0.037**
	(1.82)	(1.99)	(2.47)	(1.80)	(1.46)	(2.39)
$SIZE_{t-1}$	0.770***	0.776***	0.779***	0.743***	0.755***	0.768***
	(62.95)	(58.64)	(52.6)	(54.77)	(50.53)	(49.43)
R^2	0.63	0.65	0.66	0.63	0.64	0.66
N	5,176	4,096	3,138	5,176	4,096	3,138

$^{*}p<0.1$; $^{**}p<0.05$; $^{***}p<0.01$

This table presents OLS (columns 1–3) and GLS-RE (columns 4–6) estimates for the relations between banks' competition culture and bank lending. The dependent variable ΔLOAN is the change from the beginning of the fiscal year in the natural log of loans [Compustat item: lntal]. The value of COMP is the competition culture estimated from the bank's 10-K filings. The variable ΔCOMP represents the change in COMP over the fiscal year. The value of the variable CAP1 is the bank's tier 1 risk-adjusted capital ratio [Compustat item: capr1] at the beginning of the fiscal year, divided by 100. The variable ΔCAP1 is the change in CAP1 over the fiscal year. The variable ΔUNEMP represents the change in the employment rate over the fiscal year. The variable DEPOSITS is the lagged total deposits [Compustat item: dptc] divided by total assets [Compustat item: at]. The variable SIZE is the natural logarithm of bank's total assets [Compustat item: at]. The estimates include year dummies to control time-invariant fixed year-specific effects. All models include a constant and the standard errors are clustered at the bank-level. The t-values are given in parentheses where we first-difference Eq. (9.5) to eliminate unobserved heterogeneity and potential omitted variable bias. Then, we estimate the first-differenced model by GMM using lagged values (and differences) of ΔLOAN and the controls as instruments. By using lagged variables as instruments, we control for potential simultaneity and reverse causality.

The system GMM estimates are presented in Table 9.5, where consistent with the previous results, we find a positive relationship between banks' competition culture and change in bank lending activity. When estimating the GMM model we assume that only the year dummies are exogenous. The AR(1) and AR(2) serial correlation tests results suggest that we cannot reject the null hypothesis of no serial correlation. Further, we apply Hansen's (1982) test for overidentification, as in Arellano and Bond (1991) to assess the validity of our instruments, and based on the results we do not reject the null hypothesis that our instruments are valid. In addition, we conduct the difference-in-Hansen test of exogeneity in a manner like Bond et al. (2001) to determine whether the subset of instruments used in the level equation is exogenous. Again, we do not reject the null hypothesis that our instruments are exogenous. All told, the results of these specification tests lead us to conclude that our dynamic GMM regressions are valid and lend further support to our argument that banks' competition culture, in fact, increases bank lending activity.

9.4.2 *Bank Competition Culture and Procyclicality*

To test H2 we utilize the global financial crisis (GFC) of 2007 to 2009 and explore whether high COMP banks engage in greater procyclical lending. In particular, we explore the relationship between banks' pre-crisis period competition culture and crisis period lending where we denote, CRISIS, a variable coded one for the years 2007 to 2009 and zero otherwise. We then use, CRISIS, to consider the impact of competition culture in the year preceding the GFC, PRE_CRISIS_COMP, on the crisis period lending. To do this we estimate the following empirical model:

$$\begin{aligned}\Delta \mathrm{LOAN}_t = {} & \alpha_1 + \alpha_2 \mathrm{CRISIS}_t + \alpha_3 \mathrm{CRISIS}_t \times \mathrm{PRE\_CRISIS\_COMP} \\ & + \alpha_4 \mathrm{CAP1}_t + \alpha_5 \Delta \mathrm{UNEMP}_t + \alpha_6 \Delta \mathrm{CAP1}_t \\ & + \alpha_7 \mathrm{DEPOSITS}_{t-1} + \alpha_8 \mathrm{SIZE}_{t-1} + \varepsilon_t \qquad (9.6)\end{aligned}$$

Table 9.5 Dynamic system GMM regressions of banks' competition culture and lending

	$\Delta LOAN_t$
$COMP_t$	0.121**
	(2.06)
$CAP1_t$	−0.019
	(0.28)
$\Delta UNEMP_t$	−0.014
	(0.42)
$\Delta CAP1_t$	0.157*
	(1.84)
$DEPOSITS_{t-1}$	0.101*
	(1.91)
$SIZE_{t-1}$	0.746***
	(8.22)
$\Delta LOAN_{t-1}$	−0.001
	(0.01)
$AR(1)$ test p-value	0.00
$AR(2)$ test p-value	0.33
Hansen test for overidentification p-value	0.70
Diff–in–Hansen tests of exogeneity p-value	0.30
N	3,374

*p<0.1; **p<0.05; ***p<0.01

This table presents dynamic panel GMM estimates of the relations between banks' competition culture and bank lending. The dependent variable ΔLOAN is the change from the beginning of the fiscal year in the natural log of loans [Compustat item: lntal]. The value of COMP is the competition culture estimated from the bank's 10-K filings. The variable ΔCOMP represents the change in COMP over the fiscal year. The value of the variable CAP1 is the bank's tier 1 risk-adjusted capital ratio [Compustat item: capr1] at the beginning of the fiscal year, divided by 100. The variable ΔCAP1 is the change in CAP1 over the fiscal year. The variable ΔUNEMP represents the change in the employment rate over the fiscal year. The variable DEPOSITS is the lagged total deposits [Compustat item: dptc] divided by total assets [Compustat item: at]. The variable SIZE is the natural logarithm of bank's total assets [Compustat item: at]. The estimates include year dummies to control time-invariant fixed year-specific effects. AR(1) and AR(2) are tests for first-order and second-order serial correlation in the first-differenced residuals, under the null of no serial correlation. The Hansen test of overidentification is under the null that all instruments are valid. The Diff-in-Hansen test exogeneity is under the null that instruments used for the equations in levels are exogenous. The model includes a constant and the standard errors are clustered at the bank-level. The t-values are given in parentheses

The estimates of this model are provided in Table 9.6 where the sign and significance of the coefficients associated with the interaction term CRISIS × PRE_CRISIS_COMP are consistent with greater pre-crisis competition culture banks engaging in less GFC period lending (column 1). In particular, we find in column (1) the coefficient of our interaction term of interest to be −0.073 (t-value = 2.56), while this term in column (2) for our GLS-RE regression is −0.075 (t-value = 2.46). Also, we re-estimate Eq. (9.6) by including state dummies to control for a bank's state of origin. These results are presented in Appendix C and are similar to those provided above.

9.5 Summary

In summary, we conduct a textual analysis of banks' 10-K filings to examine the effect of competition culture on banks' lending behaviour. We find evidence that greater competition culture banks are more likely to engage in more lending. Further, we find that high competition culture banks are more likely to engage in less lending during the global financial crisis (GFC). In particular, we report that during the GFC, those banks with higher pre-crisis period levels of competition culture reduce lending more compared to other banks.

All told, this study has important policy implications, and its findings would be of interest to bank regulators, bank managers, and the research community. This is because the effect of bank's competition culture on lending has implications for the manner in which banks and other financial institutions are governed and managed. The insights provided here could be used to help banks attract capital investment especially during times of economic crisis, financial crisis, and even pandemic periods (e.g., the recent COVID-19 global pandemic period); in addition, these results could be used to help reduce systematic risk especially during crisis periods when the banking system is under increased stress. Thus, this study is of critical importance for the reasons outlined in this piece and as Federal Reserve Bank of New York President William Dudley remarked in 2014 if banks do not develop robust cultures that eliminate ethical lapses, regulators may have no choice but to step in.

Table 9.6 OLS and random effects regressions of banks' pre-crisis competition culture and crisis-period lending

	$\Delta LOAN_t$ (1)	(2)
$CRISIS_t$	−1.854***	−1.643**
	(2.64)	(2.33)
$CRISIS_t$ × PRE_CRISIS_COMP	−0.073**	−0.075**
	(2.56)	(2.46)
$CAP1_t$	−0.017	0.02
	(1.24)	(1.35)
$\Delta UNEMP_t$	0.345**	0.298*
	(2.22)	(1.91)
$\Delta CAP1_t$	−0.009	−0.01
	(0.79)	(1.09)
$DEPOSITS_{t-1}$	0.031**	0.029**
	(2.44)	(2.14)
$SIZE_{t-1}$	0.784***	0.753***
	(67.88)	(57.76)
R^2	0.63	0.63
N	5,176	5,176

*$p<0.1$; **$p<0.05$; ***$p<0.01$

This table presents OLS (column 1) and GLS-RE (columns 2) estimates for the relationship between banks' pre-crisis period competition culture and crisis-period bank lending. The dependent variable ΔLOAN is the change from the beginning of the fiscal year in the natural log of loans [Compustat item: lntal]. The variable CRISIS is coded one for the years 2007 to 2009 and zero otherwise. The variable PRE_CRISIS_COMP represents bank's competition culture estimated from the 10-K filings in the fiscal year 2006. The value of the variable CAP1 is the bank's tier 1 risk-adjusted capital ratio [Compustat item: capr1] at the beginning of the fiscal year, divided by 100. The variable ΔCAP1 is the change in CAP1 over the fiscal year. The variable ΔUNEMP represents the change in the employment rate over the fiscal year. The variable DEPOSITS is the lagged total deposits [Compustat item: dptc] divided by total assets [Compustat item: at]. The variable SIZE is the natural logarithm of bank's total assets [Compustat item: at]. The estimates include year dummies to control time-invariant fixed year-specific effects. All models include a constant and the standard errors are clustered at the bank-level. The t-values are given in parentheses

References

Acharya, V. V., Cooley, T. F., Richardson, M. P., & Walter, I. (2010). *Regulating Wall Street: The Dodd-Frank Act and the New Architecture of Global Finance*. Wiley.

Ahmed, A. S., Takeda, C., & Thomas, S. (1999). Bank Loan Loss Provisions: A Reexamination of Capital Management, Earnings Management and Signaling Effects. *Journal of Accounting and Economics, 28*, 1–25.

Altamuro, J., & Beatty, A. (2010). How does Internal Control Regulation Affect Financial Reporting? *Journal of Accounting and Economics, 49*, 58–74.

Andreou, P. C., Fiordelisi, F., Harris, T., & Philip, D. (2021). Institutional Ownership and Firms' Thrust to Compete. *British Journal of Management, 33*, 1346–1370.

Antill, S., Hou, D., & Sarkar, A. (2014). *Components of US Financial Sector Growth, 1950–2013*. Available at SSRN 2421317.

Arellano, M., & Bond, S. (1991). Some Tests of Specification for Panel Data: Monte Carlo Evidence and an Application to Employment Equations. *The Review of Economic Studies, 58*, 277–297.

Arellano, M., & Bover, O. (1995). Another Look at the Instrumental Variable Estimation of Error-Components Models. *Journal of Econometrics, 68*, 29–51.

Barth, A., & Mansouri, S. (2021). Corporate Culture and Banking. *Journal of Economic Behavior & Organization, 186*, 46–75.

Beatty, A., Chamberlain, S. L., & Magliolo, J. (1995). Managing Financial Reports of Commercial Banks: The Influence of Taxes, Regulatory Capital, and Earnings. *Journal of Accounting Research, 33*, 231–261.

Beatty, A., & Harris, D. G. (1999). The Effects of Taxes, Agency Costs and Information Asymmetry on Earnings Management: A Comparison of Public and Private Firms. *Review of Accounting Studies, 4*, 299–326.

Beatty, A., & Liao, S. (2011). Do Delays in Expected Loss Recognition Affect Banks' Willingness to Lend? *Journal of Accounting and Economics, 52*, 1–20.

Beatty, A., & Liao, S. (2014). Financial Accounting in the Banking Industry: A Review of the Empirical Literature. *Journal of Accounting and Economics, 58*, 339–383.

Becker, B., & Ivashina, V. (2015). Reaching for Yield in the Bond Market. *The Journal of Finance, 70*, 1863–1902.

Blundell, R., & Bond, S. (1998). Initial Conditions and Moment Restrictions in Dynamic Panel Data Models. *Journal of Econometrics, 87*, 115–143.

Bond, S. R., Hoeffler, A., & Temple, J. R. W. (2001). *GMM Estimation of Empirical Growth Models*. Centre for Economic Policy Research.

Bushman, R. M., Davidson, R. H., Dey, A., & Smith, A. (2017). Bank CEO Materialism: Risk Controls, Culture and Tail Risk. *Journal of Accounting and Economics, 65*, 191–220.

Bushman, R. M., Hendricks, B. E., & Williams, C. D. (2016). Bank Competition: Measurement, Decision-Making, and Risk-Taking. *Journal of Accounting Research, 54*, 777–826.

Callen, J. L., & Fang, X. (2015). Religion and Stock Price Crash Risk. *Journal of Financial and Quantitative Analysis, 50*, 169–195.

Cronqvist, H., Low, A., & Nilsson, M. (2007). *Does Corporate Culture Matter for Firm Policies?* (Working Paper). Fisher College of Business.

Fiordelisi, F., & Ricci, O. (2014). Corporate Culture and CEO Turnover. *Journal of Corporate Finance, 28*, 66–82.

Fiordelisi, F., & Ricci, O. (2021). Corrigendum to "Corporate Culture and CEO Turnover." *Journal of Corporate Finance, 70*, 102064.

Fiordelisi, F., Renneboog, L., Ricci, O., & Lopes, S. S. (2019). Creative Corporate Culture and Innovation. *Journal of International Financial Markets, Institutions and Money, 63*, 101137.

Graham, J. R., Harvey, C. R., Grennen, J., & Rajgopal, S. (2022). Corporate Culture: Evidence from the Field. *Journal of Financial Economics, 146*, 552–593.

Guiso, L., Sapienza, P., & Zingales, L. (2006). Does Culture Affect Economic Outcomes? *The Journal of Economic Perspectives, 20*, 23–48.

Guiso, L., Sapienza, P., & Zingales, L. (2009). Cultural Biases in Economic Exchange? *The Quarterly Journal of Economics, 124*, 1095–1131.

Guiso, L., Sapienza, P., & Zingales, L. (2015a). Corporate Culture, Societal Culture, and Institutions. *American Economic Review, 105*, 336–339.

Guiso, L., Sapienza, P., & Zingales, L. (2015b). The Value of Corporate Culture. *Journal of Financial Economics, 117*, 60–76.

Hansen, L. P. (1982). Large Sample Properties of Generalized Method of Moments Estimators. *Econometrica: Journal of the Econometric Society, 50*, 1029–1054.

Hanson, S. G., Kashyap, A. K., & Stein, J. C. (2011). A Macro-prudential Approach to Financial Regulation. *Journal of Economic Perspectives, 25*, 3–28.

Ivashina, V., & Scharfstein, D. (2010). Bank Lending during the Financial Crisis of 2008. *Journal of Financial Economics, 97*, 319–338.

Luu, H., Nguyen, L., & Wilson, J. O. S. (2022). *Organizational Culture, Competition and Bank Loan Loss Provisions*. Available at SSRN 3921043.

Myers, S. C., & Majluf, N. S. (1984). Corporate Financing and Investment Decisions when Firms have Information that Investors Do Not Have. *Journal of Financial Economics, 13*, 187–221.

Nguyen, D. D., Hagendorff, J., & Eshraghi, A. (2018). Does a CEO's Cultural Heritage affect Performance under Competitive Pressure? *The Review of Financial Studies, 31*, 97–141.

Nguyen, D. D., Nguyen, L., & Sila, V. (2019). Does Corporate Culture affect Bank Risk-Taking? Evidence from Loan-Level data. *British Journal of Management, 30*, 106–133.

Song, F., & Thakor, A. (2019). Bank Culture. *Journal of Financial Intermediation, 39*, 59–79.

Thakor, A. V. (2015). *Corporate Culture in Banking*. Available at SSRN 2565514.

Thakor, A. V. (2020). Ethics, Culture and Higher Purpose in Banking: Post-Crisis Governance Developments. *International Journal of Central Banking*. https://doi.org/10.2139/ssrn.3554121

Wang, Y., Farag, H., & Ahmad, W. (2021). Corporate Culture and Innovation: A Tale from an Emerging Market. *British Journal of Management, 32*, 1121–1140.

Wintoki, M. B., Linck, J. S., & Netter, J. M. (2012). Endogeneity and the Dynamics of Internal Corporate Governance. *Journal of Financial Economics, 105*, 581–606.

Zingales, L. (2015). The 'Cultural Revolution' in Finance. *Journal of Financial Economics, 117*, 1–4.

CHAPTER 10

Conclusion

10.1 Overview and Concluding Remarks

In this book, we explore the role that a specific type of corporate culture; namely, competition culture plays in corporate finance. To be sure firms' culture is a broad, intangible, and inherently complex concept (see e.g., Benabou & Tirole, 2003, 2011; Graham et al., 2022; Schein, 1990, 1992; Zingales, 2015), which is expected to be influenced by and reflect the values and practices of top management and those charged with governance. Further, this construct is expected to have a significant effect on firms' economic outcomes as it incentivizes behaviours and influences the environment within which decisions are taken. Thus, following insights provided by the competing values framework (CVF) for corporate culture, we introduce firms' competition culture as an important, economically valid, and significant empirical construct that is of increasing relevance and interest to researchers in finance and economics.

To measure competition culture, we rely on the textual analysis of firms' 10-K reports as this approach has recently been shown to be a valuable tool in finance for detecting economically relevant information from various bodies of texts (see e.g. Antweiler & Frank, 2004; Hoberg & Phillips, 2010; Kearney & Liu, 2014; Li, 2008; Loughran & McDonald, 2011, 2016, Tetlock, 2007). Specifically, we show that this approach can be applied to quantify corporate culture and although it remains debatable as to whether corporate culture is best measured using this method,

T. Harris, *Competition Culture and Corporate Finance*,
https://doi.org/10.1007/978-3-031-30156-8_10

we argue that our measure is reasonable based on the intuition that the words used by the management of a firm reflect the values that these individuals have developed over time. Further, we validate our empirical construct by relating it to alternative measures of competition culture.

Hence, using our text-based measure of competition culture we document in the first study (see Chapter 4) that firms' institutional ownership structure influences the level of competition culture. This finding provides evidence that firms' institutional ownership structure is an important determinant of firms' corporate culture. Specifically, we show that transient institutional ownership helps to promote the competition culture, while dedicated institutional ownership dampens this type of culture in firms.

In this book, we use our measure of firms' competition culture to show that firms with higher competition culture achieve superior performance as indicated by buy and hold stock returns. However, we also reveal a darker side to firms' competition culture as firms with this type of corporate culture are more prone to experience stock price crash risks. Interestingly, we document this phenomenon particularly among firms with a high proportion of transient and a low proportion of dedicated institutional ownership, and that is consistent with competition culture playing a mediating role. In addition, we find that high competition culture firms are more likely to meet and/or beat analysts' forecasts and engage in (avoid) accruals (real) earnings management activity.

In addition, we examine the effect of banks' competition culture on bank lending and find that banks with greater competition culture are likely to engage in greater lending activity. However, we report that during the global financial crisis (GFC) banks with higher pre-crisis competition culture reduce their lending more during the crisis period.

Taken together, these results suggest that dedicated institutional ownership helps to reduce managements' orientation towards the competition culture, while transient institutional ownership reinforces it and hence works as a stimulus for management to achieve superior short-term performance while engaging in opportunistic behaviour that can negatively affect firms' economic outcomes. In particular, our results suggest that institutional investors have a positive effect on a firm's orientation towards competition culture and that increased competition culture is positively linked to performance. Furthermore, our findings reveal that it is likely that managers at such firms may feel pressured to conceal "bad" news in an attempt to reach the expected levels of performance and hence firms with greater competition culture are more likely to experience large firm-specific declines in their stock prices when this "bad" news is released to the market. With these results in hand, it should come as no surprise that firms with high competition culture are more likely to meet/beat analysts' forecasts and engage in accruals-based earning management activity possibly in an attempt to meet the performance expectations of investors. What's more, it is reasonable that high competition culture in banks encourages managers to engage in greater procyclical lending activity.

All told, the results of this book have important implications of interest to academics, bank regulators, and the wider business community. This is because the effect of institutional ownership on competition culture has implications for the manner in which firms are governed and managed. In particular, our main findings should be of interest to those charged with governance, who have a responsibility to eliminate any pressures on managers from outside investors to increase their competition culture in order to achieve short-term financial objectives which may increase idiosyncratic and systematic risks.

Future research will explore the role played by other cultural orientations under the CVF in explaining firms' economic outcomes. Additionally, future work could consider the impact of recent regulatory developments (e.g., ASC 326 and IFRS 9) and the impact of the COVID-19 pandemic on the relationships between competition culture and institutional ownership, performance, crash risk, meeting/beating analysts' expectations, bank lending, among other outcomes of interest (e.g., loan loss provisioning, performance, risk-taking, CEO tenure, M&A decisions, compensation schemes, etc.). Furthermore, whether and how bank culture, particularly competition culture, plays a role in exacerbating/or mitigating bank idiosyncratic stock price crash risk and/or overall systemic risk, especially during periods of economic and financial crises could be considered in future research.

References

Antweiler, W., & Frank, M. Z. (2004). Is All That Talk Just Noise? The Information Content of Internet Stock Message Boards. *The Journal of Finance, 59*, 1259–1294.

Benabou, R., & Tirole, J. (2003). Intrinsic and Extrinsic Motivation. *The Review of Economic Studies, 70*, 489–520.

Benabou, R., & Tirole, J. (2011). Identity, Morals, and Taboos: Beliefs as Assets. *The Quarterly Journal of Economics, 126*, 805–855.

Graham, J. R., Harvey, C. R., Grennen, J., & Rajgopal, S. (2022). Corporate Culture: Evidence from the Field. *Journal of Financial Economics, 146*, 552–593.

Hoberg, G., & Phillips, G. (2010). Product Market Synergies and Competition in Mergers and Acquisitions: A Text-Based Analysis. *Review of Financial Studies, 23*, 3773–3811.

Kearney, C., & Liu, S. (2014). Textual Sentiment in Finance: A survey of Methods and Models. *International Review of Financial Analysis, 33*, 171–185.

Li, F. (2008). Annual Report Readability, Current Earnings, and Earnings Persistence. *Journal of Accounting and Economics, 45*, 221–247.

Loughran, T., & McDonald, B. (2011). When Is a Liability Not a Liability? Textual Analysis, Dictionaries, and 10-Ks. *The Journal of Finance, 66*, 35–65.

Loughran, T., & McDonald, B. (2016). Textual Analysis in Accounting and Finance: A survey. *Journal of Accounting Research, 54*, 1187–1230.

Schein, E. H. (1990). Organizational Culture: What It Is and How to Change it. In *Human Resource Management in International Firms*. Palgrave Macmillan.

Schein, E. H. (1992). *Organizational Culture and Leadership: A Dynamic View*. Jossey-Bass.

Tetlock, P. C. (2007). Giving Content to Investor Sentiment: The Role of Media in the Stock Market. *The Journal of Finance, 62*, 1139–1168.

Zingales, L. (2015). The 'Cultural Revolution' in Finance. *Journal of Financial Economics, 117*, 1–4.

Appendix A: Institutional Investors and Competition Culture

Overview

In what follows, we provide further details on the data, research design, and execution to assist with the digestibility of our results. We provide the results of supplemental analyses conducted to add support to the empirical work included in Chapter 4. In particular, we provide evidence concerning the validity of our measure, before differentiating it from product market competition. The tables are as follows:

- **Table A.1 presents the bag of words with synonyms that we use to construct our measure of competition culture.**
- **Table A.2 presents univariate and multivariate analyses of the relationship between our measure of competition culture and other indicators of corporate culture**. In Panels A and B we present comparisons between COMP and Fiordelisi and Ricci's (2014, 2021) text-based measures of corporate culture. In Panels C and D we compare COMP with a firm's profit margin, measured as earnings before interest and taxes scaled by the firm's total sales revenue. Profit margin is a theoretically (Cameron et al., 2014) and empirically valid proxy for the intensity of firms' competition culture (see e.g., Tremblay, 2020).

T. Harris, *Competition Culture and Corporate Finance*,
https://doi.org/10.1007/978-3-031-30156-8

Table A.1 Bag of words

Compete culture:
achiev*, acqui*, aggress*, attack*, budget*, challeng*, charg*, client*, compet*, customer*, deliver*, direct*, driv*, excellen*, expand*, fast*, goal*, growth*, hard*, invest*, market*, mov*, outsourc*, performanc*, position*, pressur*, profit*, rapid*, reputation*, result*, sale*, satisf*, scan*, signal*, speed*, strong*, succes*, superior*, target*, win*
Create culture:
adapt*, begin*, chang*, creat*, discontin*, dream*, elabor*, entrepre*, envis*, experim*, fantas*, freedom*, futur*, idea*, init*, innovat*, intellec*, learn*, new*, origin*, pioneer*, predict*, radic*, risk*, start*, thought*, trend*, unafra*, ventur*, vision*
Collaborate culture:
boss*, burocr*, cautio*, cohes*, certain*, chief*, collab*, conservat*, cooperat*, detail*, document*, efficien*, error*, fail*, help*, human*, inform*, logic*, method*, outcom*, partner*, people*, predictab*, relation*, qualit*, regular*, solv*, share*, standard*, team*, teamwork*, train*, uniform*, work*, group*
Control culture:
capab*, collectiv*, commit*, competenc*, conflict*, consens*, control*, coordin*, cultur*, decentr*, employ*, empower*, engag*, expectat*, facilitator*, hir*, interpers*, involv*, life*, long-term*, loyal*, mentor*, monit*, mutual*, norm*, parent*, partic*, procedur*, productiv*, retain*, reten*, skill*, social*, tension*, value*

This table reports the bag of words with synonyms that best describe the four corporate cultures (compete, create, collaborate, and control) of the competing value framework (CVF) (Cameron et al., 2014). Words ending with "*" indicate that we utilize all suffixes for those words to count as many words as possible with a close meaning. While conducting our count, we exclude negation of the lexical items by ignoring occasions when the word is preceded by "no", "non", "not", "less", "few", or "limited" by three or fewer words

Source Adapted from Fiordelisi and Ricci's (2014, 2021)

- **Table** A.3 **presents univariate analyses of the relationships between institutional ownership, corporate competition culture, and product market competition.**
- **Table** A.4 **presents OLS estimates used to investigate the relations between institutional ownership, competition culture, and Li et al.'s (2013) product market competition (PCTCOMP).** We present comparisons between COMP and PCTCOMP based on the same set of observations.
- **Table** A.5 **presents GLS-RE estimates used to investigate the relations between institutional ownership, competition culture, and Li et al.'s (2013) product market competition.** We present comparisons between COMP and PCTCOMP based on the same set of observations.

Table A.2 Univariate and multivariate analyses of the relationships between our measure of Competition culture and other indicators of firm's corporate culture

Panel A. Pearson's correlations for the relationship between COMP and Fiordelisi and Ricci's (2014, 2021) text-based measures of corporate culture

	COMP	COMPETE_FR	COLLAB_FR	CONTROL_FR
COMPETE_FR	**0.6290**			
COLLAB_FR	**−0.1877**	**0.2946**		
CONTROL_FR	**−0.2818**	**0.3619**	**0.1582**	
CREATE_FR	**−0.1439**	**0.2199**	**0.0761**	**0.2549**

Panel B. OLS and GLS-RE estimates for the relationship between COMP and Fiordelisi and Ricci's (2014, 2021) text-based measures of corporate culture

	$COMP_t$	
	(1)	*(2)*
$COMPETE\_FR_t$	0.972***	0.922***
	(33.22)	(27.13)
$COLLAB\_FR_t$	−0.387***	−0.420***
	(31.83)	(27.54)

(continued)

Table A.2 (continued)

Panel B. OLS and GLS-RE estimates for the relationship between COMP and Fiordelisi and Ricci's (2014, 2021) text-based measures of corporate culture

	$COMP_t$	
	(1)	*(2)*
$CONTROL\_FR_t$	−0.491***	−0.421***
	(7.65)	(6.18)
$CREATE\_FR_t$	−0.192***	−0.174***
	(3.96)	(3.64)
R^2	0.86	0.86
N	24,912	24,912

Panel C. Pearson's correlations for the relationship between COMP and proxies for the intensity of firms' corporate culture that are based on firms' financial numbers

	COMP	*EBIT_SALES*	*EMP_AT*	*TURNOVER*
EBIT_SALES	**0.0137**			
EMP_AT	**−0.0469**	0.0051		
TURNOVER	**−0.0143**	**0.0625**	**0.0512**	
RD_AT	**0.0388**	**−0.0585**	**−0.1722**	**−0.7591**

Panel D OLS and GLS-RE estimates for the relationship between COMP and proxies for the intensity of firms' corporate culture that are based on firms' financial numbers

	$COMP_t$	
	(1)	*(2)*
$EBIT\_SALES_t$	0.009***	0.004***
	(5.72)	(6.68)
EMP_AT_t	−0.243***	−0.155***
	(3.88)	(3.26)
$TURNOVER_t$	−0.01	−0.020*
	(0.65)	(1.80)
RD_AT_t	−0.037*	−0.042***
	(1.75)	(3.22)
R^2	0.19	0.19
N	16,695	16,695

*$p < 0.1$; **$p < 0.05$; ***$p < 0.01$

This table presents univariate and multivariate analyses of the relationships between our measure of competition culture and other indicators of the four corporate cultures (compete, create, collaborate, and control) that are theorized by the competing values framework (CVF) (Cameron et al., 2014). Panel A highlights Pearson's correlation results between our measure of competition culture and Fiordelisi and Ricci's (2014, 2021) text-based measures of corporate culture. Panel B presents OLS (column 1) and GLS-RE (column 2) estimates for the relationship between COMP and Fiordelisi and Ricci's (2014, 2021) text-based measures of corporate culture. In Panel C we provide Pearson's correlation results between the measure of competition culture and other proxies for the intensity of firms' corporate culture that is based on firms' financial numbers (see e.g., Tremblay, 2020). Panel D provides OLS (column 1) and GLS-RE (column 2) estimates for the relationship between the measure of competition culture and other proxies for the intensity of firms' corporate culture that is based on firms' financial numbers (see e.g., Tremblay, 2020). The correlation results utilize bold figures to indicate significance at the 10% level and above. The regressions all include year and industry dummies to capture year and industry-specific fixed effects. The standard errors are clustered at the firm level. The *t*-values are given in parentheses

Table A.3 Univariate analyses of the relationships between institutional ownership, competition culture, and product market competition

Panel A. Deciles analysis

		COMP		*PCTCOMP*	
		TRA	*DED*	*TRA*	*DED*
Lowest	1	0.1287	0.0501	0.1422	0.0402
	2	0.1306	0.0392	0.1396	0.048
	3	0.1333	0.038	0.1458	0.0502
	4	0.1329	0.0366	0.1453	0.0525
	5	0.1409	0.0354	0.1405	0.0535
	6	0.1451	0.0373	0.1447	0.0559
	7	0.1463	0.0367	0.137	0.0652
	8	0.1449	0.0357	0.1385	0.0616
	9	0.149	0.034	0.1368	0.0592
Highest	10	0.145	0.0406	0.1448	0.0643
Diff (10)–(1)		0.0164	−0.0095	0.0026	0.0241
t–stat		6.18***	−5.69***	0.77	11.14***

Panel B. Pearson's correlations

	PCTCOMP
COMP	**0.1389**
TRA	0.0012
DED	**0.0651**

This table presents univariate analyses of the relationships between transient (TRA) and dedicated (DED) institutional ownership, competition culture (COMP), and Li et al.'s (2013) product market competition (PCTCOMP). Panel A shows the results by deciles of competition culture, and product market competition. The significance of the difference between means in deciles 10 and 1 are indicated in the last row where, "*", "**", and "***" indicate significance at the 10%, 5%, and 1% levels, respectively. Panel B highlights Pearson's correlation results between the institutional ownership, competition culture, and product market competition. The bold figures indicate the significance that the 10% level and above

- **Table** A.6 **presents instrumental variable (IV) regressions of the relationships between transient and dedicated institutional ownership and Li et al.'s (2013) product market competition.**
- **Table** A.7 **presents fixed effects estimates used to investigate the impact of transient [Panel A] and dedicated [Panel B] institutional ownership on competition culture.** We include year and firm dummies to capture time-invariant year and firm-specific fixed effects.

Table A.4 OLS regressions of institutional ownership on competition culture and product market competition

Panel A. The effect of transient institutional ownership on competition culture and product market competition

	$COMP_{t+1}$			$PCTCOMP_{t+1}$		
	(1)	(2)	(3)	(4)	(5)	(6)
TRA_t	0.062***			0.008		
	(4.42)			(0.73)		
ΔTRA_t		0.044***	0.043***		0.006	0.005
		(4.45)	(4.49)		(0.67)	(0.60)
TRA_{t-1}		0.069***			0.007	
		(4.05)			(0.57)	
ΔTRA_{t-1}			0.059***			0.002
			(4.70)			(0.20)
TRA_{t-2}			0.068***			0.009
			(3.54)			(0.63)
R^2	0.17	0.17	0.17	0.32	0.32	0.32
N	15,242	15,242	15,242	15,242	15,242	15,242

(continued)

Table A.4 (continued)

Panel B. The effect of dedicated institutional ownership on competition culture and product market competition

DED_t	−0.028*			−0.019		
	(1.82)			(1.57)		
ΔDED_t		−0.023**	−0.023**		−0.016	−0.015
		(2.04)	(1.99)		(1.64)	(1.54)
DED_{t-1}		−0.027			−0.018	
		(1.46)			(1.25)	
ΔDED_{t-1}			−0.01			−0.009
			(0.79)			(0.79)
DED_{t-2}			−0.035*			−0.019
			(1.73)			(1.20)
R^2	0.17	0.17	0.17	0.33	0.33	0.33
N	15,242	15,242	15,242	15,242	15,242	15,242

*$p < 0.1$; **$p < 0.05$; ***$p < 0.01$

This table presents OLS estimates used to investigate the relations between transient and dedicated institutional ownership, competition culture, and Li et al.'s (2013) product market competition. All regressions include control variables, year and industry fixed effects. The standard errors are clustered at the firm level. The *t*-values are given in parentheses

Table A.5 Random effects regressions of institutional ownership on competition culture and product market competition

Panel A. The effect of transient institutional ownership on competition culture and product market competition

	$COMP_{t+1}$			$PCTCOMP_{t+1}$		
	(1)	*(2)*	*(3)*	*(4)*	*(5)*	*(6)*
TRA_t	0.031***			0.005		
	(3.27)			(0.51)		
ΔTRA_t		0.019***	0.018***		0.005	0.006
		(2.70)	(2.58)		(0.63)	(0.72)
TRA_{t-1}		0.044***			−0.001	
		(3.48)			(0.10)	
ΔTRA_{t-1}			0.031***			−0.002
			(3.14)			(0.21)
TRA_{t-2}			0.047***			0.004
			(3.22)			(0.28)
R^2	0.07	0.07	0.07	0.28	0.28	0.28
N	15,242	15,242	15,242	15,242	15,242	15,242

(continued)

Table A.5 (continued)

Panel B. The effect of dedicated institutional ownership on competition culture and product market competition

DED_t	−0.021*			−0.012		
	(1.84)			(1.09)		
ΔDED_t		−0.021**	−0.022**		−0.012	−0.012
		(2.44)	(2.55)		(1.30)	(1.26)
DED_{t-1}		−0.016			−0.008	
		(1.12)			(0.63)	
ΔDED_{t-1}			−0.013			−0.004
			(1.19)			(0.33)
DED_{t-2}			−0.02			−0.011
			(1.20)			(0.70)
R^2	0.07	0.07	0.07	0.28	0.28	0.28
N	15,242	15,242	15,242	15,242	15,242	15,242

$^*p < 0.1$; $^{**}p < 0.05$; $^{***}p < 0.01$

This table presents GLS-RE estimates used to investigate the relations between institutional ownership, competition culture, and Li et al.'s (2013) product market competition. All regressions include controls, year, and industry fixed effects. The standard errors are clustered at the firm level. The *t*-values are given in parentheses

Table A.6 Instrumental variable regressions of institutional ownership on product market competition

Panel A. IV regression first and second stage results

	1st stage: TRA_t (1)	*$PCTCOMP_t$* (2)	*1st stage: DED_t* (3)	*$PCTCOMP_t$* (4)
TRA_t		0.013		
		(0.53)		
DED_t				0.005
				(0.18)
$R2000_t$	0.263***		−0.161***	
	(6.91)		(3.78)	
$R2000_t \times RANK_t$	−0.35[illegible]***	0.152***	−0.641**	0.152***
	(10.09)	(4.45)	(2.04)	(4.44)
$MRKCAP_t$	−0.068***	−0.031***	−0.007	−0.031***
	(5.73)	(4.11)	(0.86)	(4.06)
$FLOAT_t$	0.957***	0.005	−0.039	0.005
	(5.38)	(0.29)	(0.23)	(0.29)
R^2	0.18		0.08	
N	2,440	1,808	2,440	1,808

Panel B. Stock and Yogo (2005) Weak Instruments Test

Instrumented variables	*Instruments*	*First stage F-Statistic*	*Critical value*
TRA_t	$R2000_t$	50.46	16.38
DED_t	$R2000_t$	60.21	16.38

$^*p < 0.1$; $^{**}p < 0.05$; $^{***}p < 0.01$

This table presents instrumental variable (IV) regressions of the relationships between transient (TRA) and dedicated (DED) institutional ownership and Li et al.'s (2013) product market competition (PCTCOMP) [Panel A], and the results of a Stock and Yogo (2005) weak instruments test [Panel B]. The regressions include year and industry fixed effects and the standard errors are clustered by firm. The t-values are given in parentheses

Table A.7 Fixed effects regressions of institutional ownership on competition culture

Panel A. The effect of transient institutional ownership on competition culture			
	$COMP_{t+1}$		
	(1)	*(2)*	*(3)*
TRA_t	0.014*		
	(1.83)		
ΔTRA_t		0.024**	
		(2.42)	
TRA_{t-1}			0.024**
			(2.04)
ΔTRA_{t-1}		0.005	0.004
		(0.95)	(0.70)
TRA_{t-2}			0.015**
			(2.00)
AGE_t	0.11	0.11	0.11
	(1.34)	(1.34)	(1.34)
$DTURN_t$	0.001	0	0.001
	(0.19)	(0.10)	(0.36)
LEV_t	0.023**	0.024**	0.024**
	(2.05)	(2.11)	(2.11)
MTB_t	−0.017***	−0.016***	−0.016***
	(2.90)	(2.82)	(2.78)
RET_t	−0.048**	−0.052**	−0.050**
	(2.38)	(2.56)	(2.50)
ROA_t	−0.025***	−0.025***	−0.024***

Panel A. The effect of transient institutional ownership on competition culture

	$COMP_{t+1}$		
	(1)	*(2)*	*(3)*
	(3.43)	(3.46)	(3.42)
$SIZE_t$	0.110***	0.106***	0.106***
	(5.39)	(5.14)	(5.14)
$STDEV_t$	−0.065***	−0.069***	−0.068***
	(2.78)	(2.94)	(2.90)
R^2	0.08	0.08	0.08
N	31,223	31,223	31,223

Panel B. The effect of dedicated institutional ownership on competition culture

DED_t	−0.019**		
	(2.25)		
ΔDED_t		−0.023**	
		(2.05)	
DED_{t-1}			−0.029**
			(2.20)
ΔDED_{t-1}		−0.015**	−0.015**
		(2.33)	(2.34)
DED_{t-2}			−0.014*
			(1.68)
AGE_t	0.108	0.108	0.109
	(1.31)	(1.31)	(1.32)

(continued)

Table A.7 (continued)

Panel B. The effect of dedicated institutional ownership on competition culture

$DTURN_t$	0.002	0.002	0.002
	(0.51)	(0.53)	(0.56)
LEV_t	0.023**	0.023**	0.023**
	(2.08)	(2.08)	(2.09)
MTB_t	−0.016***	−0.016***	−0.016***
	(2.82)	(2.82)	(2.85)
RET_t	−0.041**	−0.041**	−0.041**
	(2.04)	(2.04)	(2.05)
ROA_t	−0.024***	−0.024***	−0.024***
	(3.30)	(3.31)	(3.29)
$SIZE_t$	0.117***	0.118***	0.118***
	(5.86)	(5.86)	(5.87)
$STDEV_t$	−0.058**	−0.059**	−0.059**
	(2.49)	(2.51)	(2.51)
R^2	0.08	0.08	0.08
N	31,223	31,223	31,223

*$p < 0.1$; **$p < 0.05$; ***$p < 0.01$

This table presents fixed effects estimates used to investigate the impact of transient (TRA) [Panel A] and dedicated (DED) [Panel B] institutional ownership on the level of firms' competition culture (COMP). All regressions include year and firm fixed effects. The standard errors are all clustered at the firm level. The t-values are given in parentheses

Measuring Competition Culture

To construct our measure of firms' competition culture, COMP, we first convert each firm-year 10–K report in our sample into the lower case so that capitalization is ignored. Next, we replace any URLs embedded in the document with the text "HTTP". This form of URL normalization helps to ensure that our measure is not biased due to web addresses contained in the firms' 10–K. Next, all non-words and punctuations are removed and all white spaces (e.g., tabs and newlines) are trimmed to a single space. Following this necessary pre-processing, we then produce our measure of firms' competition culture, COMP, by counting the number of times the lexical items for competition appears in a firm's annual 10–K report. We account for inflections (i.e., various forms of the same word) by using the stemmed form (e.g., "compete" becomes "compet"). This helps to ensure that when we conduct our word search, we count all variants of that word. We account for negation by excluding those times when "not", "less", "few", or "limited" precede "compet" by three or fewer words. We also ignore references to the word "competent". Finally, we produce our relative measure of firms' competition culture by controlling for the other cultural types. In particular, we scale the raw word count for lexical items consistent with the competition culture by the total count of lexical items for all cultures indicated by the competing values framework (CVF). Table A.1 presents the lexical items that describe the four corporate cultures (compete, create, collaborate, and control) as theorized by CVF (please see Cameron et al., 2014).

Is Our Measure of Competition Culture Valid?

According to Kerlinger (1973) evidence of construct validity is present when the pattern of associations among variables conforms to what is predicted by theory. In this regard, we have reasons to expect that if our relative measure of competition culture, COMP is a valid measure then it should be positively and significantly related to other indicators of firms' competition culture. Hence, we posit the following proposition;

P1: There is a strong positive relationship between our measure of competition culture and other indicators of competition culture.

To investigate P1 we adopt two approaches where we first explore the relationship between our measure of competition culture and Fiordelisi and Ricci's (2014, 2021) text-based measures of corporate culture. Following this, we examine the relationship between our measure of competition culture and several non-text indicators of the firm's corporate culture that is not only consistent with theory, reasonable and intuitive, but that has been used in past empirical studies for this very purpose (see e.g. Tremblay, 2020). In all cases, we document evidence consistent with our measure of competition culture capturing firm attributes that reflect the thrust to compete. In particular, we first explore the plausibility of P1 by estimating the following model:

$$\begin{aligned}\text{COMP}_t =& \alpha_1 + \alpha_2\text{COMPETE\_FR}_t + \alpha_3\text{COLLAB\_FR}_t \\ &+ \alpha_4\text{CONTROL\_FR}_t + \alpha_5\text{CREATE\_FR}_t + \varepsilon_t \end{aligned} \quad \text{(A.1)}$$

where, the variables COMPETE_FR, COLLAB_FR, CONTROL_FR, and CREARE_FR represent the four corporate cultures; namely, *compete*, *collaborate*, *control*, and *create* as theorized by the CVF and as measured following the exact approach that is taken in Fiordelisi and Ricci (2014, 2021).

In addition, we investigate whether P1 is reasonable by estimating the empirical model presented below;

$$\begin{aligned}\text{COMP}_t =& \alpha_1 + \alpha_2\text{EBIT\_SALES}_t + \alpha_3\text{EMPLOY\_AT}_t \\ &+ \alpha_4\text{TURNOVER}_t + \alpha_5\text{R\&D\_AT}_t + \varepsilon_t \end{aligned} \quad \text{(A.2)}$$

where the variable EBIT_SALES is a firm's profit margin measured by a firm's income before interest and taxes divided by the firm's total sales. The variable EMPLOY_AT denotes the number of employees of the firm scaled by the firm's total assets. TURNOVER is the firm's total sales scaled by total assets. The variable R&D_AT represents the firm's research and development expenditure divided by the firm's total assets. As suggested in past studies (see e.g., Tremblay, 2020), the variables EBIT_SALES, EMPLOY_AT, TURNOVER, and R&D_AT can be used as indicators of firms' intensity of the CVF's *compete culture*, *collaborate culture*, *control culture*, and *create culture*.

Table A.2 Panel A presents the Pearson correlations between COMP, and Fiordelisi and Ricci's (2014, 2021) text-based measures of corporate culture (COMPETE_FR, COLLAB_FR, CONTROL_FR, and CREARE_FR). And, consistent with P1, we find that our relative measure of firms' competition culture COMP is positively and significantly related to Fiordelisi and Ricci's (2014, 2021) text-based measure of competition culture; namely, COMPETE_FR (correlation = 0.6290). Further, Panel B of Table A.2 provides OLS (column 1) and GLS-RE (column 2) estimates of Eq. (A.1). In keeping with P1, we find a positive and significant relationship between COMP and COMPETE_FR as indicated by the coefficient term on COMPETE_FE of 0.972 (t-value = 33.22) in column (1) and 0.922 (t-value = 27.13) in column (2).

Pearson correlations for the relationship between COMP and indicators of the intensity of the firm's corporate culture that are based on the firm's financial numbers are presented in Table A.2 Panel C. We find that our relative measure of competition culture COMP is positively and significantly related to EBIT_SALES (correlation = 0.0137), a proxy of firm's competition culture (see e.g., Tremblay, 2020). In addition, we present in Panel D of Table A.2 OLS (column 1) and GLS-random effect (column 2) estimates of Eq. (A.2) and consistent with P1, we find a positive and significant relationship between COMP and EBIT_SALES as indicated by the coefficient term on EBIT_SALES of 0.009 (t-value = 5.72) in column (1) and 0.004 (t-value = 6.68) in column (2).

Competition Culture and Product Market Competition

We present further analyses aimed at supplementing the results and findings previously presented. Even though the COMP measure is designed to capture firms' competition culture under the CVF it is plausible that it may have an association with measures indented to capture firms' product market competition through textual analysis. In this regard, we explore whether our measure of firm's competition culture is indeed distinct from Li et al.'s (2013) product market competition measure, as they measure the intensity of firms' product market competition in a manner that is seemingly close to our approach. Specifically, they count the number of times the words "competition(s)", "competitor(s)", "competitive(s)", "compete(s)", "competing(s)", appear in the firm's 10-K filing minus those occasions when these words are proceeded by "not", "less", "few", or "limited" by three or fewer words. They then control for the length of the 10-K by scaling by the number of words in the report.

However, unlike Li et al. (2013) we compute COMP using a more comprehensive bag of words that captures corporate values relevant to a firm's operating philosophy under the CVF, particularly the *compete*, *create*, *collaborate*, and *control* corporate cultures. We then scale the number of competition culture words by the total number of words characterizing all four corporate cultures (as opposed to the total number of words in the 10-K). This approach allows us to construct an intensity measure of a firm's competition culture, which is consistent with the CVF that theorizes a context in which the four different corporate cultures vie with each other. Nevertheless, if our measure simply reflects variations in product market competition then it is possible that the relationship that we discover between TRA (DED) and COMP is driven by the intensity of firms' product market competition as opposed to the intensity of firms' competition culture. To preclude such a possibility, we analyse in Table A.3 the relations between TRA (DED), our measure of competition culture, COMP, and product market competition, PCTCOMP, as computed in Li et al. (2013).[1] Table A.3 Panel A presents mean scores for TRA (DED) by deciles of COMP and PCTCOMP, respectively, inclusive of the results of t-tests conducted to assess the significance of the difference in means between the highest (10th) and the lowest (1st) deciles. Panel B of Table A.3 highlights Pearson correlations between COMP, TRA, DED, and PCTCOMP. Interestingly, we find that while our prior results suggest that transient institutional ownership (TRA) is strongly positively related to competition culture as measured by COMP, transient institutional ownership *is not* related to product market competition as measured by PCTCOMP.

In addition, we estimate the following models to present comparisons between COMP and PCTCOMP based on the same set of observations.

$$\begin{aligned}\mathrm{COMP}_{t+1}(\mathrm{or PCTCOMP}_{t+1}) = {} & \alpha_1 + \alpha_2\mathrm{TRA}_t(\mathrm{or DED}_t) + \alpha_3\mathrm{AGE}_t \\ & + \alpha_4\mathrm{DTURN}_t + \alpha_5\mathrm{LEV}_t + \alpha_6\mathrm{MTB}_t \\ & + \alpha_7\mathrm{RET}_t + \alpha_8\mathrm{ROA}_t + \alpha_9\mathrm{SIZE}_t \\ & + \alpha_{10}\mathrm{STDEV}_t + \varepsilon_t \end{aligned} \tag{A.3}$$

$$\begin{aligned}\mathrm{COMP}_{t+1}(\mathrm{or PCTCOMP}_{t+1}) = {} & \alpha_1 + \alpha_2\Delta\mathrm{TRA}_t(\mathrm{or}\,\Delta\mathrm{DED}_t) \\ & + \alpha_3\mathrm{TRA}_{t-1}(\mathrm{or DED}_{t-1}) + \alpha_4\mathrm{AGE}_t \\ & + \alpha_5\mathrm{DTURN}_t + \alpha_6\mathrm{LEV}_t \\ & + \alpha_7\mathrm{MTB}_t + \alpha_8\mathrm{RET}_t + \alpha_9\mathrm{ROA}_t \\ & + \alpha_{10}\mathrm{SIZE}_t + \alpha_{11}\mathrm{STDEV}_t + \varepsilon_t \end{aligned} \tag{A.4}$$

[1] Li et al. (2013) product market data are obtained from: http://webuser.bus.umich.edu/feng.

and

$$
\begin{aligned}
\mathrm{COMP}_{t+1}(\mathrm{or PCTCOMP}_{t+1}) = & \alpha_1 + \alpha_2 \Delta \mathrm{TRA}_t (\mathrm{or} \Delta \mathrm{DED}_t) \\
& + \alpha_3 \Delta \mathrm{TRA}_{t-1} (\mathrm{or} \Delta \mathrm{DED}_{t-1}) \\
& + \alpha_4 \mathrm{TRA}_{t-2} (\mathrm{or DED}_{t-2}) \\
& + \alpha_5 \mathrm{AGE}_t + \alpha_6 \mathrm{DTURN}_t \\
& + \alpha_7 \mathrm{LEV}_t + \alpha_8 \mathrm{MTB}_t + \alpha_9 \mathrm{RET}_t \\
& + \alpha_{10} \mathrm{ROA}_t + \alpha_{11} \mathrm{SIZE}_t \\
& + \alpha_{12} \mathrm{STDEV}_t + \varepsilon_t
\end{aligned} \tag{A.5}
$$

The OLS estimates for Eqs. (A.3–A.5) are shown in Table A.4. The results suggest that COMP measures something that is distinctly different from PCTCOMP. In particular, our findings indicate that COMP has a significant positive (negative) relationship with transient (dedicated) institutional ownership, while PCTCOMP does not have any relationship with institutional ownership structure whatsoever. In addition to the OLS estimates presented in Table A.4, we provide RE estimates of for Eqs. (A.3–A.5) for completeness in Table A.5. These estimates also suggest a statistically significant relationship between COMP and our measures of institutional ownership, while being unable to detect any significant relations for PCTCOMP.

What's more, we further test the relationship between TRA (DED) and PCTCOMP directly by estimating the following instrumental variable model:

$$
\begin{aligned}
\mathrm{PCTCOMP}_t = & \alpha_1 + \alpha_2 \widehat{\mathrm{TRA}}_t \left(\mathrm{or} \widehat{\mathrm{DED}}_t\right) + \alpha_3 \mathrm{R2000}_t \times \mathrm{RANK}_t \\
& + \alpha_4 \mathrm{MRKCAP}_t + \alpha_5 \mathrm{FLOAT}_t + \varepsilon_t
\end{aligned} \tag{A.6a}
$$

$$
\begin{aligned}
\mathrm{TRA}_t (\mathrm{or DED}_t) = & \gamma_1 + \delta_1 \mathrm{R2000}_t + \beta_1 \mathrm{R2000}_t \times \mathrm{RANK}_t \\
& + \beta_2 \mathrm{MRKCAP}_t + \beta_3 \mathrm{FLOAT}_t + \mu_t
\end{aligned} \tag{A.6b}
$$

where R2000 is a dummy variable that is equal to one if the firm is a member of the Russell 2000 index and is zero if the firm is assigned to the Russell 1000 index, RANK is the firm's rank within the Russell index based on the firm's market capitalization, MRKCAP is firms' market capitalization on May 31st each year, and FLOAT is the difference between rank implied by the observed market capitalization and the rank assigned by Russell in June.

The estimates of the two-stage model Eqs. (A.6a) and (A.6b) are presented in Table A.6. The coefficient of interest, α_2, of Eq. (A.6a) is insignificant.

Taken altogether, our findings imply that the relationship between TRA (DED) and our measure of competition culture is not driven by managers' perception of firms' product market competition. Rather, they are consistent with COMP measuring corporate attributes pertaining to the competition culture, which is reflected in the choice of words used to construct firms' 10-K reports.

Appendix B: Competition Culture and Crash Risk

Overview

This appendix provides further details on the research design and execution to assist with the digestibility of our main results. As such, we present the results of supplemental analyses conducted to add support to the main empirical work included in Chapter 6. These tables are as follows:

- Table B.1 **presents GLS-RE estimates used to investigate the relationship between competition culture and stock price crash risk.**
- Table B.2 **presents OLS estimates used to investigate the relationship between competition culture and stock price crash risk.** These estimates include additional controls for managerial short-termism.
- Table B.3 **presents GLS-RE estimates used to investigate the relationship between competition culture and crash risk for subsamples of firms.**

T. Harris, *Competition Culture and Corporate Finance*,
https://doi.org/10.1007/978-3-031-30156-8

Table B.1 Random effect regressions of competition culture on stock price crash risk

	$DUVOL_{t+1}$	$ESIGMA_{t+1}$	$NCSKEW_{t+1}$
	(1)	*(2)*	*(3)*
$COMP_t$	0.018**	0.029***	0.024***
	(2.34)	(3.62)	(3.13)
AGE_t	−0.041***	−0.037***	−0.047***
	(4.85)	(4.29)	(5.63)
$DTURN_t$	0.024***	0.018**	0.021***
	(3.12)	(2.37)	(2.73)
LEV_t	−0.028***	−0.013*	−0.025***
	(3.54)	(1.70)	(3.13)
MTB_t	0.008	0.008	0.009
	(1.06)	(1.07)	(1.14)
RET_t	0.129***	0.079***	0.132***
	(4.75)	(2.89)	(4.88)
ROA_t	0.066***	0.041***	0.047***
	(7.90)	(4.57)	(5.33)
$SIZE_t$	0.188***	0.097***	0.178***
	(20.03)	(10.22)	(18.80)
$STDEV_t$	0.139***	0.089***	0.168***
	(4.62)	(2.93)	(5.56)
R^2	0.04	0.02	0.03
N	18,654	18,654	18,654

*$p < 0.1$; **$p < 0.05$; ***$p < 0.01$

This table presents GLS-RE estimates used to investigate the relationship between competition culture and crash risk. All regressions include year fixed effects and the standard errors are clustered at the firm level. The *t*-values are given in parentheses

Table B.2 OLS regressions of competition culture on stock price crash risk

	$DUVOL_{t+1}$	$ESIGMA_{t+1}$	$NCSKEW_{t+1}$
	(1)	*(2)*	*(3)*
$COMP_t$	0.025**	0.029***	0.028***
	(2.34)	(2.67)	(2.64)
AGE_t	−0.034***	−0.034***	−0.039***
	(2.80)	(2.89)	(3.27)
$DTURN_t$	0.022**	0.016	0.018*
	(2.26)	(1.56)	(1.80)
LEV_t	−0.016	0.018	−0.008
	(1.43)	(1.62)	(0.70)
MTB_t	0.006	−0.003	0.007
	(0.60)	(0.27)	(0.77)
RET_t	0.167***	0.091***	0.172***
	(4.77)	(2.59)	(4.98)
ROA_t	0.079***	0.078***	0.064***
	(7.27)	(7.06)	(5.77)
$SIZE_t$	0.180***	0.093***	0.166***
	(14.46)	(7.66)	(13.35)
$STDEV_t$	0.199***	0.121***	0.235***
	(5.02)	(3.07)	(5.96)
RDC_t	−0.014	−0.032	−0.011
	(0.62)	(1.42)	(0.47)
RDI_t	0.006	0.018	0.01
	(0.58)	(1.56)	(0.81)
$RDII_t$	−0.058	0.006	−0.061
	(0.96)	(0.09)	(0.96)
ΔGDP_t	0.602*	−0.958***	0.42
	(1.70)	(4.21)	(1.43)
R^2	0.06	0.03	0.05
N	11,343	11,343	11,343

$^*p < 0.1$; ** $p < 0.05$; *** $p < 0.01$

This table presents OLS estimates used to investigate the relationship between competition culture and crash risk with additional controls for managerial short-termism. These additional controls are as follows: RDC, equal to 1 if the firm experiences a cut in R&D expenditure over the past year; RDI, the firm's R&D intensity measured as total R&D expenditure for the fiscal year scaled by sales; RDII, industry R&D intensity measured as total R&D expenditure for all firms in the industry for the fiscal year scaled by total industry sales; ΔGDP, the natural logarithm of the change in US GDP. All regressions include year and industry fixed effects and the standard errors are clustered at the firm level. The *t*-values are given in parentheses

Table B.3 Subsample analyses of competition culture on stock price crash risk

	HIGH TRA & LOW DED			*HIGH* TRA *& HIGH* DED		
	DUVOL$_{t+1}$	*ESIGMA*$_{t+1}$	*NCSKEW*$_{t+1}$	*DUVOL*$_{t+1}$	*ESIGMA*$_{t+1}$	*NCSKEW*$_{t+1}$
	(1)	*(2)*	*(3)*	*(4)*	*(5)*	*(6)*
Panel A. The effect of competition culture on crash risk for subsamples of high transient and low (or high) dedicated ownership firms						
COMP$_t$	0.047***	0.061***	0.053***	0.006	0.013	0.013
	(2.83)	(3.48)	(3.15)	(0.34)	(0.69)	(0.70)
AGE$_t$	−0.029	−0.012	−0.036*	−0.048**	−0.036*	−0.053***
	(1.54)	(0.67)	(1.95)	(2.57)	(1.81)	(2.80)
DTURN$_t$	0.042***	0.034**	0.041***	0.040**	0.021	0.038**
	(2.77)	(2.16)	(2.66)	(2.38)	(1.24)	(2.31)
LEV$_t$	−0.036**	−0.038**	−0.037**	−0.031*	−0.001	−0.028
	(2.17)	(2.11)	(2.16)	(1.71)	(0.05)	(1.50)
MTB$_t$	0.009	0.016	0.011	0.035**	0.025	0.034**
	(0.46)	(0.81)	(0.56)	(2.49)	(1.58)	(2.23)
RET$_t$	0.057	−0.034	0.034	0.125*	0.104	0.118
	(0.37)	(0.49)	(0.52)	(1.67)	(1.33)	(1.60)
ROA$_t$	0.039**	0.032	0.027	0.043*	0.016	0.016
	(2.06)	(1.50)	(1.28)	(1.86)	(0.58)	(0.64)
SIZE$_t$	0.165***	0.093***	0.136***	0.141***	0.067**	0.122***
	(5.90)	(3.23)	(4.82)	(5.72)	(2.47)	(4.83)

	HIGH TRA & LOW DED			HIGH TRA & HIGH DED		
	$DUVOL_{t+1}$	$ESIGMA_{t+1}$	$NCSKEW_{t+1}$	$DUVOL_{t+1}$	$ESIGMA_{t+1}$	$NCSKEW_{t+1}$
	(1)	(2)	(3)	(4)	(5)	(6)
Panel A. The effect of competition culture on crash risk for subsamples of high transient and low (or high) dedicated ownership firms						
$STDEV_t$	0.083	0.006	0.089	0.158**	0.140*	0.165**
	(1.16)	(0.08)	(1.27)	(2.06)	(1.71)	(2.16)
R^2	0.04	0.03	0.03	0.04	0.02	0.04
N	4,011	4,011	4,011	3,575	3,575	3,575

	LOW TRA & LOW DED			LOW TRA & HIGH DED		
	$DUVOL_{t+1}$	$ESIGMA_{t+1}$	$NCSKEW_{t+1}$	$DUVOL_{t+1}$	$ESIGMA_{t+1}$	$NCSKEW_{t+1}$
	(1)	(2)	(3)	(4)	(5)	(6)
Panel B. The effect of competition culture on crash risk for subsamples of low transient and low (or high) dedicated ownership firms						
$COMP_t$	0.012	0.012	0.016	0.008	0.031*	0.01
	(0.80)	(0.81)	(1.07)	(0.46)	(1.73)	(0.58)
AGE_t	−0.014	−0.018	−0.018	−0.043**	−0.048**	−0.046**
	(0.86)	(1.12)	(1.10)	(2.24)	(2.49)	(2.43)
$DTURN_t$	−0.005	−0.011	−0.02	−0.037	−0.037	−0.044*

(continued)

Table B.3 (continued)

	LOW TRA & *LOW* DED			*LOW* TRA & *HIGH* DED		
	$DUVOL_{t+1}$	$ESIGMA_{t+1}$	$NCSKEW_{t+1}$	$DUVOL_{t+1}$	$ESIGMA_{t+1}$	$NCSKEW_{t+1}$
	(1)	*(2)*	*(3)*	*(4)*	*(5)*	*(6)*
Panel B. The effect of competition culture on crash risk for subsamples of low transient and low (or high) dedicated ownership firms						
	(0.31)	(0.71)	(1.21)	(1.54)	(1.43)	(1.82)
LEV_t	−0.007	0.009	0.001	−0.02	−0.023	−0.02
	(0.45)	(0.63)	(0.09)	(1.04)	(1.23)	(1.03)
MTB_t	−0.001	0.002	0.002	0.018	0.016	0.01
	(0.06)	(0.11)	(0.10)	(0.99)	(0.86)	(0.53)
RET_t	0.053	0.056	0.059	0.134*	0.019	0.146**
	(1.06)	(1.15)	(1.20)	(1.82)	(0.26)	(2.06)
ROA_t	0.066***	0.039***	0.049***	0.073***	0.048**	0.051**
	(4.46)	(2.64)	(3.36)	(3.54)	(2.26)	(2.36)
$SIZE_t$	0.214***	0.130***	0.205***	0.119***	0.047**	0.117***
	(10.35)	(6.35)	(9.85)	(5.60)	(2.26)	(5.53)
$STDEV_t$	0.053	0.047	0.092*	0.103	−0.007	0.152**
	(0.94)	(0.86)	(1.65)	(1.33)	(0.10)	(2.01)
R^2	0.07	0.04	0.05	0.04	0.02	0.03
N	4,505	4,505	4,505	3,088	3,088	3,088

$^*p < 0.1$; $^{**}p < 0.05$; $^{***}p < 0.01$

This table presents GLS-RE estimates used to investigate the relationship between competition culture and crash risk for subsamples of firms. All regressions include year and industry fixed effects and the standard errors are clustered at the firm level. The t-values are given in parentheses

Appendix C: Competition Culture and Bank Lending

Overview

In this appendix, we provide the results of further analyses designed to assist with the interpretation of the main results of Chapter 9. These tables present these supplemental analyses as follows:

- Table C.1 **presents OLS and GLS-RE estimates used to investigate the relationship between banks' competition culture and bank lending**. These results include year and state dummies to time and state fixed effects.
- Table C.2 **presents OLS and GLS-RE regressions of banks' pre-crisis competition culture and crisis period bank lending.** These results include year and state dummies to capture time and state fixed effects.

T. Harris, *Competition Culture and Corporate Finance*,
https://doi.org/10.1007/978-3-031-30156-8

Table C.1 OLS and random effects regressions of banks' competition culture and lending

	$\Delta LOAN_t$					
	(1)	*(2)*	*(3)*	*(4)*	*(5)*	*(6)*
$COMP_t$	0.037***			0.023**		
	(3.47)			(2.20)		
$\Delta COMP_t$		0.019*	0.025**		0.01	0.018*
		(1.85)	(2.30)		(0.86)	(1.65)
$COMP_{t-1}$		0.028**			0.01	
		(2.25)			(1.06)	
$\Delta COMP_{t-1}$			0.040***			0.030**
			(2.81)			(2.07)
$COMP_{t-2}$			0.025*			0.02
			(1.73)			(1.13)
$CAP1_t$	−0.016	−0.050***	−0.054***	0.02	0.01	0.01
	(1.18)	(3.56)	(3.19)	(1.28)	(0.56)	(0.55)
$\Delta UNEMP_t$	−0.026	0.005	0.009	0.20	0.32	0.493*
	(1.11)	(0.18)	(0.33)	(0.87)	(1.21)	(1.84)
$\Delta CAP1_t$	−0.008	−0.002	0.012	0.01	0.00	0.01
	(0.76)	(0.11)	(0.84)	(0.97)	(0.25)	(0.34)
$DEPOSITS_{t-1}$	0.012	0.016	0.025*	0.01	0.01	0.027*
	(0.9)	(1.19)	(1.69)	(1.02)	(0.70)	(1.71)
$SIZE_{t-1}$	0.766***	0.770***	0.768***	0.739***	0.749***	0.757***
	(60.6)	(55.07)	(49.17)	(51.01)	(46.45)	(45.79)
Year dummies	YES	YES	YES	YES	YES	YES
State dummies	YES	YES	YES	YES	YES	YES
R^2	0.63	0.65	0.66	0.64	0.66	0.67
N	5,176	4,096	3,138	5,176	4,096	3,138

$^*p < 0.1$; $^{**}p < 0.05$; $^{***}p < 0.01$

This table presents OLS (columns 1–3) and GLS-RE (columns 4–6) estimates for the relations between banks' competition culture and bank lending. The dependent variable ΔLOAN is the change from the beginning of the fiscal year in the natural log of loans [Compustat item: lntal]. The value of COMP is the competition culture estimated from the bank's 10-K filings. The variable ΔCOMP represents the change in COMP over the fiscal year. The value of the variable CAP1 is the bank's tier 1 risk-adjusted capital ratio [Compustat item: caprl] at the beginning of the fiscal year, divided by 100. The variable ΔCAP is the change in CAP1 over the fiscal year. The variable ΔUNEMP represents the change in the employment rate over the fiscal year. The variable DEPOSITS is the lagged total deposits [Compustat item: dptc] divided by total assets [Compustat item: at]. The variable SIZE is the natural logarithm of bank's total assets [Compustat item: at]. The estimates include year and state dummies to control time-invariant fixed year and state-specific effects. All models include a constant and the standard errors are clustered at the bank-level. The t-values are given in parentheses

Table C.2 OLS and random effects regressions of banks' pre-crisis competition culture and crisis period lending

	$\Delta LOAN_t$	
	(1)	(2)
$CRISIS_t$	0.382***	−1.146
	(3.36)	(1.07)
$CRISIS_t$ × PRE_CRISIS_COMP	−0.069**	−0.075**
	(2.39)	(2.40)
$CAP1_t$	−0.015	0.018
	(1.15)	(1.27)
$\Delta UNEMP_t$	−0.097***	0.198
	(5.99)	(0.87)
$\Delta CAP1_t$	−0.009	−0.01
	(0.85)	(1.04)
$DEPOSITS_{t-1}$	0.018	0.018
	(1.37)	(1.29)
$SIZE_{t-1}$	0.779***	0.749***
	(63.69)	(53.08)
Year dummies	YES	YES
State dummies	YES	YES
R^2	0.65	0.64
N	5,176	5,176

*$p < 0.1$; **$p < 0.05$; ***$p < 0.01$

This table presents OLS (column 1) and GLS-RE (columns 2) estimates for the relationship between banks' pre-crisis period competition culture and crisis period bank lending. The dependent variable ΔLOAN is the change from the beginning of the fiscal year in the natural log of loans [Compustat item: lntal]. The variable CRISIS is coded one for the years 2007 to 2009 and zero otherwise. The variable PRE_CRISIS_COMP represents bank's competition culture estimated from the 10-K filings in the fiscal year 2006. The value of the variable CAP1 is the bank's tier 1 risk-adjusted capital ratio [Compustat item: caprl] at the beginning of the fiscal year, divided by 100. The variable ΔCAP1 is the change in CAP1 over the fiscal year. The variable ΔUNEMP represents the change in the employment rate over the fiscal year. The variable DEPOSITS is the lagged total deposits [Compustat item: dptc] divided by total assets [Compustat item: at]. The variable SIZE is the natural logarithm of bank's total assets [Compustat item: at]. The estimates include year and state dummies to control time-invariant fixed year and state-specific effects. All models include a constant and the standard errors are clustered at the bank-level. The t-values are given in parentheses

References

Cameron, K., Quinn, R., DeGraff, J., & Thakor, A. (2014). *Competing Values Leadership*. Edward Elgar Publishing.

Fiordelisi, F., & Ricci, O. (2014). Corporate Culture and CEO Turnover. *Journal of Corporate Finance, 28*, 66–82.

Fiordelisi, F., & Ricci, O. (2021). Corrigendum to "Corporate Culture and CEO Turnover." *Journal of Corporate Finance, 70*, 102064.

Kerlinger, F. (1973). *Foundations of Behavioral Research*. Holt, Rinehart and Winston.

Li, F., Lundholm, R., & Minnis, M. (2013). A Measure of Competition Based on 10-K Filings. *Journal of Accounting Research, 51*, 399–436.

Tremblay, A. (2020). *Cultural Differences, Synergies and Mergers and Acquisitions*. Available at SSRN 2895110.

Index

T. Harris, *Competition Culture and Corporate Finance*,
https://doi.org/10.1007/978-3-031-30156-8

D

CPSIA informat
at www.ICGtesti obtained
Printed in the US
LVHW02140029
745667LV0000

9 783031 30155

CPSIA information can be obtained
at www.ICGtesting.com
Printed in the USA
LVHW021400290423
745667LV00002B/90

9 783031 301551